Praise for

101 Best Home-Based Businesses for Women, 3rd Edition

"A phenomenal resource for any woman with an entrepreneurial spirit! Priscilla has made it easier than ever for women to find their ideal home-based career. If you're interested in launching a successful business from home, this book is a must!"

—Debra M. Cohen, founder, Homeowner Referral Network (HRN) Business, and president, Home Remedies of NY, Inc.

"Six years ago I was scared I would never be able to be with my baby. I bought one of Priscilla Huff's books. Now I have my own successful home business. I cannot believe I now offer advice to others who want their own home businesses. If you want to be successful, buying this book is very important."

—Jennifer Dugan, Dugan's Travels

"If you are looking to start a home business, you won't be disappointed in the abundance of information Priscilla has compiled. This book covers everything a woman needs to know about what types of home businesses are available and how to get a home business started. Starting a home business can be a tremendous amount of work, but with Priscilla's book, you can be on your way to home-based success in no time at all."

—Lesley A. Spencer, founder, Home-Based Working Moms (www.hbwm.com)

"The unlimited resources provided literally take you through the process step by step and make obtaining the home biz dream a possible reality."

—Kim Essenmacher, independent telecom agent, Cognigen

Also by Priscilla Y. Huff

101 Best Home-Business Success Secrets for Women

101 Best Small Businesses for Women

HerVenture.com

More 101 Best Home-Based Businesses for Women

The Self-Employed Woman's Guide to Launching a Home-Based Business

101 Best Home-Based Businesses for Women

3rd Edition

Priscilla Y. Huff

PRIMA PUBLISHING

Published by Prima Publishing, Roseville, California. Member of the Crown Publishing Group, a division of Random House, Inc., New York.

PRIMA PUBLISHING and colophon are trademarks of Random House, Inc., registered with the United States Patent and Trademark Office.

Disclaimer
This book contains information of a general nature regarding starting and operating a business. It is not intended as a substitute for professional, legal, or financial advice. As laws may vary from state to state, readers should consult a competent legal or financial professional regarding their own particular business. In addition, readers should understand that the business world is highly dynamic and contains certain risks. Therefore, the author and publisher cannot warrant or guarantee that the use of any information contained in this book will work in any given situation.

Third Edition

ISBN 0-7394-2911-6

Printed in the United States of America

For my husband and sons for their encouragement and patience; and for my mother, Helen, whose courage, spirit, and joy of living have inspired her family and many others who have come to know her. Thanks, again, to the many women entrepreneurs who took their time to share valuable success tips with my readers.

Contents

Introduction

In the 21st century, women-owned businesses continued the growth rate that was started in the 1980s and 1990s. Here are just a few statistics to support this:

- The U.S. Census Bureau's "1997 Survey of Women-Owned Business Enterprises" shows that the growth in the number of women-owned firms, employment, and revenues exceeds the rate of growth of all businesses.
- The number of women-owned businesses continues to grow at twice the rate of all U.S. firms, and those businesses show significantly greater increases in employment and revenues, according to a report from the Center for Women's Business Research <www.womensbusinessresearch.org> (founded as the National Foundation for Women Business Owners). Between 1997 and 2002, the center estimates that the number of majority-owned, privately held women-owned firms will have grown by 14 percent (compared to 7 percent nationwide) and will stand at 6.2 million in 2002.
- Sales generated by women-owned firms increased by 40 percent nationwide during the period, nearing $1.15 trillion. These firms will employ nearly 9.2 million workers in 2002, up 30 percent from 1997, which reflects a growth rate that is one and a half times the national average.
- According to the American Association of Home-Based Businesses <www.aahbb.org>, 24 million Americans have home businesses, and the U.S. Census Bureau <www.census.gov> estimates that women own approximately 66 percent of these home-based businesses.

I first began writing about women entrepreneurs and their home businesses in the 1980s when my sister-in-law, Donna, and her friend Cindy started a business called Educational Clowning. Both were teachers who had put their teaching careers on hold while starting families, and they came up with the idea to partner together when they had clowns come to entertain at a camp for children with special needs that Donna and Cindy codirected.

At first, they began to entertain at children's birthday parties, but when their former school principals asked them to perform some skits for their schools' classes, Donna and Cindy began to write skits about fire safety, health units, and other topics related to the students' curriculums. They were so well received by the students, teachers, and administrators that Donna and Cindy were soon in demand by their surrounding public and private schools. They had found a niche in their clowning services, based on their professional knowledge and teaching backgrounds. Like Donna and Cindy, many home-based business owners often profit by meeting the needs of a niche market—a smaller, yet profitable customer base whose needs were not being met.

The home-based businesses in this book are, of course, not the only ones you can run out of your home, but they are some of the more successful and highly recommended ones by the women who own them. This is not a get-rich-quick book. It gives an overview of certain home-based businesses and lists important resources to use to get more information. Some have criticized me for being too elementary in the information that I have included, but this book is for those searching for home business ideas. It is only one step of many on the road to owning a successful home business. Business experts advise would-be entrepreneurs to thoroughly research any and all business ventures they are contemplating. This book is only one of many other books and resources, such as government agencies, business Web sites, business organizations, radio and television shows, and other women home-business owners, that you should investigate in order to learn not only how to start a home business but how to manage it so it grows into a profitable venture. It is up to you to achieve whatever business goals you plan.

The women mentioned in this book are just a few of the millions of women who are working from their homes, both part-time and full-time. You, too, can start your own business if you do your research and make the commitment to persist and make it happen.

It is my hope (and 101 wishes) that you, too, will find a satisfying and fulfilling home business that enables you to achieve both your professional and life goals! Good luck!

Explanation of Business Features

Each business profiled in this book contains most or all of the following details, depending on what information was available:

- **Description of the Business**—Describes the activities involved in conducting the business featured.
- **Start-Up Costs and Financing Sources**—Estimates what it will cost to get a business going and suggests some financing options.
- **Pricing Guidelines**—Provides an idea of what to charge for your business's services or products.
- **Marketing and Advertising Methods and Tips**—Offers suggestions for getting customers.
- **Essential Equipment**—Lists the basic materials and technology you need to start the business featured.
- **Recommended Training, Experience, or Needed Skills**—Describes the knowledge or background needed as well as tips for gaining experience.
- **Income Potential**—This is a general idea of the *potential* a woman can earn operating this business. You might note, however, that a business's profits are determined by the demand for a service or product by its customers. Two women operating the same type of home business may experience a large difference in the income their venture produces, depending on a variety of factors, such as region in which they operate, the income level of the customers they serve, and other such variables. See "What will you charge for your services?" in chapter 3, "Your Business Plan."

- **Type of Business**—Lists whether it is an "in-home" business or an "out-of-the-home" business, the latter meaning you have a home office yet do the work away from your home.
- **Target Market**—Describes the customers who will most likely use your products or services.
- **Success Tips**—Practical advice from home business owners themselves on what has made them successful. Note: The business owners quoted and profiled *do not* have business start-up information (such as a book, a publication, or an e-newsletter) *unless* otherwise noted in their credit information.
- **Franchises, Distributorships, and Licenses**—Lists related commercial business opportunities or ventures. (Listings are for general advice and suggestions only and do not constitute an endorsement by the author or publisher.) See chapter 4, "Franchises, Distributorships, Network Marketing, and Other Home Business and Work-at-Home Opportunities" for more information about investing in these opportunities.
- **For More Information**—Lists publications, books, trade associations, home study courses, business start-up guides, and other helpful resources. Note: Many associations *do not* have start-up business information, but, rather, they exist primarily for membership networking. To ensure a reply to your requests for information, please send a first-class long self-addressed, stamped envelope (LSASE). Many associations are nonprofit and are staffed by volunteers.
- **Additional Business Ideas**—Lists related business ventures.

If you have additional questions about a specific business start-up, please feel free to send me (the author) an e-mail at <pyhuff@hotmail.com> and write "Reader Question" in the subject line.

Part I

Home-Based Business Considerations

1

Before You Start Your Business

Several years ago, Pam, a mother of two, quit her job as a bookkeeper. "I liked my job but was tired of the looks I'd get from management if I missed work because one of my children was sick. Plus, after my expenses I was only clearing an extra $20 a week!" Pam decided to start her own bookkeeping service, which now grosses more than $40,000 a year. As busy as her business is, though, she still is able to arrange her business around her first priority—her family.

Pam is one of the millions of women and men who have begun home-based businesses since the 1980s and that continue to start them each and every day now in the 21st century. According to the U.S. Small Business Administration, the number of home businesses grew 20 percent between 1997 and 2000, and the American Association of Home Businesses <www.aahbb.org> says that more than 24 million Americans are home business owners.

It seems that more women are home business owners. The Center for Women's Business Research <www.womensbusinessresearch.org> (formerly the National Foundation for Women Business Owners) findings indicate that approximately 66 percent of home-based businesses are owned by women. Women have begun working from their homes for many reasons: high-quality day care, though improving, can be difficult to find and is costly; the need for both spouses to work to maintain a medium standard of living is almost a necessity; and technological developments and advances in computers, fax machines, and other office equipment have enabled the average person to set up an affordable home office.

In addition, in the 1970s women learned they could neither do it all nor have it all. Trying to balance their careers with family obligations and relationships with their husbands just did not work—except for the few superwomen who had some magic formula to make it all happen! Many women were tired of climbing the corporate ladder, having to do twice as much as their male counterparts just to be recognized.

Shannan Hearne-Fortner, an eBusiness marketing specialist and president of Success Promotions <www.successpromotions.com>, explains why she returned to a home business: "The main reason I returned to a work-at-home status was the outrageous cost of day care. It was becoming harder and harder to actually come out ahead each week with four kids in day care and after-school care. Also, I had to put a value on parenting. How much money did I have to make away from home to equal the value of raising our daughters myself instead of them being raised by someone else during most of their waking hours? And the third thing was, I'm a pretty good boss. It was hard to find a company to work for that was as understanding and flexible about my needs as a parent as I am. Hopefully, the day will come that I can offer employment to other parents who need flexibility as well."

Instead of surrendering all their goals and aspirations, women in the 1980s began to use their educations and previous work experiences to start their own businesses, many of which are still being run out of their homes. This is not to say, however, that everything is easier for the home-based business owner. The time spent on a home business may well exceed the "normal" 40-hour workweek; there can be endless distractions, including interruptions from family and relatives (usually when you are in the middle of a very important telephone conversation!); and your customers may think you are never closed and call you at all hours, day or night.

For example, Pam works about 50 to 60 hours a week, with approximately 20 hours of that time spent at clients' offices. Her daughter is in school, but Pam still has to make arrangements to have her son watched while she makes office visits. Pam says, "I try to work at the businesses when my son is in preschool. Luckily for me, I've just hired my mother to do part-time office work for me. This works out great because I not only have dependable help, but also a built-in babysitter if one of the children is sick."

Though a home-based business may lead to a more hectic home life, home-based businesses have the important element of flexibility not usually found in a regular 9-to-5 job. Home-based business owners can tailor their businesses to fit their needs as well as their families' needs. They also have the freedom to work in their offices at any hour, run their businesses according to their philosophies, and pursue any new opportunities their businesses may offer.

Most find the advantages of a home-based business far outweigh those of a "regular" job. As Pam says, "I'll never work for anyone else again!" Jerrie, who owns a gift basket business, takes her three-year-old son with her when she makes deliveries. She says, "I do not apologize for bringing my son. I believe with so many women beginning businesses who have small children, people are just going to have to accept that children will sometimes help or accompany their mothers."

Home-based business owners (whose numbers are increasing every year) usually start at the top. They are the presidents, the bosses, and the board of directors of their businesses, all in one. Unlike employees of other companies, every action they take affects their businesses in some way. They are responsible for all aspects of their businesses, which include financing and budgeting, marketing and advertising, dealing directly with customers and suppliers, keeping accurate records, and maintaining production of services or products.

Many women entrepreneurs formerly worked in the corporate world and concluded they could be more effective running their own businesses. Their business skills, honed while working for outside companies, greatly contributed to their successful business ventures. In fact, many business experts recommend first working in a business outside the home that is similar to the one you would like to create.

To some, running their own businesses becomes overwhelming, and they go out of business in less than a year. For those who persist (often working other jobs while starting their businesses), the rewards are great. As you will read in the examples in part II, women business owners have a distinct pride in what they have accomplished.

What types of businesses are run from the home? In the past, women babysat or ironed and mended clothes or made crafts from their homes to earn pin money, yet they were not seen as being business owners or entrepreneurs. At present, however, the types of home-based businesses are as varied as any list of established businesses. They include everything from catering to clowning and from garden consulting to cleaning. They are traditional and untraditional, with many more professionals opening home offices.

The home-based businesses featured in this book are owned and run by women. Some are full-time, some part-time, depending on the type of business and the time the woman has to put into her business. This book also can help any interested men, because today jobs are performed interchangeably by women and men, and often wives and husbands are either partnering in a home business or each one operates her and his own separate home business under one roof. I chose to focus on women's home-based businesses, however, because so many women are seeking alternative ways to balance their careers with their families and personal goals.

By featuring the women's businesses found in this book, I hope women who might have been hesitant about starting a business will be encouraged to go ahead with their ventures. For this reason, too, I have tried to be realistic in describing each business. There are no get-rich-quick stories here or magic formulas for instant success—only actual facts about real women working very hard to establish and run their own businesses.

Many of these businesses are service-oriented, because this type of business usually requires less start-up capital than others. Service businesses are increasingly needed to help meet the needs of the millions of dual-income families as well as for the burgeoning number of single-parent and single-income families. The expected growth in the number of senior citizens in the United States as the baby boomers age will also create a demand for in-home and other services.

What is a service business? It is one that fills a need in your community. How can you determine what people need? Listen! If you hear people saying over and over, "I wish there were someone who could help me . . ." or "I hate doing . . . !" or "I wish I could hire someone to do it for me!" there might be an opportunity for a service-type business.

Once you have an idea for one or two businesses, determine how many similar businesses are offered in your community. If there are others like the one you want to start, think how you could improve or interpret such a business in your way. You could offer better rates, offer better hours, target a wider (or smaller) age group, improve customer service, or offer door-to-door delivery. The next chapter goes into more detail about how to choose the best business for you.

Questions to Ask Yourself Before You Start

Where Will You Work?

Where you work will depend on whether your service involves going to your customers' homes or offices or their coming to you. With a cleaning business, for example, you (or your workers) will be going to clients' homes; but if you have a tax or financial service where your customers come to you, you will need adequate parking spaces and a home office, preferably with a separate entrance (or one that can be shut off from the rest of your house so that your customers do not hear the cartoons your children are watching or, worse, their squabbling!).

Your home office may be a corner, closet, room, or other space that can be used exclusively for your business. Pam's office is now in her dining room, but she has plans to remodel her garage into an office. She says, "I'd like my office moved where I can shut the door on it at the end of the day. Whenever I walk by [my dining room] now, I'm reminded of work."

Setting up an office—in no matter how small a space—will help establish your business as a serious venture to yourself and your family. If you plan to have your business be more than just a hobby, your work area will have to look professional. Determine what basic equipment you need, and purchase it new or used. You can always upgrade later as your business grows (and it will, if you are determined enough!).

Installing a separate telephone line for your business (with an answering machine or service or voice mail) is almost a necessity if you have a family. Just one teenager can tie up a phone for hours! You will lose business if your customers cannot reach you. A cellular phone is a good investment because it can be used from your home office but it also frees you from your home office because it allows your customers to reach you anywhere, anytime.

Establishing your own office or space will help you to set in your mind that you are "going to work." It may take some self-discipline, especially at first, to walk away from household distractions, but to succeed in your business, remind yourself to save that wash or tape that TV program to see later, after your business is closed.

Is It Permissible to Work from Your Home?

Before you open for business or begin to advertise, check with your local authorities about having a home business. Honey, who has a silk flower business, first checked with her township. She was given permission to open a home business as long as customer traffic and deliveries did not get so heavy that neighbors would complain. Honey says, "I also went to my neighbors to tell them what I was planning to do. They said they would not mind and thought it was a neat idea. One even gave me some orders!"

Your state may have regulations and licensing requirements for running certain businesses, such as catering; caring for animals, children, or the elderly; or operating a beauty salon. Check with your state department of health or social services, or call your local state representative or senator to get a listing of state agencies that issue small business licenses.

Your regional Small Business Development Center (SBDC) <www.sba.gov/sbdc>, a local Women's Business Center <www.onlinewbc.gov>, or a local SCORE office <www.score.org> will also have information about your state's business regulations and offer free or low-cost business counseling and seminars. (See "Government Resources" in part III.)

Who Should You Talk to Before You Start?

1. A good accountant can be worth his or her weight in gold! He or she can show you how to set up a good bookkeeping system and keep vital records for tax purposes. Two women who run a party business have this to say about their accountant: "We send him our quarterly statements, and he tells us how much money we are making and if we should even be in business!"
2. A lawyer who specializes in small business matters is a valuable resource. He or she can legalize your business name (even though you can do this yourself) and can give counsel on steps to take to protect yourself and your business from possible lawsuits.

   If you can only afford one hour of a lawyer's time, take it. Even a brief appointment may help save you time and prevent future costly legal mistakes. Good legal advice can give you the peace of mind you may need, especially if this is your first business venture. As your business grows, you can always hire a lawyer for more information.
3. A licensed property and casualty agent can evaluate your business insurance needs. These agents, unlike accountants or lawyers, usually do not charge a fee. They are paid a percentage of the policy premiums you pay. Start with the agent who handles your homeowner's policy. If he or she cannot help you, ask for a referral to another agent who can.
4. A growing number of financial advisers and home-based business and professional practice consultants provide

services for individuals and small businesses. A number of experienced business owners have become professional business coaches. These professionals can help set up your business: find start-up money, help with the bookkeeping, and suggest ways to manage and expand your business.

5. Of course, you should do some of your own research before you hire any expert's services. Check with these sources first:

    - Local chamber of commerce
    - Local women's business club(s)
    - State association of insurance agents
    - State bar association
    - Your bank
    - Local library for county business and professional directories
    - Other women with home-based businesses

    Talking to women who run home-based businesses may be one of your best research sources. These women can recommend the services of those who understand and have had experience in helping home-based business owners. It will pay off to look around for the best people to help you in your business. Remember to ask all the questions you can think of before you hire any experts. If you are not satisfied with their services, try someone else. After all, it is your business, and you know best what goals you want to achieve.

What Kind of Insurance Does a Service Business Need?

According to independent insurance agent Kathy Delp, "It depends on the type of business. For example, you may need more liability coverage if you have customers come to your home office, additional insurance to cover equipment if you produce a product, or insurance covering accidental breakage or damage if you work in clients' homes."

She recommends you check your homeowner's policy to see if it contains any personal business coverage. After you decide what you want covered, your agent can modify your present policy with an extension to adequately cover your business needs. If your present policy cannot be extended, your agent can recommend a company that will offer the coverage you need.

Kathy also believes that an independent insurance agency may be the best type of agency to ask about business coverage because it deals with many insurance companies. An independent insurance agency, which has flexibility because it's not affiliated with just one large company, can recommend the best carrier at the best price.

When purchasing insurance, home-based business owners should make sure they have adequate liability coverage and, second, enough business property coverage. If your car, truck, or van will be used in your business, check with your agent to make sure you are properly covered. Other types of insurance you may need include health, business interruption, disability, and life insurance.

Study your business insurance policy—know what is covered and to what extent—before you start up your business. Keep copies of your policies in a safe place. Also keep a listing of your agents and their phone numbers close at hand so you can easily call them if the need arises.

Will You Work Alone or with a Partner?

This is a good question to discuss with your attorney. He or she can tell you the advantages and disadvantages of a sole proprietorship (a business owned by one individual) and a partnership (a business owned by two or more persons).

Three out of four businesses are sole proprietorships. If you start a business by yourself, you are the sole proprietor. You make all the decisions; you decide which direction your business is to take; and you get any related tax savings and, of course, all the profits. In other words, it's your "baby."

As with a baby, though, a sole proprietorship is also the full responsibility of the parent (owner). You have to pay any business debts, and anything you own can be subject to liquidation if you cannot pay the debts off. You have to learn to handle all aspects of your business. You should have plans in place should you die or become incapacitated.

Most of the businesses featured in part II are sole proprietorships, and their owners have loved the challenges involved in their business ventures. If they were not sure how to handle certain aspects of their businesses, these sole proprietors went to people who could help them or they figured out their own methods through trial and error.

A partnership has the advantages of combining the skills, expertise, and capital of two or more persons. Partners share the responsibilities and the costs. Whether you have been friends for 25 years or just met recently, you should have a written legal agreement drawn up by your lawyer. Why? Unfortunately, two-thirds of all partnerships dissolve, many due to unresolvable differences between the partners.

The owners of one of the businesses featured in this book ran into difficulties and were ultimately unable to hold their partnership together. The partnership of two women who had been friends ever since childhood worked well until one of them got married. The husband was jealous of the time his wife gave to the business, so to placate him, she put in less time. Her partner became resentful that she was doing all the work. The married woman dropped out of the business to start one with her husband. As a result, the women's friendship has never been quite the same!

A lawyer can draw up a partnership agreement containing information such as how much each partner invests; division of salaries, duties, and responsibilities; participation of each partner in the profits and losses; what happens if one partner wants to sell out or dies; and other details to equally protect each partner's interest. A partnership must be based on trust, but people are only human, and a legal agreement can help prevent future hassles if you go your separate ways. (See "Legal Structure," in chapter 3, "Your Business Plan."

How Much Time Will You Need for Your Business?

Whether your business will be full- or part-time is, of course, a factor. Regardless of your choice, it is better to start small and grow with your business than to take on a full-size endeavor—unless you are completely prepared to do so.

Careful planning will save you time in the long run. There are scores of books and motivational tapes that can help you manage your time. Here are some basic time-management tips:

- Keep a record of a week's worth of day-to-day activities to see how many free hours you have per day.
- Set your priorities. Family, business, and volunteer work should each have its place. You may have to cut back on your volunteer activities or settle for a less-than-perfect house, but you will need all the extra hours you can find to get your business started while still having time for your family.
- Make goals and set tentative deadlines for meeting them. Decide what steps it will take to reach each goal and schedule them, one by one, on your calendar.
- Sit down with your family and tell them what you are going to do. Tell them you love them, but you are going to be busy starting a new business and so would appreciate all the help and understanding they can give. They'll probably be enthusiastic about your new job until the morning comes when you've forgotten to do the "white" wash. If you involve your family in your business from the start, they will be less apt to feel resentful.
- Be realistic. Remember that everything will take longer to accomplish than you expect. Be flexible and learn to make the most of whatever blocks of time are available during the day, especially if you have a family. One divorced mother of four has her own wallpapering and painting business. She says, "I work four days a week, leaving one for errands or family matters. I let my customers know that my family is first in my life and that there may be interruptions from time to time. If they cannot handle that, I will refer them to someone else."
- Get organized. At the beginning of each month, one mother, who has a basket and chair caning business, marks down her and her children's activities in different colors on a calendar. She writes down due dates for long-term projects (hers and her children's) so things are not let go until the last minute. She laughs as she says, "If anyone ever stole my calendar, I

would be lost! It would be far easier to replace a TV or VCR than it would be to remember everything that has been scheduled and written on that calendar!" She also plans a month's worth of meals for her family so she doesn't "have to think when making the weekly shopping list."

All schedules are subject to unexpected changes, of course, whether due to family illnesses, weather conditions, car or appliance breakdowns, and so forth. But by having a home-based business, the owner often has the advantage of being able to work around these crises.

If you are a woman with children, you will have to make the most of your free time. Keeping your office or work area organized will help you save time in picking up where you left off, whether to start a meal or take your turn carpooling. Write yourself a note to help you remember where you stopped. Periodically, file your papers to help keep your office in order.

A professional organizer says if it takes you longer than a minute to find something in your home office, you should take a few minutes to reorganize. The old adage "Time is money" applies to a home business, because any time you waste takes money from your pocket.

Will Your Business Be Full-Time or Part-Time?

Unless you have substantial savings put away or someone else to support you, starting a business full-time is usually not the best way to go. Many of the women business owners featured in this book are still working part-time in their businesses. Others went full-time after their part-time business warranted it.

According to the Small Business Administration (SBA), millions of people work at home part-time. Many of them work for other companies, but the number who work for themselves is increasing every year. Working part-time in your business will give you time to learn how to run a business. You can take courses as needed or work in a similar business to get the experience and know-how you will need in your own. Working at home part-time in addition to your regular job will also enable you to save money to invest in your business. Plus, in some cases you can maintain your health benefits. With the present health care crisis, you need health insurance, especially if you and your spouse are self-employed. It only takes one severe medical crisis to bankrupt an uncovered person or family! (Note: There are business owner associations, both local and national, such as the National Association for the Self-Employed [NASE], as well as specific industry organizations that offer health insurance for small business owners.)

Your business will dictate when it is time to go full-time, though you may decide you still like it just part-time. Either way, it's your decision, and you will have to decide what's best for you.

Will Your Business Be an "In-Home" Business or an "Out-of-the-Home" Business?

Some home-based businesses involve out-of-home work, such as landscaping, cleaning, and entertaining. Others involve more "in-home" work, such as writing, handicrafts, upholstery, and computer businesses. Many require that you go out to customers and then also do related work in the home office, as with a bookkeeping service.

In your chosen business venture, be aware of what percentage of your time will be spent doing in-home or out-of-home work. Knowing this will help you decide matters such as your wardrobe (professional image or working clothes), your child care needs, your home office hours, coverage of your office when you are away, and other needs of your business.

How Will Your Family Be Affected or Involved?

As mentioned earlier, discuss your business venture with your family. Let them know how much you need their support. Consider the following:

- *Expect an adjustment period.* Your family may have a hard time accepting that you really are working from home. They will interrupt you at any time, even when you may have an important business call. Let them know you are always there for them, but you have to do your work, too. It will take time to find the right balance between your family and business obligations.

- *Emphasize the positive.* Let your family know that you are flexible—you can arrange business hours so that you can be a classroom mother or take summer picnics, and so forth.
- *Involve your family whenever you can.* Linda, a freelance photographer, often takes her 10-year-old son on assignments whenever he is home from school. Linda says, "Justin acts as my assistant, carrying my tripod and camera bag and getting extra film for me. Sometimes, he even gets into the photos, like when I photographed a local herpetologist for a magazine article. I needed a shot of the man showing his snakes and lizards to someone, so I used my son. Justin got to hold a 25-pound python and a large iguana and now he has pictures to prove it!"

Lesley Spencer, mother and founder-director of Home-Based Working Moms <www.hbwm.com>, says, "I feel it is important to consider and reconsider your family relationships when you have your own business. As wives and mothers, I feel it is very important that we not put our businesses before our family and relationships. As mothers, we also have to be aware of the amount of time and energy children and a business can take from us. We need to remember that our spouses also need our time and attention. It's a balancing act that needs constant attention and evaluation."

If family members want to help out, give them responsibilities they are capable of handling, such as answering the phone, collating papers, or even creating designs or logos for brochures or pamphlets. JoAnn, who has a painting and wallpaper business, hires her high school daughter to help her in the summer. She lets her younger children paste paper that is ready to be hung.

If you have infants or preschoolers, it may be difficult to run a home-based business without help. Some women pay babysitters to come into their home to watch the children while they work. Others barter sitting time with friends who are home with their own small children or form neighborhood play groups.

These options allow home business women some uninterrupted time to make business calls and complete other home business tasks. And some work when their husbands come home.

It's not easy to have a home-based business and a family, and at times you may feel you are performing a crazy juggling act. JoAnn says, "My business has helped support myself and my family and I feel good about what I do. My children are proud of me, and I know I can be there when my kids need me. Need I say more?"

For More Information

Business Insurance

Insuring Your Business—What You Need to Know to Get the Best Insurance Coverage for Your Business, by Sean Mooney (New York: Insurance Information Institute, 1993). For the current price and ordering information, contact the Insurance Information Institute <www.iii.org>, 110 William Street, 24th Floor, New York, NY 10038; (212) 346-5500. The I.I.I. also offers free brochures (send an SASE): *Insuring Your Business Against a Catastrophe—Instructions on How to Develop a Catastrophe Plan Now to Avoid Losses Should a Disaster Strike* and *Insuring Your Home Business—A Guide to Help Home Business Owners Understand Their Insurance Needs.*

To Find an Independent Insurance Agent

Independent Insurance Agents & Brokers of America
127 South Peyton Street
Alexandria, VA 22314
E-mail: <info@iiaba.org>

Home Business and Family

C-E-O & Mom: Same Time, Same Place, 2nd ed., by Rochelle B. Balch <www.rbbalch.com> (Glendale, AZ: RB Balch & Associates, 2000).

The Entrepreneurial Parent: How to Earn Your Living from Home and Still Enjoy Your Family, Your Life, and Your Work, by Paul and

Sarah Edwards < www.workingfromhome.com > and Lisa M. Roberts < www.en-parent.com > (New York: Putnam Publishing Group, 2002).

How to Raise a Family and a Career Under One Roof, by Lisa Roberts. (Moontownship, PA: Brookhaven Press, 1997).

Let's Go into Business Together: Eight Secrets for Successful Business Partnering, expanded ed., by Azriela Jaffe < www.isquare .com/crlink.htm > (Franklin Lakes, NY: Career Press, 2001).

Mom Inc: Taking Your Work Skills Home, by Neale S. Godfrey with Tad Richards (New York: Simon & Shuster, 1997).

Mompreneurs: A Practical Step-by-Step Guide to Work-at-Home Success, rev. ed., by Patricia Cobe and Ellen H. Parlapiano < www .mompreneursonline.com > (New York: Berkley Publishing, 2002).

The Stay-at-Home Mom's Guide to Making Money from Home: Choosing the Business That's Right for You Using the Skills and Interests You Already Have, rev. 2nd ed., by Liz Folger < www .bizymoms.com > (Roseville, CA: Prima, 2000).

The Women's Home-Based Book of Answers: 78 Important Questions Answered by Top Women Business Leaders, by Maria Bailey < www.bluesuitmom.com > (Roseville, CA: Prima, 2001).

The Work-at-Home Mom's Guide to Home Business: Stay at Home and Make Money with Wahm.com, by Cheryl Demas (Naples, FL: Hazen Publishing, 2000).

Working at Home While the Kids Are There, Too, by Loriann Hoff Oberlin (Franklin Lakes, NJ: Career Press, 1997).

Organization and Setup

Home Management 101: A Guide for Busy Parents, by Debbie Williams (Vancouver, WA: Champion Press, 2001).

The Home Office and Small Business Answer Book: Solutions to the Most Frequently Asked Questions About Starting and Running Your Business, 2nd ed., by Janet Attard (New York: Henry Holt, 2000).

Home Office Life: Making a Space to Work at Home, by Lisa Kanarek (Gloucester, MA: Rockport Publishers, 2001).

The Home Office Planner: Hundreds of Great Ideas for Your New Office, by Barty Phillips (San Francisco: Chronicle Books, 2002).

Web Resources—Organizational Experts' Web Sites

< www.homeofficelife.com >

Lisa Kanarek's HomeOfficeLife.com.

< www.organizedtimes.com >

Debbie Williams's Organized Times.com.

Recycled Office Furniture

Independent Office Products and Furniture Dealers Association
(formerly Business Products Industry Association)
301 North Fairfax Street
Alexandria, VA 22314
(703) 549-9040
< www.iopfda.org >

Provides names of the nearest recycled furniture dealers in your area.

2

Choosing the Best Business for You

Do You Have the Right Personality for a Home-Based Business?

Many financial experts note that successful small business entrepreneurs have certain characteristics in common. How do you compare to their findings?

- ☐ Are you an independent-type person, not afraid to go in one direction while others go in another?
- ☐ Do you believe in yourself? When others ask, "Why?" do you ask, "Why not?"
- ☐ Do you know how to set goals for an objective and persist until you have achieved them, even if you make mistakes along the way?
- ☐ Are you well organized? Can you juggle numerous projects simultaneously? (Most women and mothers do this very well!)
- ☐ Do you have experience and/or knowledge in the business you are pursuing? If not, are you willing to take the time to learn the needed skills?
- ☐ Do you know where you can get professional help in running your business? (The resources listed in part III can be a start.)

- ☐ Were you or one of your parents ever self-employed before? Many people have a fear of starting their own business. Those who have grown up with self-employed family members usually understand what it means to run a home-based business.
- ☐ Are you a good money manager? Are you willing to start small and expand as you go along, instead of overextending your business before you become established?
- ☐ Do you have good people skills? Even though you work by yourself, you may be in the business of satisfying other people's needs. Do you have the ability to understand, communicate, and deliver what each customer wants?
- ☐ Are you flexible and adaptable with your business goals? Many entrepreneurs start out in one direction with their business, only to go in another, unexpected direction later. Successful business owners are wise enough to recognize a promising trend and follow it.
- ☐ Do you have the energy, drive, and patience to make your business work? The SBA estimates the average small business takes one to two years (or more) even to show a profit. Most likely you will have to make time for your business while trying to maintain your other activities (another job, family matters, and so on). You may end up working many hours over the "normal" 40-hour-a-week job!

How Do You Decide Which Business Is the One for You?

Think hard about what goals you want to achieve and what is important in your life. Then write them down. Visualize what you see yourself doing six months from now, a year from now, and five years from now.

If you don't have a definite idea of what type of business to start, assess your skills and interests to narrow your business choices. Filling out the chart on page 22 may help you determine what business is right for you. Copy the chart onto a wide piece of paper and fill in your responses.

	Education/Training	*Achievements*	*Skills Acquired*	*What I Liked Best About the Job. Why?*
Jobs				
Volunteer Positions				
Military Service Positions				
Hobbies				
Interests				

1. **Jobs**—List all the jobs you've ever held. Include part-time jobs and jobs held while you were in school.

   Education/Training—If you needed a degree, certification, or special training for any of your jobs, list them here. Having credentials can help establish you as an expert or a professional to your customers. Print your credentials on your business cards and promotional materials if they apply.

   Deborah Schadler's bachelor of science and master's degrees in education and her 10 years' teaching experience were the basis for the successful tutoring center she began from her home.

   Achievements—This is the time to brag about what you accomplished in each of your jobs! If you increased sales, started a new product line, organized a new program, or were responsible for any other important achievement, write it down. This process will help you analyze your strengths and give you more self-confidence as you list the results of all your work.

   Skills Acquired—On-the-job training can be as valuable as completing courses in the same subject—in fact, even more so if you are able to transfer those skills to your business. Why? You have had firsthand experience and have seen what works and what does not.

   What You Liked Best About the Job. Why?—You may have hated a job but not everything about it. If you add up all the things you liked about your jobs, you may get a better picture of what you like to do. It usually follows that if you like what you do, you will work harder at it—and so the better chance you will have to succeed in your business.

2. **Volunteer Positions**—Just because you were not paid does not mean you did not accomplish something. Volunteering your time shows dedication and direction of purpose. Write down any volunteer positions you've held and fill in the columns as you did with your paid jobs.

   In the past, women have traditionally been the volunteers in communities (which is one of the reasons they have been

willing to work for less than men) and often have been responsible for starting organizations. School parent-teacher groups, family support groups, and church committees are commonly directed by women. Fund-raising, organizing support, and leading the groups are just a few of the many activities an active volunteer contributes to an organization. Skills acquired and achievements made in your volunteer work are just as significant as those acquired in a paying job.
3. **Military Service Positions**—Relate any military experience, training, and education you've had to civilian occupations.
4. **Hobbies**—What starts out as a hobby for some people often turns into a full-time business. One woman made custom lampshades as a hobby, then turned it into a part-time job. When her husband was injured in a car accident, she was able to increase her business to full-time to cover their expenses until he recovered.
5. **Interests**—Write down your interests and examine them to see if you have the knowledge to adapt them to a service business. In selecting a business, feel free to think up new and different businesses or a new twist on a standard idea. One woman developed a sewing service for the physically disabled after a disabled friend requested clothing that would be easy to take on and off. Sometimes our interests can lead us into related hobbies or work. For example, Linda always liked to take pictures. As her interest grew, she read everything she could on photography and, of course, kept taking lots of pictures. She later went to work at a photo store and also took a night photography course. Now a mother of young children, she has a home studio specializing in children's portraits and takes freelance photos for businesses and writers. Linda says, "I love being able to earn money doing something I enjoy!"

Remember, don't be afraid to brainstorm for business ideas and to search for your particular niche. You just might find yourself in a business that is both special and successful!

A business niche is an untapped market of potential customers whose needs are not being met. For example, a husband and wife started a lawn-mowing business but found that most of the grounds of larger companies and the bigger lawns of homeowners were already being mowed by other landscaping and mowing contractors. But an owner of one of these larger landscaping businesses suggested the husband and wife approach owners of townhouses and other small properties—properties he was too busy to take on. The husband and wife marketed to these owners and found a lucrative niche market catering to people with smaller properties.

When Ami White, owner of an online party supply business, SweeterCelebrations.com, and an online gift business, MySONflower.com, was asked how she found her business niches, she replied, "I have had several business ideas and a few that I actually tried out for awhile such as gift baskets, candy bouquets, and handmade soaps that I did for a short time. I just kept working and searching until I found what I was happiest doing. Some people know exactly what they want to do but when they start doing it, they find out it's really not for them. Or it can work the opposite way when they try business ventures that they do not think they will like and discover they are really good at doing these. I am now pleased to say that I have found some great suppliers for *both* of my businesses. I found out, through trial and error, that I am not the creative type. I love to connect with people. The Internet has helped me find others who make or sell what I like and I can then provide it for my customers."

For More Information

Books, Home Business Ideas

The Best Home Businesses for the 21st Century: The Inside Information You Need to Know to Select a Home-Based Business That's Right for You, rev. ed., by Paul and Sarah Edwards <www.workingfromhome.com> (New York: Putnam Publishing Group, 1999).

The Shoestring Entrepreneur's Guide to the Best Home-Based Businesses, by Robert Spiegel (New York: St. Martin's Press, 2000).

Books, Choosing a Home Business

Finding Your Perfect Work: The New Career Guide to Making a Living, Creating a Life, by Paul and Sarah Edwards (New York: Putnam Publishing Group, 1995).

Turn Your Passion into Profits: How to Start a Business of Your Dreams, by Janet Allon (editor of *Victoria* magazine) (New York: Hearst Books, 2001).

Which Business? Help in Selecting Your New Venture, by Nancy Drescher (Grants Pass, OR: PSI Research/The Oasis Press, 1996).

Online Course

"How to Find the Perfect Home Business for You," by Liz Folger <www.bizymoms.com>.

3

Your Business Plan

Taking Care of Legalities and Other Preopening Business Matters

Discuss starting your business with experts—your lawyer, accountant, bookkeeper, insurance agent, business consultant, and financial adviser, as well as local, state, and federal agency offices that oversee business practices. Because laws for home-based and small businesses vary from town to town, county to county, and state to state, you need to follow proper steps to avoid possible future legal conflicts.

Networking with other home-based women entrepreneurs can also be a great help in getting start-up information. Some cities, counties, and states have organizations or offices specifically funded to help women get started in their own businesses. Do your research—there may be more resources out there than you thought!

Selecting a Business Name

Experts suggest using a word or words that describe what you do in your business name. For example, the business Karen's Custom Cushions lets prospective customers know that Karen, the owner, will do just what her business name says—sew custom-made cushions for chairs, outdoor furniture, benches, and so forth. With Deborah's Teach Me Tutoring Service, you assume students who need help with their studies will use her services.

At the same time, it is wise to have a name that is not too specific and can cover a number of related services. Often a person starts a business in one direction and then finds an opportunity to go into another. For example, with the Teach Me Tutoring Service, Deborah began tutoring high school students who were having difficulty in certain subjects. Today, she has expanded her services to include coaching students to qualify for scholarships; offering a reading-readiness summer camp; teaching English to new citizens; helping newly promoted company executives improve their grammar and writing skills; and helping brain-trauma patients relearn basic reading and writing in a local hospital's rehabilitation center. If Deborah had named her business Smith's Algebra Tutoring, technically she would only have offered algebra remedial instruction and thus have closed off other business opportunities.

When you decide on a name, register it with both your county and state officials. This registration—also known as DBA, "doing business as"—protects you from someone else using your name for their business (assuming the name you picked has not already been registered by someone else) and permits you to conduct business using that name. Contact your county clerk's office and your state business office for the procedure. You then can open a bank account, cash business checks, arrange for a separate business telephone line, and conduct general business activities under your business name.

Before you decide on and register a name, it is also a good idea to conduct a trademark search to ensure your name is not being used by anyone else and also is not used as a registered trademark. It will help you avoid any possible legal conflicts. You can do this in several ways:

1. Visit one of the Patent and Trademark Depository Libraries (PTDL), which have directories of federally registered trademarks plus an online database of registered marks and appli-

cations for trademarks awaiting approval. To find a PTDL in your state, visit the Web site of the U.S. Patent and Trademark Office (PTO) <www.uspto.gov> or call the PTO's Trademark Assistance Office at (703) 308-4357.

2. Use your favorite Internet search engines.
3. Hire a professional trademark service or expert.

Legal Structure

Your business will fall under one of the following legal structures:

- A *sole proprietorship* is a business that is owned and operated by one person. It is the least costly way—in terms of registering and legal fees—of starting a business.
- A *partnership* is a business formed by two or more people. Because many partnerships dissolve, it is best to have legal agreements drawn up by your attorney to prevent unforeseen business disputes.
- A *corporation* is a more complex business association in which the business becomes a legal entity in itself with powers and liabilities independent from the persons who own it. Some states now permit individuals to establish limited liability companies, known as LLCs. LLCs are less costly to create and maintain than incorporating and still limit the risk to your personal assets. Business experts recommend a sole proprietor look into incorporating when their business profits reach or exceed $100,000 a year. When you first start your venture, it is much more likely that your home-based business will take one of the other two forms. As always, consult with a lawyer who is familiar with business law.

Permits, Licenses, and Resale Tax Number

Depending on where you live and the kind of business you will be conducting, you may have to get a permit, a license, a resale tax number, or all three to operate. Locally, check with your city, town, or borough as to zoning and other regulations regarding a home business. For county regulations, contact the office of your county clerk. Please note also that some state and national laws exist that regulate and/or prohibit certain types of home businesses such as commercial cooking, sewing apparel, making toys and dolls, and some others. Contact your state's department of commerce and the U.S. Government's Department of Labor to determine if there are any legal restrictions regarding your specific business. (See part III, "Resources," for contact information).

The business identification numbers you must get in order to conduct business include the following:

- A *resale tax number*—If you sell any product to consumers, most states require you to collect sales tax. Your resale tax number is also your tax exemption number, which allows you to buy supplies wholesale without paying sales tax. Contact your state department of revenue to get a number and sales tax filing procedures.
- A *tax exemption number*—If you sell products wholesale only, you do not need to collect sales tax, but you do need a tax exemption number, which also allows you to buy wholesale supplies without paying sales tax. If you sell wholesale, you must record the resale tax number of the shop that buys from you for your tax records.

Establish a Business Bank Account

When you are ready to open for business, you should also open a business bank account. This will keep your start-up money and income earned separate from your personal account. If your business is not a corporation, you will need a Social Security number or a federal employee identification number (if you plan to hire employees) from your local Internal Revenue Service (IRS) office. If you are a sole proprietor of your business and do not employ others, your Social Security number can be used as your federal identification.

Talk to other women business owners in your area and ask what financial institutions they use and why. Shop around and compare the services of a number of banks and see which one best fits the needs of your business.

Your Business Plan

Just as you need a map to help you find the route to an unknown destination, you need a plan to help you determine which direction(s) to go to get your business up and running. Your first plan should estimate your goals, expenses, and how much you plan to charge for your services, as well as show how you plan to attract and keep customers. After you actually begin your business, you will find you will need to revise your plan yearly, or even monthly, as your business grows.

There is no right or wrong way to write a business plan, but you do need to write one. Putting your plans on paper takes your dream of owning a business and begins to turn it into reality. There are no guarantees that your business will succeed, but a well-written and researched business plan plays an essential role in a business's success.

How do you write a business plan? Check your local library for books on business plan basics. Contact your local chamber of commerce or Small Business Development Center (SBDC) to help you draw up a plan. (See "Government Resources" in part III.) You may also want to contact a professional business consultant to help you write a business plan. (See "Business Plan Consultant" in part II.)

Some important questions to consider as you write your plan follow. This list of questions is not all-inclusive. You may have additional questions to ask. Remember that the more questions you ask, the more complete your research will be. And the more complete your plan, the fewer surprises you'll have as you start out—and the more successful you are likely to be!

1. **What is your business?**
   First, write a broad definition, such as cleaning, entertainment, or child care. Then specify, for example, what type of cleaning you will be doing—homes? offices? both? Or what

kind of child care—daytime? evening? drop-off? It is important to keep both your broad and specific definitions in mind when your business starts. Your business may stay in the same broad category such as cleaning, but it may change directions as to the specific kind of cleaning you do, depending on what is most in demand in your area.

2. **What are your objectives?**
   Be honest with yourself and list everything you hope to achieve, both businesswise and personally. Also list both short-range and long-range objectives. Short-range objectives may include setting up your home office or applying for a loan to purchase basic equipment. Long-range objectives may include getting a certain number of customers in the first year or making a profit (for many small businesses, it may take two years before any profit is seen).

   Review your objectives daily, weekly, monthly, and yearly to see if your business is headed in the right direction. You may need to add (or delete) some objectives as your business grows.

3. **How do you research your market?**
   For your business to be successful, you have to know (a) if people have a need for your service and (b) if they are willing to pay for it. Big businesses hire marketing research firms for thousands of dollars to find this out for them. You, however, can do your own smaller market survey. Here is a list of criteria that should be included:
   - *Who will use my services or products?* Identify your potential customers so you can target your business at them. Your local chamber of commerce can tell you the income level of your town's residents, the average number of people in a household, age levels, spending trends, and other economic details. Other service business owners in your area can also tell you about their customers. With products, you can do some test-marketing with free samples to get some initial feedback. Do not be discouraged if your preliminary research shows that the people in your area will

probably not use your services or products. Check out nearby communities. Their residents, even though close in distance, may have completely different profiles, such as college students or military personnel.

- *Do they need my services or products?* Ask people you know (and those you do not) if they would use your service or product and find out why or why not. If they use a similar service or product or they have in the past, ask them what they would like to see improved.
- *What would they be willing to pay for my business services?* Survey similar businesses, both in your area and in other communities, to get an idea of what prices are charged. Then decide (based on your projected start-up costs and monthly expenses) how much you will need to charge to meet your financial objectives.
- *Is the market growing for my services or products?* You need to know if the sales potential for your business will be increasing. Contact your local chamber of commerce and nearest SBDC to find out how many service businesses are in your area. Also find out how many other businesses like yours are in existence and if they are busy. Check with county offices dealing with small businesses, women's advisory councils, or the U.S. Department of Labor's *Occupational Outlook Handbook* to track down statistics on business growth in your area.
- *Examine competing businesses.* Interview customers from a competing business. Can you offer something unique and possibly better? Many businesses begin to lose customers when they grow because they forget the adage "Satisfied customers are repeat customers." You may be able to attract customers by learning from your competitors' mistakes. But rather than criticize your competition, focus instead on the unique benefits that your business offers its customers. It is more professional and you may even get referrals from competitors for a market they really do not serve.

4. **How will you get your customers?**
Now that you have a pretty good idea who your customers are (be aware that your typical customer may change as you discover who really uses your business services), you will want to (a) tell them what services or products you provide, (b) emphasize what sets your business apart from the competition and how they will benefit from patronizing your business, and (c) explain how they can engage your business services.

Going back to your definition of your business will help you when you want to list the services your business offers in your advertising and promotional materials or in answer to queries about your business. You may add or subtract to these services, depending on what your customers want. Pam started her business by providing routine bookkeeping. She soon expanded her business services to include billings, mailings, correspondence, and other business management matters as her customers asked her to do more. You should also create promotional materials such as a one-page, résumé-type business sheet or flyer to hand or send out in response to inquiries about your business services or post on community bulletin boards around town.

Ask yourself what your business offers customers that the competition cannot provide. Be specific. Can you offer a better price? Better service? Faster service? Will your business handle an aspect other businesses will not (odd hours, small jobs, etc.)? Emphasizing your business's unique features in your advertising will help you draw customers to try your business services. Then it is up to you to keep them!

Using the information from your preliminary research, you now have an idea of the customers you want to direct your business promotion toward. For example, if your research reveals your best prospective customers are young, married couples, you would choose different methods of promotion than if your customers are single, professional businesswomen. You will want to decide the most effective means to promote your business, so the target customers will be aware of your business and how they can engage your services.

5. **Which promotional and marketing methods will you use?** Promotion is essentially communication. The better you communicate to your prospective customers, the more business you will receive. Knowing which advertising will be the most effective may take a period of trial and error. Business promotion falls into two categories: paid and free.

Paid promotion or advertising comprises classified and display ads in newspapers, magazines, community booklets, and so forth; radio and television (network and cable) ads; promotional ads including those on signs, vehicles, pencils, and business cards and in telephone and/or business directories and direct mailings.

Paid advertising, next to equipment, can be the biggest expense of your new business. Some business experts estimate your advertising costs could be anywhere from 2 percent to 10 percent of your annual gross income, so you want every advertising dollar to count and to reach those who are likely to patronize your services.

Before you spend a single penny on advertising, list all the local advertising sources and find out their rates. Ask whoever is in charge of advertising what types of people read or listen to (if it's radio) their advertising. Spend time reading and listening to business ads, especially those offering business services. Notice how many are repeat ads from week to week. You might even call some of the businesses that advertise and ask them about the number of responses they get to their ads.

When you are ready to advertise, begin placing your ads where they will be read by prospective customers based on your research. If you are not confident about writing a classified or display ad, ask the advertising representative for help. Most offer free assistance in copywriting and layout.

Run your ad for as long as you can afford and feel it will be effective. Keep track of the response to each ad, in terms of the number of responses and number of customers who actually hire your services. You can then gauge whether it is worth it to continue that specific ad or not.

As your budget allows, try different types of media advertisements. Radio and television will reach several communities. With the rapid increase of cable television, it is worth trying their advertising. "Free" newspapers may also get good responses. Eventually, you'll know which method brings the best results for your business.

Free promotion or advertising includes public talks and appearances, press releases, feature articles in local newspapers or on Web sites, demonstrations, promotional events, or donations of your services to fund-raising auctions that help people know your business exists.

Free publicity, especially for a service business, is one of the best ways to get business with just a minimum expense and a little effort and ingenuity. You can begin by sending out a press release to local newspapers and to editors of related online publications and Web sites announcing your business start-up. You can also use press releases later when your business is established to announce the sponsorship of a special event or expansion of your business services.

Editors will be more likely to print your release—or follow up with a feature article—if you stick to the proper format (check sources in your library on how to write press releases). A press release must be neatly typed, doubled-spaced, concise, and written on your business stationery. You might also want to include a black-and-white photograph of you conducting business.

Do not forget to include the basics of news stories—who, what, why, when, where, and how. Make sure the answers to these questions appear in the first couple paragraphs of your release. Do not forget to include how people can reach you for more information about your business services. Some other free methods of publicity include:

- *Word of mouth.* A good recommendation by a customer to a potential customer is one of the best ways to get people to know your business is up and running. Begin by telling friends, relatives, and anyone you talk to that you have started your business. Always carry your business cards to hand out, and give several to your friends and relatives to pass on. Network with other men and women in businesses (professional women's clubs, members of chambers of commerce, other home-based business owners, etc.). They may even give you tips to help your business grow—as long as your business does not compete with theirs. Then always give the best possible service as you conduct your business. Word of mouth can keep your business going if you give that little extra to your customers. Remember, however, that word of mouth can also spread negative comments about your business, so never forget your customer, no matter how much your business grows!

- *Community bulletin boards.* You see these everywhere—in stores, banks, restaurants, and so forth. Ask permission to post your business cards or flyers (sometimes only nonprofit organizations are permitted to post notices). Then post your cards or flyers on the board, preferably at eye level. Check back periodically to see if you need to replenish or rearrange your notices (sometimes accidentally or purposely, your materials may be covered up by other flyers). Make sure, too, that your notices look professional and not something hastily scrawled and put together.
- *Offer a seminar or be a speaker.* Patricia Gallagher offers short courses for an adult education program on how to run a day care center, based on her own former home-based business. She gets paid as an expert on this subject, plus she sells her book *So You Want to Open a Profitable Day Care Center.* She also has been a guest speaker for many community groups and has appeared on radio and television shows.
- *Have a "happening."* Hold a special occasion in connection with your business. You can announce it in a press release and either invite the newspapers to take photos or take your own. Elizabeth, who owns a garden consulting business, conducted a children's gardening workshop in

the spring. The children learned planting basics, and Elizabeth had free publicity for her business.

- *Donate your services to a charitable event.* Auctions for nonprofit organizations, raffles, and other fund-raising events provide opportunities to publicize your business, not to mention being tax-deductible as well.

6. **What will you charge for your services?**

This depends on a number of factors: your expenses and your time; the quality of your service; your potential market; your competition's prices; how long you have been in business (you may charge more as you improve your business expertise and get a reputation for excellence); and what your customers are willing to pay.

A national or professional trade association connected with your business may offer current rate information and other helpful sources in establishing pricing and billing. Check with your library for business directories and the *Encyclopedia of Associations.*

Some service businesses may have price-charging guidelines, but if your business is unique or the only one in your community, you may have to set your own prices to make what you believe—and what your accountant or your bookkeeper tells you—to be a reasonable profit.

To find out if you are making a profit, you have to know your break-even point—when your projected income just covers your costs. At this point, you do not make or lose any money.

The SBA's pamphlet *Business Plan for Small Service Firms* gives this formula to find the break-even point:

$$\text{Break-even point (in sales dollars)} = \frac{\dfrac{\text{Total fixed costs}}{1 - \text{Total variable costs}}}{\text{Corresponding sales volume}}$$

Once you know your break-even point, then you can begin to set a price for your services, knowing that you must at least charge a certain amount to reach this point. A service price for each job can be determined by using the following formula:

material/supply costs + labor (your time) + overhead + the percentage of profit you want to make = your price.

Overhead costs include all costs other than materials used and your labor. If your business is your sole source of income, do not forget to include costs such as health insurance, Social Security, taxes, loan payments, monthly utilities' bills, and other expenses in your overhead calculations.

Make sure you also charge for your labor. One of the biggest mistakes women business owners make is that they charge too little for their time. Women are the ones who traditionally have done volunteer work and so may not be used to charging for their time. Some women who have not been in the business world do not put a value on their work the way their male counterparts do. Thankfully, these attitudes have changed since the 1970s, with more women having worked outside the home, having obtained more higher education and training, and holding executive positions with their companies. Pam explains what she says to her clients when they raise a question about her bookkeeping fees: "I tell them I have two children I am helping to support and this business is not just a hobby to me! That usually stops any complaints. My clients know I offer good service at competitive prices."

What percentage of profit do you include in your price? Some women use the service price equation above and double the total for their final price. Their price formula would be:

[material/supply costs + labor (per project or hour) + overhead] × 2 = price

Once you've arrived at a price, compare your price to your competitors' prices and see if potential customers would pay what you need to charge. It may take some time before you come up with the right price for you and your customers. With a service business, prices often change based on a particular job or extenuating circumstances. Keep careful records of your time and expenses, and your business's cash flow, the amount of money paid out for expenses compared with the money you received for your services and/or products. When in doubt, consult with your bookkeeper or accountant for help in determining what to charge.

The women profiled in this book each have their own methods of determining their prices based on their experience with their business. For example, Donna Kramer, a wedding and party consultant, charges 20 to 25 percent of the gross cost of whatever part of the plans she handles, plus the cost of supplies she uses.

Judi Wagner, who has a balloon decorating service, followed the price guidelines in a how-to video purchased through a balloon supply catalog. She also uses her own planning and estimation sheets to help determine the costs for each event.

For certain service businesses such as Kramer's and Wagner's, it is important to ask for a deposit when you are hired for a project. Wagner asks for a nonrefundable deposit, which will at least cover her costs in case her client backs out.

The pricing guidelines and formulas given in this book will not guarantee you a profit in your business. On average, a small business takes two years to show a profit. By carefully monitoring your records and seeking professional advice when you need it, your business can become self-supporting and profitable. The women who have successful businesses have done just that.

7. **How will you get repeat customers?**

"The best customers are satisfied customers." This adage applies to all businesses, especially small ones. You need your customers and cannot take any of them for granted, at any time. Following are some tips to keep your customers coming back:

- *Be professional.* Treat your customers fairly, honestly, and with courtesy. Use business cards, stationery, forms, or brochures to help establish your business as official. Return phone calls and reply to letters and other inquiries promptly. Follow the ethics and etiquette of your business and avoid underhanded tactics.

✤ *Be flexible.* Jackie, who has a successful catering business, says, "Don't be afraid to go the extra mile for your customer by being competent in your business and complimentary in dealing with your customers."

Going the extra mile might mean fulfilling a special request for a customer or helping out in a way another business would not have time to do. As long as it does not interfere with the workings of your business or cause conflicts with your family or coworkers, you may find it advantageous to help out your customers in special ways. For example, Pam Baker will sometimes see clients on Saturday mornings or other unscheduled times, but she reciprocates by occasionally taking time off from her business to attend to family matters.

Small businesses can often be more flexible with clients' needs than larger businesses, and every client likes to be treated with special attention. Clients will show their appreciation with repeat business and referrals to others.

✤ *Provide top-quality service or product.* You may not be the biggest provider in your service area, but you can do your best for each client, and the word will spread to other prospective clients. Providing top-quality service and/or a product requires understanding what your client wants or needs. You can better understand a client's expectations by asking the following questions:

Have you ever used a similar service or product?

If so, why are you considering changing?

What do you expect (generally) from my service or product?

What do you need most from my service or product? (Please be specific.)

Whom do I contact if I have questions or problems that might arise?

What is your payment schedule?

How long will you need my service? (Year-round? Seasonal?)

Do you use the services or products of any other independent businesses?

What questions do you have about my service or product?

This list gives you an idea of what you might want to ask new clients before and after they patronize your business. No doubt, you will develop your own list or survey questions based on your own experiences. Take careful notes of your clients' answers, and make a copy of them for future reference. Conduct surveys on a regular basis to ensure your business is continuing to meet the needs of your customers and clients.

If you have questions when you begin working, do not assume you know what your client wants—ask more questions. It's better to clarify something in the beginning than to do work a client does not want or need.

- *Evaluate your business.* When you first start up your business, you will want as much feedback as possible from your customers. Ask them if they were satisfied with your service or product. Why or why not? Did they have any suggestions for improving your service or product? Are there any additional services or products they would like your business to provide? Would they use your business services or products again? Would they recommend your business services or products to another business or person?

  You can ask these questions in person, over the phone, or in the form of a questionnaire. If your customer is extremely satisfied with your service, ask if they will write a letter stating the reasons they are satisfied. Then ask permission to use this testimonial to attract prospective customers.

  When you have a number of testimonials, you can put them into a promotional notebook or packet like Carol has. Carol, the owner and president of an organizational business, put together more than 30 articles and letters of satisfaction about her business into a portfolio that she gives to prospective customers. To each portfolio, Carol attaches plastic holders that contain her business cards and brochures. The result is a professional-looking and complete promotional package that both advertises and describes in detail Carol's business services.

Even if your business becomes successful to the point that your customers seek out your services or products, you should keep assessing your business. By monitoring your customers' needs and satisfaction levels, you can keep your business up to date. If you lose touch with your customers, you may find them stolen away by competitors.

✣ *Know how to handle customer complaints.* No matter how many satisfied customers you have, someday you will probably have to handle a customer complaint. If you are the sole proprietor of your business (and actually do your business services), it is hard not to take complaints personally.

JoAnn Kaiser, who has her own wall decorating business, says, "When I had my first complaint, I was devastated! It really upset me that my customer was not satisfied. Fortunately, after I talked to my customer, I realized I had misunderstood what she really wanted. I changed what she wanted at no cost and my customer was happy again."

It's good business to adhere to the motto "The customer is always right" (even if they really aren't). If you are courteous, are diplomatic, and really listen to the customer complaint, you should be able to handle most problems. Of course, some customers are easier to work for than others. If you get repetitive complaints from one person or business and you believe you (or your employees) are doing the best possible job, you might suggest, politely, that you will help them find another service business similar to yours.

It is good, too, to have a service contract, especially for larger jobs. This protects both you and your customer should problems develop. If you are unsure how to word such an agreement, consult your lawyer.

8. **How will you financially plan your business?**
This is one of the most important parts of your business plan. A good financial plan includes information such as start-up costs, sources of financing, a balance sheet showing your assets and liabilities, and a budget for each month of your first year of operation, along with a profit-and-loss projection, break-even point determination, and a cash-flow prediction. Financing will be discussed further in chapter 5, "Financing Options for Your Home-Based Business and When Is Venture Capital Right for Your Business?"

A business plan takes time to research and put together, but the better defined it is, the better you will be able to follow the right path toward success.

For More Information

Books, Start-Up Information

The Complete Idiot's Guide to Starting a Home-Based Business, 2nd ed., by Barbara Weltman (New York: Macmillan Publishing, 2000).

Homemade Money: How to Select, Start, Manage, Market and Multiply the Profits of a Business at Home, 5th ed., by Barbara Brabec (Cincinnati, OH: F & W Publications, 1997).

The Small Business Start-Up Guide, 3rd ed., by Robert Sullivan (Great Falls, VA: Information International, 2001).

Books, Business Plan

Anatomy of a Business Plan: A Step-by-Step Guide to Building a Business and Securing Your Company's Future, 5th ed., by Linda Pinson (Chicago, IL: Kaplan Professional Company, 2001).

Business Plans Made Easy, rev. ed., by Mark Henricks (Irvine, CA: Entrepreneur Media, 2002).

Your First Business Plan: A Simple Question and Answer Format Designed to Help You Write Your Own Plan, rev. ed., by Joseph Covello and Brian J. Hazelgren (Naperville, IL: Sourcebooks, 1997).

Software, Business Plan

Automate Your Business Plan, version 10, by Linda Pinson <www.business-plan.com> 2002.

Business Plan Pro 2002, by Palo Alto <www.paloalto.com>.

BizPlan Builder 8, by Jian <www.jian.com>.

Web Sites, Business Plan

<www.jian.com>

Jian—Developer of business plan software. Includes an online "Business Planning Workshop" <www.jian.com/workshop/index.htm>.

<www.bplans.com>

Palo Alto—Software company, maker of business, marketing, and Web site planning software. Provides more than 60 free sample business plans you can view online.

<www.business-plan.com>

Web site of Linda Pinson—Business plan expert. Lists her book and companion business planning software, *Automate Your Business Plan.*

<www.onlinewbc.gov/docs/starting/basics.html>

Women's Online Business Center document—"Business Plan Basics."

Books, Naming Your Business

Names That Sell: How to Create Great Names for Your Company, Product or Service, by Fred Barrett (Portland, OR: Alder Press, 1995).

Trademark: Legal Care for Your Business and Product Name, by Kate McGrath, Stephen Elias, and Sarah Shena (Berkeley, CA: Nolo Press, 2001).

Books, Legal Structure

INC. Yourself: How to Profit by Setting up Your Own Corporation, 9th ed., by Judith H. McQuown (New York: Broadway Books, 2001).

Nolo's Quick LLC: All You Need to Know About Limited Liability Companies, by Attorney Anthony Mancuso (Berkeley, CA: Nolo Press, 2000).

The Partnership Book: How to Write a Partnership Agreement, 6th ed., by Attorneys Denis Clifford and Ralph Warner (Berkeley, CA: Nolo Press, 2001).

Partnerships: Laws of the United States, by Daniel Sitarz (Carbondale, IL: Nova Publishing, 1999).

Sole Proprietorships, by Daniel Sitarz (Carbondale, IL: Nova Publishing, 2000).

Web Sites, Business Legalities

<www.corporate.com>

The Company Corporation—Details on incorporation services for businesses, plus information and business tips.

<www.easyas123.com/insidestory.htm>

Article by Judith Dacey, CPA—"The Inside Story on Incorporation: Is It Right For You?"

<www.llcweb.com>

The Limited Liability Company—Provides information about this business form, including a comparison chart of business structures.

Books, General Business Management

Guerrilla Saving: Secrets for Keeping Profits in Your Home-Based Business, by Jay Conrad Levinson <www.gmarketing.com> (New York: John Wiley & Sons, 2000).

Software for Monitoring and Predicting Your Cash Flow

Microsoft Excel, by Microsoft, Inc. <www.microsoft.com/office/excel>.

Up Your Cash Flow, by Granville Publications Software <www.upyourcashflow.com>.

4

Franchises, Distributorships, Network Marketing, and Other Home Business and Work-at-Home Opportunities

For years, women have been earning money from home in business enterprises such as distributorships, network marketing, and home business ventures. If these options interest you, make sure you thoroughly investigate any companies connected with these ventures to be sure (1) they are legitimate (See sidebar, "Buyer Beware"); (2) they are a good match with your business and marketing skills; and (3) they have the best potential for *you* to make the money to meet your needs and goals.

Franchises

Instead of starting a business independently, you may want to look into the options of franchises or distributorships.

What is a franchise? With a franchise, you pay someone else for the right to sell and distribute their products and use their trade name or trademark. A franchise fee is charged and, depending on the franchise, there may or may not be ongoing royalty fees, advertising costs, or the mandatory purchase of the company's supplies needed to run the franchise.

Franchises are now a popular way of being in business for oneself. According to the Franchise Opportunities' Web site <www.franchiseopportunities.com>, there are more than 750,000 franchise businesses in North America, generating in excess of $1 trillion in sales. The advantages to owning a franchise include the following:

- Risks and failures are fewer than when starting an independent business.
- Franchises can provide product name recognition.
- Franchisors often provide a location and professional start-up advice.
- Franchisors will monitor franchises and help with any operating difficulties.

The disadvantages include the following:

- Franchises can be expensive to acquire.
- A franchise is not really your business. What you really have is a contract to operate the franchise, usually for 10 years, which may or may not be renewed.

Although a franchise may be an attractive option for starting a home-based business, it is not something to rush into. For any of the business ideas given in this book, thoroughly research the business or franchise in which you may be planning to invest your time and money. This may take months or even years. Because a contract is mandatory in a franchise, it is wise to hire a lawyer who is familiar with franchise legalities to protect your investment.

Fortunately, the Women's Franchise Committee, part of the International Franchise Association (IFA), is a good source of information for women interested in starting a franchise business (see later in this chapter for the IFA's address). Franchise experts suggest that women should think about the following questions before buying a franchise:

- ✤ What are your personal strengths and how can you use them in each franchise?
- ✤ What hours do you want to work? (9 to 5?) Does working nights and weekends bother you?
- ✤ Do you like working directly with customers or would you rather work behind the scenes?
- ✤ How much capital do you have to invest? Or how can you obtain the capital you need?

And women should ask the franchisors these questions:

- ✤ Based on my investment, what rate of return and break-even point can I expect?
- ✤ What costs should I expect to pay before I make a profit for myself: fees, rents, wages, and so forth?
- ✤ What is a typical day in the business really like?
- ✤ What regular support can I expect from the franchisor? Between regular visits, how accessible is the franchisor when I have a problem?
- ✤ What ongoing training for employees, managers, and owners does the franchisor provide?
- ✤ What is the length of the franchise contract and how easy is it to renew?
- ✤ What are the reasons for disenfranchising, that is, reasons that I can leave the franchise and the reasons that the company can ask me to leave its systems?
- ✤ Does the home office compete with me for business?
- ✤ What is the company's regional and national five-year expansion plan and what role can I play in it?
- ✤ At what cost and under what criteria can I expand to additional locations or add more territories?

- What is the required advertising budget and how will it be used to benefit me directly?
- What is the franchisor's mission statement and what does it say about its relations with franchises?

It is also very important to request from franchisors their Uniform Franchise Offering Circular (UFOC), which they are required to provide you by law. Note that it is recommended that you consult with a lawyer familiar with franchise contracts *before* you enter into any franchise agreement.

For More Information

Associations

American Association of Franchises and Dealers (AAFD)
P.O. Box 81887
San Diego, CA 92138
<www.aafd.org>

"The AAFD is a national nonprofit trade association representing the rights and interests of franchisees and independent dealers throughout the United States."

International Franchise Association (IFA)
1350 New York Avenue, Suite 900
Washington, DC 20005
(202) 628-8000; (202) 628-0812 fax
<www.franchise.org>

The IFA is a membership organization of franchisors, franchisees, and suppliers. Also publishes the magazine *Franchise World* and such franchise-related publications as the *Franchise Opportunities Guide, Buying Your First Franchise, How to Be a Franchisor,* and *CFA Franchise Canada: The Official CFA Directory.* Its Women's Franchise Committee seeks to help women understand and take advantage of the diverse opportunities that franchising offers to women.

Government Resource

The Federal Trade Commission (FTC)
CRC-240
Washington, DC 20580
< www.ftc.gov >

The FTC provides online articles concerning buying a franchise and general franchise and business opportunities.

Books

The Franchise Bible: How to Buy a Franchise or Franchise Your Own Business, 4th ed., by Erwin J. Keup (Grants Pass, OR: PSI Research/The Oasis Press, 2000).

Franchises and Business Opportunities: How to Find, Buy and Operate a Successful Business, by Andrew Caffey (Irvine, CA: Entrepreneur Press, 2002).

The Shoestring Entrepreneur's Guide to the Best Home-Based Franchises, 1st ed., by Robert Spiegel (New York: St. Martin's Press, 2000).

Tips & Traps When Buying a Franchise, rev. ed., by Mary E. Tomzack (Oakland, CA: Sourcebook Publications, 1999).

Web Sites, Magazines

Following are just two of many print publications offering business start-up and management information including franchises and business opportunities. These are available online or at local bookstores or newsstands.

< www.entrepreneur.com >
Entrepreneur magazine.

< www.homebusinessmag.com >
Home Business magazine.

Web Sites, Franchising Information

< www.betheboss.com >
Be the Boss—Features a franchise directory, informative articles, and worksheets.

< www.sourcebookpublications.com >
Sourcebook Publications—Offers franchising books, databases, and consulting services.

Distributorships and Network Marketing

Generally, a less-expensive way to be affiliated with another established business is to be a distributor for them. As a distributor, you are a wholesaler who has purchased the rights to market one company's goods (not numerous companies' products as an independent sales rep would do) to customers within a given (though not always exclusive) territory. For example, each Hallmark store is run by the person who bought the rights. You buy the company name, but you pick and choose the products you wish to sell at that particular location. A distributorship may also be a franchise held by a distributor. A distributorship differs from a franchise in that all you are doing is purchasing the rights to run the company; however, you can run it any way you wish. With a franchise, you must generally follow the business operations' guidelines as stipulated by the franchisor.

With multilevel marketing (MLM; also known as network marketing), a distributor not only sells the company's products but will enlist others to sell these products or services under their supervision—called downline. You, as the recruiter, would then receive a percentage of the enlistees' sales.

According to the Direct Selling Association, 65 to 70 percent of direct sales are made through MLM, but MLM accounts for only 3 percent of all retail sales. Whether you sell cosmetics or baskets, there are thousands of distributors who have made money with direct sales with legitimate companies such as Mary Kay Cosmetics or Longeberger Baskets. Unfortunately, there have been many bogus network marketing programs that were nothing more than pyramid scams, and the people who were on the "bottom" of the pyramid lost all their money.

As a distributor in network marketing, you are in business for yourself and set your own hours. Generally, you purchase the

Buyer Beware

Here are three resources that provide information about business scams you should avoid:

- The Better Business Bureau (BBB). Look in your local telephone directory or search the Web site <www.bbb.org> for the office nearest to you.
- The Federal Trade Commission (FTC), CRC-240, Washington, DC 20580; (202) 326-2222. This federal office publishes a number of reports about business and consumer scams. You can also register a complaint. Though the FTC cannot resolve individual disputes, it can take action if there is evidence of a pattern of deceptive or unfair practices. Write, call, or visit their Web site <www.ftc.gov> to access this information.
- The National Consumers League's National Fraud Information Center and Internet Fraud Watch. For information about this nonprofit consumer advocacy organization's publications, the latest information about business and consumer scams, or to report a suspected fraud, call (800) 876-7060, or visit their Web site <www.fraud.org>.

starter kit with order forms, samples, and supplies that you sell directly to the consumer. Here are some questions and guidelines to ask yourself and to follow concerning network marketing:

- Do I like or use the products or services I will be selling?
- Do I like the persons with whom I will be dealing? Do my instincts say to trust them?
- How long has this company been in business and can I talk to a number of other distributors with this company?
- Is the company product-oriented rather than recruitment-oriented?

The Direct Selling Association alerts you to avoid the following:

- Salespeople who deprecate other products, firms, or salespersons.
- Salespeople who take advantage of your lack of experience.
- Salespeople who falsely tell you that you have won a contest or that they are taking a survey.
- Companies that charge an entry fee much more than the cost of a sales kit.
- Companies that pressure you to purchase a large number of supplies and products but will not repurchase them if you should decide to withdraw from the business.
- Companies that sell few or no products to customers.

If you work with a legitimate company and feel confident to handle the decisions required as a distributor and network marketer, you can be a success at this home-based, money-making, alternative business venture.

Jackie Ulmer, founder of Street Smart Wealth <www.streetsmartwealth.com> says, "Network marketing is a solid way for entrepreneurial women (and men) to build a lucrative business from home, using many of the skills learned in the business world. It is *not* a get-rich quick scheme, but rather a unique way to achieve success, both personally and financially."

Ulmer adds, "To be successful, it helps to start with a business plan and a mission statement for your business. The business plan would consist primarily of day-to-day marketing activities and steps to promote your business. It is important to gain a solid base of both customers and representatives. It is also very important to note, that like any business, it takes time, patience, a budget, and persistence to create a profit and, eventually, a substantial income."

"Network marketing is really a business of sharing a unique product line with others, and then focusing on those who have an interest and can truly benefit from what we offer," concludes Ulmer.

Other Home Business Ventures

Besides franchises, distributorships, and multilevel marketing, some other ways to sell another company's products are through licensing and just general business opportunities (packages, wholesale buying, and so forth). Many home business opportunities are advertised in magazines, in newspapers, on radio, and on television. As with the previously discussed business ventures, you should approach any opportunity with a skeptical attitude before signing any checks. Here are several important questions to ask yourself or the seller:

- ✤ As an owner of this business opportunity, what will my daily business activities involve?
- ✤ How much money do I want to earn?
- ✤ How much time do I have to give to this new venture?
- ✤ What is the asking price of the opportunity and is it negotiable?
- ✤ Can I pay by credit card (making it much less of a danger of losing money than when paying by cash or check)?
- ✤ Can I talk to other buyers of the business opportunity?

You can look into home business opportunities that interest you, but be skeptical of ones that promise big bucks and little work. There is no substitute for business success other than hard work and persistence—unless someone gives you a ready-made business complete with manager and employees. Plus it's much more thrilling to succeed through your own efforts, but make sure to be educated and know all the angles about what you are venturing into!

Whichever way you sell another's products or services, be cautious and investigate the business thoroughly before you invest even one dollar.

For More Information

Opportunities for distributorships and franchises (as well as licensing) can be found in advertisements and articles in larger business newspapers, such as the *Wall Street Journal,* or in the annual business opportunity issues of business magazines such as *Entrepreneur* and *Home Business* and others.

Associations
American Business Opportunity Institute, Inc.
c/o Andrew A. Caffey
3 Bethesda Metro Center, 700
Bethesda, MD 20814

Send an LSASE for information about publications, programs, and services.

Direct Selling Association (DSA)
1275 Pennsylvania Avenue, NW, Suite 800
Washington, DC 20004
<www.dsa.org>

Nonprofit trade association for companies who sell their goods and services directly to consumers. Members include Avon Products, Mary Kay, and others whose goods and services are sold directly to consumers. Members abide by a code of ethics; Web site has a listing of members, a calendar of events, and other information about direct selling and what it is about.

Multi-Level Marketing International Association (MLMIA)
119 Stanford Court
Irvine, CA 92612
<www.mlmia.com>

Membership comprises companies as well as distributors that are involved in the multilevel marketing (MLM) aspect of direct selling. Write or visit the Web site for membership information and a listing of books, videos, and other products.

Books
Dream Big! A Woman's Book of Network Marketing by Cynthia Stewart-Copier (Holbrook, MA: Adams Media Corp., 2000).

Home Businesses You Can Buy: The Definitive Guide to Exploring Franchises, Multi-Level Marketing, and Business Opportunities Plus: How to Avoid Scams, by Paul and Sarah Edwards and Walter Zooi (New York: Putnam Publishing Group, 1997).

E-Book: *Bizy's Guide to Building a Successful Network Marketing Business* by Jackie Ulmer; for ordering information, visit the BizyMoms Web site <www.bizymoms.com>.

Magazines

Step into Success, P.O. Box 712, Lakeland, MI 48143. Magazine founded by Belinda Ellsworth, editor-in-chief, written for women involved in direct sales and other businesses, offering resources, helpful articles, and motivational tips. Write or visit the Web site <www.stepintosuccess.com> for more information about the publication and books and related products.

Work-from-Home Options: Finding Legitimate Work-from-Home Jobs

Many persons ask about (legitimate) work-from-home options for various reasons: they do not have the funds, time, or inclination to start a home business; their health is poor or they have a limiting disability; they are the primary caregiver of children or elderly relatives who need constant care; or for some other reason that requires them to stay at home. Telecommuting—working at home for an employer—has been and continues to be a growing trend, but that is usually a working arrangement between an employer and an already-employed worker. So the question is whether you can find *legitimate* work-from-home jobs (such as stuffing envelopes or assembling products) if you are not already employed by a company. The answer: "Maybe, but these jobs are difficult to find!" Here are several reasons why:

- *Certain types of home work are illegal.* Some regulations by the federal and state governments forbid companies from hiring home workers for certain jobs involving sewing, jewelry making, and other industries. These laws are the result of past home worker abuses by employers. For information, contact your local and state officials and visit the Department of Labor's site <www.dol.gov> and search for "home work."

- *IRS independent contractor (IC) guidelines can be confusing.* Employers may wish to avoid hiring home workers because of the complicated IRS guidelines they must follow as to who is and who is not an IC or an employee, especially someone working from their home. For more information, visit the Nolo Press Web site <www.nolo.com> for articles in the section "Working as An Independent Contractor."
- *Employers are hesitant to hire an unknown worker.* Few employers will trust a person they do not know with company materials or responsibilities. Those new workers employers do hire often come from referrals by present (trusted) workers and only after an interview and a trial working period. That is why when seeking a home work job, people should first search in their own area for home work opportunities. Note, too, that it just makes more practical sense for employers to have employees in one location in terms of such issues as quality control, cost, health and safety, and, of course, liability rather than having workers scattered about in private dwellings.

Thus, if you are seeking a home working job, you should first take an assessment of your own skills. And second, you should ask around your own neighborhood for businesses that may need part-time help. If you become a valued employee and the job can be performed (legally) in a home setting, then your employer may permit you to take the job home. Many companies these days will often "outsource" certain kinds of work to independent contractors, depending on their skills and qualifications.

Another question would be, "What types of work are people doing from home?" Just a few of the many ingenious ways people are earning money working from their homes and homes of others are waiting in people's homes for repair persons or deliveries; being a greeter at Realtors' open houses; being a mystery shopper (posing as a shopper for a company in order to evaluate their employees' customer service); and other unique ways of earning money on one's own. You could also approach women home business owners who might need assistance with their business's management tasks such as mailings, answering e-mails, telemarketing, or customer service.

Remember: *There are many, many work-at-home scams.* Scam artists abound everywhere, including on the Internet, to take money from those who wish to work from home. Follow the adage "If it sounds too good to be true, it probably is" and *never* send any money for information. However, there are *legitimate* work-from-home jobs out there—but as with any venture, it will take some effort to find (or create) your ideal work-from-home situation!

For More Information

Book

The Work-At-Home Sourcebook, 8th ed., by Lynie Arden (Metairie, LA: Live Oak Publications, 2002).

Support Organizations for Moms Who Work from Home

Home-Based Working Moms <www.hbwm.com>.
Work-At-Home Moms <www.wahm.com>.

5

Financing Options for Your Home-Based Business and When Is Venture Capital Right for Your Business?

Financing Your Home Business

Financing your new business venture(s) is one of the biggest obstacles you will face in your start-up phase. Adequate financing can either make or break your business's success and future growth. The quest for you is to determine the total amount you will need to open and operate your new venture. It bears repeating to emphasize the importance of writing an effective business plan to reveal two major categories of expenses: *one-time start-up costs* for equipment, legal and accounting fees, business promotional materials, business phone hookup, advertising, and so forth; and *basic operating expenses,* which will help you figure your profit margin.

After determining your venture's estimated expenses, you need to decide what type of capital your business needs. Basically, there are three types of business financing: equity, debt, and alternative financing (or a combination of these). In *equity financing,* individuals or institutions put money into your business and in turn receive either some control over your business's operations or are repaid through profit sharing or when a company is sold. With *debt financing,* you borrow from a bank or an alternative financial institution that usually expects to be repaid over a specified length of time and with interest. Lastly, there is *alternative financing,* which can include everything from accounts receivable financing, leasing, and credit cards to a home-equity line of credit or severance package money. Many new entrepreneurs also use *creative financing,* which is a combination of any of these methods plus possibly some original ones of their own.

Here are some popular alternative financing methods:

- **Part-Time Profits or Job**—More than three-quarters of all home ventures are started part-time. Most of these earnings are put back into the business to meet its capital needs. Or you can moonlight at a part-time job for cash.
- **Credit Cards**—A few years ago more than half of all women used credit cards to finance new businesses because there were fewer financial resources than exist for women today. Credit cards are still good for fast cash, but look for ones with the lowest interest rates and then pay off the balance before rates increase.
- **Selling Personal Assets**—The sale of personal items such as antiques, jewelry, and stocks may provide extra funds.
- **Early Inheritance**—Check with your accountant or tax specialist to see how much money can lawfully be given to you.
- **Barter**—A barter exchange is still a taxable sale or income (keep careful tax records) but can provide a product or service exchange.
- **Grants, Awards, Contests**—Grants, which are not as readily available as some sources would have you believe, may be given to qualifying businesses. Some business associations

and nonprofit organizations may help with loans or give cash awards. Check, too, in entrepreneurial publications for announcements of programs that come with cash awards, prizes, or in-kind products and services.

In continuing the discussion about finding financing for your business, equity financing—having an individual or institution venture capitalist "invest" in your company—usually pertains to businesses that have high profit margins, the potential for rapid growth, and the possibility of giving these investors a high return if the business should "go public" or be acquired by a larger corporation. The advantage of this financing is that the infusion of working capital does not have to be repaid like a loan. The disadvantage is that these investors (venture capitalists) often have the right to review your management decisions and make strategic decisions concerning your business.

The Online Women's Business Center recommends that if you need less than $500,000 in equity you should go to private investors such as ACE-Net (the Angel Capital Electronic Network), which is a new SBA computer matching service for investors and business owners. (You can find further discussion of ACE-Net later in this chapter.)

Debt financing involves loans, line of credit, and special loan programs such as those offered by the SBA or by state or city governments. Other variations of debt financing are loans from friends and family (make sure, though, that you treat them like a professional lender with a contract and interest payments!); borrowing against your house (home equity line of credit or second mortgage), retirement, pension, or life insurance; or a personal bank loan. Again, your business plan will be a deciding factor in your getting many of these loans.

Federal Government Sources

- Contact the U.S. Small Business Administration. Call (800) UASKSBA for SBA offices nearest you for more information on guaranteed loans to small businesses such as LowDocumentation

Loans (Lowdoc), FASTRAK Loans, Microloans, the Women and Minority Prequalification Pilot Loan Program, and the Certified Development Company Program.

- Visit the Web sites of the Online Women's Business Center <www.onlinewbc.gov> and Service Corps of Retired Executives (SCORE) <www.score.org> to locate centers and SCORE chapters nearest you for information and assistance.

State Government Sources

All 50 states have programs and services that provide various means of support for small businesses, including minority or women's opportunities. Contact the offices of your local state senator and state representative for referrals and information.

Local Government Sources

Besides the federal and state offices in your area, ask your local government if any business funding or support programs exist.

Other Sources

- Local business groups and associations are excellent sources of networking information about lending institutions and existing community entrepreneurship programs.
- Local foundations, colleges, and business schools may also sponsor business counseling and support.
- National associations, such as the National Association of Women Business Owners (NAWBO) <www.nawbo.org> and Women Incorporated (WI), 1401 21st Street, Suite 310, Sacramento, CA 95814, also provide members with information on funding programs they may sponsor.

Thoroughly research all possible financing resources available to you and then decide which ones will best help your business get the backing it needs to start and succeed. Once you have obtained financing, concentrate on your marketing plan for continued growth and profits. Set up a business budget, scrutinize every purchase, and you may never need to seek financing again.

Additional Resources

Books

Free Money for Small Businesses and Entrepreneurs, 4th ed., by Laurie Blum (New York: Wiley, 1995).

Start-Up Financing: An Entrepreneur's Guide to Financing a New or Growing Business, by William J. Stolze (Franklin Lakes, NJ: Career Press, 1997).

Venture Capital: What Is It and Is It the Right Financing Option for Your Business?

With the much-publicized rocket growth in recent years of tech companies financed with venture capital (VC), plus the dramatic increase of venture capital funds over the last 20 years, it may seem to many entrepreneurs that millions are to be had just for the asking. Not quite! Statistics show that only a very small percentage of companies receive venture capital, and most of those are for expansion activities, not start-ups. Venture capitalists may interview hundreds of applicants before investing in only a few selected companies with favorable investment opportunities.

What Is Venture Capital and Who Are Venture Capitalists?

"The Venture Capital Industry: An Overview," an article posted on the National Venture Capital Association's site <www.nvca.org>, states, "Venture Capital is money provided by professionals who invest alongside management in young, rapidly growing companies that have the potential to develop into significant economic contributors."

Venture capital is usually not mentioned in conjunction with home-based businesses primarily because this type of financing is most often sought by already-established businesses with a proven track record of solid profits and potential growth. However, with more women-owned companies acquiring venture capital, it is important that a woman entrepreneur be aware that this type of financial resource is available for her, especially if her home or small business grows to the point that she will be seeking money for expansion. To help clarify what venture capitalists are and are not, here is some additional information:

- Venture capitalists are "active" financiers, helping to guide and foster the growth in the companies in which they have invested.
- Venture capitalists do invest in companies at all stages of a business's life cycle.
- Venture capitalists may specialize in one or two industry sectors (such as health care, computer services, and so forth), may limit their funding to a certain geographical area, or may invest in a variety of companies.
- Venture capital companies generally do not invest in oil, gas, or mining; real estate; or retail companies.
- Venture capitalists do not generally seek a permanent arrangement but rather eventually seek to exit the investment, depending on their firm's investment goals and strategies, through initial public offerings (IPOs; the most visible type of exit for a venture investment) or through mergers or acquisitions (the most common).
- Some venture capitalists *do* invest in non- or low-tech companies, not just the well-publicized high-tech companies, but business experts say that entrepreneurs will have to do a thorough search to find them.

What Kinds of Venture Capital Exist?

Venture capitalists can make up several types of firms, including the following:

- Private independent firms, which have no affiliations with any other financial institutions.
- Affiliate or subsidiary firms, which make investments on behalf of banks, insurance companies, outside investors, or the parent firm's clients or which are direct investors or corporate venture investors, subsidiaries of nonfinancial, industrial corporations, making investments on behalf of the parent firm itself.

Some other types of investment groups include the following:

- Angel groups, which are informal or formal private (wealthy) investor groups that help to fund businesses that are yet too small to attract professional venture capital. These "angels" do not usually require a large piece of your company in exchange for their money.

  One resource is the ACE-Net, the Access ("Angel") to Capital Electronic Network <http://ace-net.sr.unh.edu/pub>, a Web-based service sponsored by the Office of Advocacy, U.S. Small Business Administration, which helps angel investors and small businesses looking for early-stage financing find one another. A fee is charged and companies must register their offering with the appropriate federal and state securities trading agencies as well as submit a Small Corporate Offering (SCOR) form for approval to be listed.
- Government-affiliated investment programs such as Small Business Investment Companies (SBICs), which are venture capital firms licensed by the SBA to provide either long-term debt or equity financing to qualified small businesses. According to an SBIC fund director, an SBIC's average investment in a company is $1.5 million (compared to the average investment of $9 million by other venture capitalists). SBICs are generally located more in smaller towns and rural areas of the United States. Note, though, that these private equity firms are for *already-established businesses in later stages*. For information about SBICs, contact your nearest SBA office or visit <www.nasbic.org>.

  There are now several SBICs that are SBA-backed women-owned venture capital companies, like Capital Across America <www.capitalacrossamerica.org>, which is based in Nashville, Tennessee, that was founded by Whitney Johns Martin; the Women's Growth Capital Fund <www.womensgrowthcapital.org>, founded by Patty Abramson; and others that you can find listed on the Women's Business Center site <www.onlinewbc.gov>. These women-owned SBICs generally differ from other VCs in that they loan the money to the women business owners in such a way that allows them to retain control of their companies. They also fund primarily already-established businesses and not start-up ventures.

Is It the Right Funding Option for My Business?

If you think your business has reached the growth stage that it would be a good prospect for an equity investment, experts advise you to research and learn the different types of venture capital funds available, especially those that invest in companies similar to yours.

While each venture capital company or investor will have its own criteria that companies have to meet, here are just a few of the considerations they'll want to see in a prospective company:

- Significant returns over a relatively short time period.
- A company with a definite "edge" over competitors.
- Adequate access to existing distribution channels.
- Potential for significant growth and profits in the next several years.
- Companies with a strong management team, character, and commitment.

What Questions Should Small Business Owners Ask Themselves Before They Seek Venture Capital?

Before beginning a search for venture capital, financial experts recommend you ask yourself if you are ready to share in the ownership of and the control over your company that usually is required of you if venture capitalists invest in your company. This may be both psychologically and emotionally challenging to you, especially if you were the sole founder and creator of your business. Business experts say you should also ask yourself additional questions like:

- Why am I seeking venture capital?
- What are my business's financial goals?
- In what stage of development is my company?

What Are the Steps Involved in Finding and Applying for Venture Capital?

If you have decided that seeking venture capital for your home or small business is an option you wish to pursue, there are a number of steps involved. *Before* you approach a venture capital firm, experts advise that you should:

- Consult with an attorney, an accountant, and others familiar with venture capital arrangements and securities for possible referrals and ongoing advice.
- Research and make a listing of prospective investors that match your needs and company profile.
- Prepare a complete and well-documented proposal, including a comprehensive business plan.

In your venture capital search, business experts especially caution you to:

- Avoid investors who want a money-back guarantee on their investment should the venture fail. It is a risk for you both.
- Avoid any person or firm that requires you to give them money in the beginning. Check out any company's background, too, and get references to see if it is truly legitimate.
- Avoid wasting valuable management time if your business is not a good candidate for venture capital funding. Neglecting your daily business's operations may lead to business failure!

The Bottom Line

Venture capital financing is not essential for your company's success. Many businesses have prospered very well without it, by using alternative (and often creative) financing strategies. Home business owners are generally advised by experts to pursue virtually every other financing source other than venture capital funding. Depending on the success and growth of your business, though, it may be a viable option someday in the future. You may reach the point someday that you believe your company has the right combination of a unique idea with a large-scale market and a high (and rapid) profit potential so that it would be worth the effort it would take for you to obtain this type of financing.

As with any business decision, take the time first to conduct the preliminary research in order to be knowledgeable about what you would like to do, and of course, consult with reputable and qualified experts to help you avoid costly mistakes.

For More Information

Associations

Associations and their staff do not "match" companies seeking financing with venture capitalists. It is recommended that you do your own research about venture capital companies that interest you and approach them directly with your ideas.

Canadian Venture Capital Association (CVCA) <www.cvca.ca>. CVCA's directory is available as a PDF file that can be downloaded at no charge from the Web site. Note: CVCA does not provide a matching service, recommend, or in any way get involved with any deals between their members (investors) and people seeking venture capital financing (investees). You must contact directly any of the funds that you are interested in speaking to about their respective plans and, please, no phone calls.

The National Venture Capital Association <www.nvca.org>. Educational and networking opportunities for people who wish to learn more about equity investment.

Books

Angel Investing: Matching Startup Funds with Startup Companies—a Guide for Entrepreneurs and Individual Investors, by Mark Van Osnabrugge and Robert J. Robinson (New York: John Wiley & Sons, Inc., 2000).

The Insider's Guide to Venture Capital, 2002: Who the Key Players Are, What They're Looking for, and How to Reach Them, by Dante Fichera (Roseville, CA: Prima, 2001).

Pratt's Guide to Venture Capital Sources, by Stanley E. Pratt (editor) (Westport, CT: Greenwood Publishing). Check for the latest edition in your public or local college library's reference section.

Web Sites

< www.businessfinance.com >
America's Business Fund Directory.

< www.financehub.com >
FinanceHub: Venture Capital on the Web—Includes articles and database of investors with links to venture firms.

< www.startupbiz.com >
StartUpbiz.com—Includes a number of relevant links to investment capital sources and to leading VC firms.

< www.vfinance.com >
Venture Capital Resource Library—Features a bookstore, a glossary of terms, news, and so forth.

Part II

101 Best Businesses

Special Event Services

1
BALLOON DECORATING

This service business provides balloons to decorate clients' homes or offices for special occasions such as birthday, theme, and company parties; or celebrations for newborns, anniversaries, graduations, retirements, and so forth. Other services may include creating special table centerpieces, balloon deliveries in clown or character outfits, and balloon "drops," in which balloons filled with ordinary air are suspended in large nets from the ceiling and are released in a colorful cascade. You may also combine this service with other event-planning services.

As the business owner, you meet with clients in your home or theirs and fill out a planning sheet to agree on the kind and placement of balloons (sketches by clients are helpful). Then you give a cost estimate with the aid of an order form you've had printed up and take a nonrefundable deposit that will at least cover your initial costs if the customer should cancel. Your telephone number (or a contact person's) should be listed on the customer's copy of the order form in case there are any questions.

Start-Up Costs and Financing Sources

- Approximately \$500 to \$1,200 for basic supplies, rental fees, and brochures and flyers.
- Personal funds, loans from family or friends, small business loan.

Pricing Guidelines

Follow industry recommendations. Professional balloon decorators usually offer their customers several balloon packages with set prices, plus an a la carte price list of extras like table centerpieces and/or arches and trellises that customers may order. One balloon decorator recommends that after you provide your customer with an estimate, you ask for a nonrefundable deposit 60 to 90 days prior to the event to at least cover the cost of your supplies if your customer should cancel.

Marketing and Advertising Methods and Tips

- Place advertisements on community bulletin boards, attach business cards to balloon arrangements, pass out flyers with your business description, sign up with local newspapers' business directories, take a booth at bridal shows, post a signboard outside events, and encourage word-of-mouth referrals. Advertising in the business section of your local phone directory is advised for this type of business.
- Send direct mailings to newly engaged couples, school districts that hold formal dances, and various organizations. This is an effective way of getting business.
- Put together a portfolio or photo album of your work to show to potential customers.
- Offer to donate your balloon decorating services at a community nonprofit organization's event.
- Les Wigger of Balloon Wrap, Inc., recommends having a Web site and listing your e-mail address. He says, "[E-mail] is a great way to do this solicitation. It is quick and easy to respond to."

Essential Equipment

Balloons, mylars (foil-like balloons), curling iron to seal the mylars, netting, assorted marbles (to anchor balloons), helium tanks, a hand truck, air and gas fillers, and other miscellaneous supplies (such as scissors, string, ribbon, tape, client order forms).

Optional: forms for arches and trellises.

Recommended Training, Experience, or Needed Skills

- Have a flair for decorating, and, as one decorator says, "Know how to tie balloons!"
- Study how-to videos, and, if possible, apprentice with another balloon decorator.
- Attend balloon artists' conventions.

Income Potential

$250 to $400 per booking.

Type of Business

Out-of-the-home.

Target Market

Engaged couples, families of retirees, companies and organizations that hold regular banquets, new parents, schools, community organizations and businesses celebrating anniversaries, grand openings, and other special events.

Success Tips

- Try different methods of advertising so potential customers can hear about your service.
- When you order supplies, try to order for several bookings at one time. It saves on shipping costs, and usually discounts are given for larger orders.
- Be considerate. Make sure you know what and if you are supposed to remove or clean up after you decorate a customer's home or a hall. For example, use tape or bags of marbles to anchor your balloons and decorations to avoid leaving thumbtack holes in linens, tables, or walls.
- The National Balloon Center suggests the following: develop a game plan, keep good records, attend classes, study manuals and videos, and practice.
- In marketing another balloon business idea—balloon delivery (see "Additional Business Ideas")—Joyce Gowens, author of

the BizyMom's e-book *Making Money with Balloons* and founder of the Rainbow Deliver-Eez <www.rainbowdelivery.com>, says, "If you want to stay successful in the balloon business you need to advertise! Whether it is passing out flyers or business cards or putting an ad in a church newsletter, a school newspaper, or a weekly mailing such as the *Penny Saver.* You have to let people know that you are at their service. I hear this so often, 'Wow! I didn't know I could have balloons delivered! Great!'"

Gowens continues, "Getting your business name 'out there' truly does not have to be costly. The best way I have found is to add a magnet to my business cards and then stick the card to mailboxes. In this business, your product is not needed 'at that moment,' so your card will be placed on the refrigerator and when an occasion rolls around your number will be right there! One last quick tip . . . Do not let any event or occasion pass you by! Never 'assume' that people will just call you because it is graduation day. Put those flyers out there, get your business cards out there and *tell* them to order balloons!"

Franchises, Distributorships, and Licenses

Balloon Wrap, Inc.
18032 Lemon Drive, #C-144
Yorba Linda, CA 92686
(714) 993-2295
Contact: Les Wigger
<www.balloonwrap.com>

Offers free consulting services and lifetime licenses. Dealerships range in price from $495 to $1,595. Video training, supplies, and inventory are all available from BWI.

For More Information

Books

Festivities Publications, 815 Haines Street, Jacksonville, FL 32206; <www.festivities-pub.com>. Balloon design and business books, industry magazines, videos.

Magazines

Amy Stewart's Balloon Journal, P.O. Box 6250, Beverly Hills, CA 90212. Send an LSASE for subscription information.

Balloons and Parties Magazine, Partilife Publications, LLC, 65 Sussex Street, Hackensack, NJ 07601. E-mail: <info@balloonsandparties.com>.

Supplies

The Anderson Balloon Company
P.O. Box 16788
Cleveland, OH 44116
<www.a-balloon.com>

Balloons Everywhere, Inc.
16474 Greeno Road
Fairhope, AL 36532
<www.balloons.com>

Web Sites

<www.balloonhq.com>

Balloon HQ—Offers "everything you ever wanted to know about latex and foil balloons for parties and entertainment," including details about starting and growing your own balloon business, along with decorating ideas and information on the history and science of balloons. Members promote their artistic skills online through Balloon HQ's user member portfolios. Balloon HQ also serves as a community for balloon artists and ballooning entrepreneurs.

Additional Business Ideas

- Balloon Delivery Service. Refer to—*Bizy's Guide to Making Money with Balloons,* by Joyce Gowens. Visit <www.bizymoms.com> for ordering information.
- Balloon Entertainment. Refer to—Balloon Magic, 4291 Chapel View Circle, Provo, UT 84604; <www.balloonmagic.com>; (801) 377-0878; (801) 377-0848 fax; balloons, gifts, retail, balloon decorating; balloon and magic entertainment; balloon delivery; balloon instruction and training.

2
GIFT BASKETS

The gift basket industry is a billion-dollar-plus industry. According to *Gift Basket Review,* nearly 100 percent of gift basket start-up business owners are in fact women. Giving gift baskets is a unique idea that has grown in popularity over the past 20 years and that is offered by commercial businesses, florists, specialty shops, and many small home-based operations. Baskets can be filled with an assortment of specialty foods and gifts and can be tailored for almost any occasion, such as births, birthdays, housewarmings, or ice cream sundae-making. You need an ample work and storage area, plus a method of delivery. In addition, a toll-free telephone number and the ability to take credit card orders help increase business.

Start-Up Costs and Financing Sources

- From $4,000 for small operations to $12,000 to $15,000 and up, depending on the type of baskets offered, the availability of products (wholesale), and the type of customer you are serving.
- Personal savings, small business loan.

Pricing Guidelines

Follow the industry guidelines (baskets usually range from $25 to $85 +).

Marketing and Advertising Methods and Tips

- Print up business cards and brochures (illustrated or with photos) describing baskets offered.
- Take out display ads in the local newspapers before major holidays.
- Donate some of your gift baskets to fund-raising auctions.
- Conduct demonstrations for community groups on putting together gift baskets.
- Rent a table at local craft shows and let people make up their own baskets (say, for Mother's or Father's Day).

- Rent a booth at gift buyers' trade shows.
- Drop off complimentary jars filled with candies to local businesses and organizations along with your business cards and brochures.
- Use a Web site to show off examples of your baskets. Many local chambers of commerce offer their members a Web page on the chamber site.

Essential Equipment

Baskets (purchase wholesale or at yard sales or from basket makers), ribbons, straw filler, shrink-wrap machine (or shrink-wrap and hair dryer), basket items, table space for assembly, storage shelves for supplies and inventory, car or van for delivery.

Recommended Training, Experience, or Needed Skills

- Work at a gift basket shop or a floral design studio.
- Subscribe to trade magazines and buy how-to videos.
- Follow start-up guides and manuals.
- Attend trade shows.
- Have a talent for creating arrangements.

Income Potential

Depending on the volume of baskets you sell and your profit margin, annual income can range from $25,000 to $50,000. It is not uncommon for gift basket business owners to earn $100,000 to $200,000 per year!

Type of Business

Primarily an in-home business except for deliveries.

Target Market

Companies that send gifts to valued customers and other corporate executives. Individuals wishing to send a special gift or "thank you." This is a growing market, especially during holidays.

Success Tips

- Offer free delivery within a certain mile radius, and then charge so many cents per mile beyond that.
- Concentrate on your marketing and what makes your baskets special as compared to the competition's.
- One woman with a gift basket business says she finds it easier to make a basket for a woman than for a man. "Women," she says, "for the most part like things that are feminine, no matter what their occupation. Men vary widely in their likes, hobbies, and jobs."

For More Information

Association

Gift Basket Professionals Network
446 South Anaheim Hills Road, #167
Anaheim Hills, CA 92807
<www.giftbasketbusiness.org>

Membership consists of gift basket designers, home-based business owners, retail store owners, gift consultants, writers, seminar presenters, wholesalers, and affiliates.

Books

The Art of Creating Great Gift Baskets, by Sherry Frey. It's Write Here! Publications, 441 Hickory Lane, Chambersburg, PA 17201.

How to Start a Home-Based Gift Basket Business, 2nd ed., by Shirley George Frazier (Old Saybrook, CT: Globe Pequot Press, 2000).

Publication

Gift Basket Review, Festivities Publications, 815 Haines Street, Jacksonville, FL 32206; <www.festivities-pub.com>. Monthly trade magazine covering issues of interest for owners of gift basket businesses. Also offers helpful trade books, videos, and trade show information.

Start-Up Guide

Entrepreneur's Start-Up Guide, *How to Start a Gift Basket Service.* For pricing and ordering information, visit <www.smallbiz-books.com> or call (800) 421-2300.

Supplies, Wholesale

Gift Concepts
151 Millard Avenue
West Babylon, NY 11704
Attn: Jackie Connelly
<www.giftconcepts1.com>

Additional Business Ideas

- College student gift baskets—All students love to eat, especially while studying for midterms and finals. Put out cards and brochures on campus during homecoming and parents' weekends.
- See the regular issues of such print publications as *Entrepreneur* <www.entrepreneur.com> and *HomeBusiness* <www.homebusinessmag.com> magazines (available at newsstands and bookstores) and their Web sites for listings of related business opportunities and franchises.

3
GIFT REMINDER SERVICE

In this business you get paid for reminding clients of important dates for special days—birthdays, anniversaries, graduations, and so forth—and for shopping for appropriate gifts. If you are knowledgeable about fashion and trends, you could shop for the best buys for men and women executives who have little time to comparison shop.

Start-Up Costs and Financing Sources

- $3,000 minimum.

- Small business loans, personal savings, credit card purchases, loans from friends or family.

Pricing Guidelines

You could charge a monthly fee averaging about $75 to $100 per client, depending on the number of calls and services you would provide. If shopping, you would base your prices on mileage to and from stores and a percentage of the cost of the items you purchase.

A reminder service can charge $35 to $65 an hour or a one-time set-up fee with a monthly maintenance charge.

Marketing and Advertising Methods and Tips

- Encourage referrals by friends and satisfied customers.
- Send direct mail to company executives.
- Give "shopping tips" lectures to professional groups.
- Run display ads in business trade papers and local newspapers' annual business supplements.
- Leave brochures, business cards, or pamphlets at clothing and gift shops.

Essential Equipment

Answering machine, fax machine, separate telephone line, filing system (manual or computer system to keep dates and clients organized), computer, PDA (personal digital assistant) record-keeping sheets or billing software, reliable vehicle.

Recommended Training, Experience, or Needed Skills

- Start small with one or two clients, or volunteer to do it for family or friends for a period of time to see if you can manage this business.
- Have a retail background in clothing or gift merchandise, as well as knowledge about fashion.
- Follow start-up guide recommendations.

Income Potential

Annual earnings can range from $10,000 a year part-time to $45,000 full-time.

Type of Business

About one-third in-home for scheduling, planning, and calls; two-thirds out-of-the-home for shopping.

Target Market

For shopping—working couples, business executives. For reminder service—professional practices that schedule regular appointments (doctors, dentists, etc.); salespersons who send out regular thank-yous; car dealers, auto service shops.

For More Information

Software

Check your local computer store for scheduling and management software.

Additional Business Ideas

Other reminder services: medical appointments, wake-up calls at prearranged times.

4
PARTY AND EVENT PLANNER

A party and event planner hires caterers, florists, and decorators; rents party supplies; reserves halls or banquet rooms; books entertainment; and helps with just about anything the client needs for a special occasion. Party planners might organize an entire event or just a part of it. Donna of Decorations to Dessert says, "I tell my customers, 'Tell me what you want,' and then I start from there."

Tally Attaway, president of Distinctive Events <www.distinctive-events.com> employs a four-person staff full-time and has as many as 25 freelancers to help with weddings and other functions. Attaway's expertise in these areas relieves clients' anxiety prior to and during their events. "It's one-stop shopping," she says. "All they do is hire me and then arrive at the party. They can have a fabulous time without any worries."

Start-Up Costs and Financing Sources

- From $1,000 to $6,000.
- Personal savings, small business loans, loans from family.

Pricing Guidelines

Hourly rates from $50 to $70; 15 percent to 20 percent of the cost of the arrangements the planner handles.

Marketing and Advertising Methods and Tips

- Encourage word-of-mouth referrals.
- Print up business cards, brochures, and flyers to post on community bulletin boards.
- Take out an ad in the local newspaper's classified section.
- Join or attend business organizations' networking and business card exchange events and industry trade shows.
- Patty Sachs <www.pattysachs.com>, party planning expert and author of the *Pick a Party* books, says, "Instead of spending time and money trying to find new customers, you get better results by the same efforts in cultivating new business from your existing customers by keeping in touch with newsletters, planning tips and greetings via e-mail or snail mail, on their special occasions."

Essential Equipment

Filing system (manual or computer), answering machine or service, fax machine, separate telephone line, printed promotional materials, cellular phone, pager.

Recommended Training, Experience, or Needed Skills

- Volunteer (or charge a small fee to cover expenses) to help set up parties for friends or relatives.
- Work in a catering business.
- Have excellent organizational skills, work well under stress, and be able to handle people tactfully but assertively (especially your suppliers).
- Communicate well with your clients and understand their wants and needs.

Income Potential

Experienced, full-time planners can earn annual incomes in the six figures!

Type of Business

Two-thirds in-home, coordinating and planning; one-third out-of-the-home, making sure everything runs as planned on the day before and the day of the special event.

Success Tips

- Donna offers two addtional tips: "Act as if this event were your affair," and "Pay attention to the smallest details and ask many questions—do not assume anything!"
- Attaway says, "When you are dealing with someone's most important day, you have to be there for them."

For More Information

Association

International Special Events Society (ISES)
401 North Michigan Avenue
Chicago, IL 60611
< www.ises.com >

ISES is dedicated to serving all the disciplines of the special events industry, offering networking opportunities, professional development and certification, and books.

Books

The Complete Idiot's Guide to Throwing a Great Party, by Phyllis Cambria and Patty Sachs (Indianapolis, IN: Alpha Books, 2000).

Dollars and Events: How to Succeed in the Special Events Business, by Joe Goldblatt and Frank Supovitz (New York: John Wiley & Sons, 1999).

Publications

Special Events magazine, P.O. Box 12914, Overland Park, KS 66282; <www.specialevents.com>. A resource for event professionals. Contact for subscription information.

Start-Up Guide

Entrepreneur's Start-Up Guide, *Event Planning Service.* For pricing and ordering information, visit <www.smallbizbooks.com> or call (800) 421-2300.

Supplies

MeadowLark Party Shoppe
The Beistle Company
One Beistle Plaza
Shippensburg, PA 17257
<www.party-here.com>

Additional Business Ideas

- Plan company picnics.
- MeetingsNet <www.meetingsnet.com> is the meeting industry's portal for information and resources related to planning meetings and events.

5
PARTY RENTALS

In this business you supply party items that people do not normally own, such as outdoor tents, extra folding chairs, large coffee-makers, silverware, china, and even sports equipment for volleyball or croquet, for example. Large party rental businesses have huge warehouses stocked with inventory. Your storage area may not be so large, but you could start small and use space in your garage or even rent a storage unit. Consider specializing in certain types of parties or picnics to keep your business manageable.

Start-Up Costs and Financing Sources

- $5,000 to $10,000 minimum.
- Personal savings, small business loans, credit cards.

Pricing Guidelines

Follow the trade industry guidelines; call or visit party rental stores or showrooms and price their items.

Marketing and Advertising Methods and Tips

- Send out flyers to caterers.
- Place classified and display ads in local newspapers, especially before holidays, graduation times, and during the summer.
- Set up a Web site.
- Place an ad in the phone book's business pages under "Parties" and "Rentals."
- Purchase local radio and cable television ad time.

Essential Equipment

Phone, fax machine, inventory sheets, party equipment and supplies, hand trucks, a storage area, and a reliable truck or van.

Recommended Training, Experience, or Needed Skills

- Work in a party rental store or business.
- Volunteer to set up parties for charities, friends, and relatives.

Income Potential

$18,000 to $40,000.

Type of Business

About three-fourths of your time is spent in-home, planning, organizing, and meeting with clients; about one-fourth of your time is spent delivering and picking up the rented items.

Target Market

Caterers, event planners; families of brides, families with babies; customers holding special celebrations indoors and out-of-doors.

Success Tips

Decide if you want to rent party supplies for specific events (children's parties, company or family picnics, outdoor wedding receptions, graduations, religious ceremonies, and other occasions unique to a culture, organization, and so forth), or for formal or informal occasions. (You could sell paper products, too, if you specialize in informal events.) Then target your customers accordingly.

For More Information

Association

American Rental Association
1900 19th Street
Moline, IL 61265
<www.ararental.org>

Membership benefits; resource products including manuals and forms.

Magazine

Special Events magazine, P.O. Box 12914, Overland Park, KS 66282; <www.specialevents.com>. A resource for event professionals. Contact for subscription information.

Additional Business Ideas

Specialize in renting moving trucks, tools, formal wear, costumes, home improvement (such as wallpaper removal tools, paint sprayers, garden equipment).

6
REUNION PLANNING

Reunion planners arrange get-togethers for high schools, colleges, or other institutions, as well as for families and members of former military units. Reunions may be held annually or every five to 10 years. One school alone could have as many as eight to 10 reunions each year.

Because many people no longer have the time to plan these events themselves, professional reunion-planning businesses have sprung up. The owner of a reunion-planning business organizes all the events leading up to the reunion day, including locating class members, mailing the invitations, hiring the entertainment, finding a location, and taking reservations. Reunion services also offer to provide such items as memory books, photo name tags, liability insurance for the event, and public announcements to locate family or class members.

Start-Up Costs and Financing Sources

- $5,000 to $15,000.
- Personal savings, small business loans.

Pricing Guidelines

The industry recommends charging a per-person fee based on the number that attend the reunion.

Marketing and Advertising Methods and Tips

- Send out direct mailings to schools and institutions.
- Ask your suppliers (caterers, photographers, banquet hall owners, florists, etc.) to recommend your service.
- Press releases and announcements in both print publications and online reunion Web sites.

Essential Equipment

Computer with a modem (connection to the Internet) as well as database and desktop publishing software, answering machine or service, fax machine, filing system.

Recommended Training, Experience, or Needed Skills

- Volunteer to help plan your own or your spouse's class reunion.
- Have excellent organizational skills.
- Use research skills to locate missing class members.
- Pay close attention to details and learn what was current for each group's graduation year or time period.

Income Potential

$3,000 to $5,000 per event.

Type of Business

In-home, except when consulting with class members and overseeing the event, if that is requested by your clients.

Target Market

High school and college class members, large families, former military units.

Success Tips

- Send out attractive, attention-getting mailings. Make sure names and addresses on mailings are spelled correctly.
- Schedule appropriate entertainment.
- Make sure the space you rent is large enough to handle the number of attendees.
- Plan activities that will include everyone in the reunion.
- The Internet has drastically changed this business in that it is much easier to find people using the many online resources.

For More Information

Association

National Association of Reunion Managers
P.O. Box 23211
Tampa, FL 33623
< www.reunions.com >

Nonprofit organization promoting standards and a code of ethics among its membership. Benefits include a conference, a newsletter, and networking for professional reunion managers.

Book

Family Reunion, by Jennifer Crichton. (New York: Workman Publishing Company, 1998).

Software

Reunion Planner Software <www.reunionplanner.com>. Software plus articles, tips, links.

Training

Reunion Business Consultants
P.O. Box 21127
Tampa, FL 33622
<www.ReunionCelebrations.com>

Professional high school reunion-planning company; also offers a business opportunity with a complete training course.

Web Sites

<www.family-reunion.com>

Family-Reunion.com—Resource site for planning family reunions; software, books, links.

<www.reunions.com>

National Association of Reunion Managers (NARM)—professional networking association.

Additional Business Ideas

Set up a home-based research business to help locate missing persons for families, friends, or reunion planners.

7
VIDEOTAPING SERVICE

Industry experts say the demand for video production services is expanding by a minimum of 25 percent per year and is expected to continue to do so for the next decade. A videotaping service usually concentrates on weddings, parties, recitals, and other special events but may also involve videotaping a person's or business's items for insurance purposes. In states permitting videotaping of some legal proceedings, lawyers may use your services as needed.

Start-Up Costs and Financing Sources

- Costs may range from $5,000 to $25,000, depending on if you use rented equipment or purchase your own.
- Personal savings, small business loans, loans from friends and family.

Pricing Guidelines

Follow industry standards; call other video services to get an idea of their fees.

Marketing and Advertising Methods and Tips

- Print up business cards and flyers; post them on community bulletin boards.
- Display magnetic signs on your vehicle.
- Purchase classified and display ads in your local newspapers.
- Ask party and wedding planners and suppliers to refer you to their customers.
- Send direct mailings to dance studios, schools, and preschools, theater groups, local clubs and organizations; lawyers and other professionals; home insurance companies; real estate companies.
- Purchase ads on your local cable television channel.
- Rent a booth at trade shows (home, bridal, sports, general business).

- ✤ Take out an ad in the business telephone directory under "Video Production Services."

Essential Equipment

Video camera, tripod, VCR, color monitor, cell phone, separate telephone line with fax machine, car or van to transport equipment, computer with video capabilities.

Recommended Training, Experience, or Needed Skills

- ✤ Work in media department of schools or video businesses.
- ✤ Take courses at local schools and colleges for technical knowledge and advanced video skills.
- ✤ Volunteer to videotape family, club, or sports events.
- ✤ Have a working knowledge of videotaping techniques. It is helpful to work with a commercial service or expert before you start out on your own.
- ✤ Have good people skills and an artistic eye.

Income Potential

Depends on your expertise, the number of clients, and the number of tapings you do per week. In taping live events—sports, dance recitals, and other occasions—you can sell copies to relatives or the individuals themselves, or to any institutions or organizations that may contract you on a regular basis.

Type of Business

Your time should be about equally divided between out-of-the-house taping and in-house paperwork and marketing.

Success Tips

- ✤ Know the lighting conditions and environment in which you will be filming.
- ✤ Ask customers what they want highlighted during the event before you film.

Franchises, Distributorships, and Licenses

VideoMasters (formerly Video Data Services)
2200 Dunbarton Drive, Suite D
Chesapeake, VA 23325
< www.videomasters.org >

Write for prices or visit the Web site for more information.

For More Information

Books

Basics of Video Production, 2nd ed., by Des Lyveer and Graham Swainson (Newton, MA: Butterworth-Heinemann, 1999).

Video Production, by Herbert Zettl (Boston, MA: Wadsworth Publishing Company, 2000).

Publication

Videomaker magazine, P.O. Box 4591, Chico, CA 95927; < www .videomaker.com > . Offers information for video producers. Write or visit the Web site for subscription information.

Web Site

< http://videouniversity.com >

Video University—Features articles such as "Finding the Right Video Business," and others; books; and additional excellent resources for the professional videomaker.

8
WEDDING PLANNER AND CONSULTANT

The wedding industry estimates that in 1997, $32 billion was spent on weddings in the United States. Bridal couples want their day to be special, but at the best price. A wedding or bridal consultant helps the couple establish a budget and finds the best suppliers to fit that budget. Once primarily used by the rich, wedding planning consultants today offer services at prices most every bride can afford. These experts use their knowledge and expertise to help the bride and her family save time and money, and they even, at times, help to keep peace between the families—with the goal to have that "perfect" wedding day.

Start-Up Costs and Financing Sources

- $5,000 to $12,000 average.
- Personal savings, small business loans, credit cards.

Pricing Guidelines

Industry standards suggest a flat fee, 10 percent to 15 percent of the wedding budget; an hourly rate, $50 to $70; or a per diem rate, $300 to $1,200.

Marketing and Advertising Methods and Tips

- Encourage referrals from clients and suppliers.
- Run classified ads in the business directory of local telephone companies and the local newspapers, especially in their wedding supplements that often appear once or twice a year.
- Put together a portfolio to show prospective clients the weddings you have planned.
- Print up business cards and brochures.
- Rent booths at bridal shows.
- Send direct mailings to engaged couples.

Essential Equipment

Answering machine or service, business telephone line, fax machine, filing system (manual or computer), marketing materials (business cards, brochures, portfolio). Packy Boukis, a professional wedding consultant and owner of Only You Wedding and Event Consulting <www.clevelandwedding.com>, says "You'll need several pairs of good shoes because you'll wear them out running around town on your clients' behalf!" Boukis also recommends you have a variety of outfits, from business suits to evening wear, as you meet with suppliers and also attend formal weddings.

Recommended Training, Experience, or Needed Skills

- ✤ Volunteer to help plan friends' or relatives' weddings.
- ✤ Attend bridal trade shows.
- ✤ Join a professional association.
- ✤ Read trade and consumer magazines and newsletters to note the current trends.
- ✤ Attend training seminars and workshops (see "For More Information," later in this section).
- ✤ Have excellent organizational skills and assertiveness to get your suppliers to deliver on time and to obtain high-quality service.
- ✤ Have an ability to be tactful, even under trying circumstances!

Income Potential

Rates vary in the different regions of the country. Consultants commonly charge 10 to 15 percent of the total wedding expenses.

Type of Business

Approximately two-thirds in-home, organizing the wedding; about one-third out-of-the-home, consulting with the bridal couple and family and visiting the suppliers and places where the wedding and reception will be held.

Success Tips

- ✤ Having reliable and caring suppliers will help make you a success.
- ✤ Project confidence so that your clients will trust you to handle their plans, but avoid being too bossy.
- ✤ Packy Boukis says about getting started, "Get to know local caterers, owners of bridal shops and others who can influence potential clients."
- ✤ LaShonda White, owner of a wedding and event-planning business, Parties, Weddings, Etc. <www.partiesweddingsetc

.7h.com >, says, "I think that one of the best tips that I have learned is 'Never give up.' Owning a business can be rewarding in many ways. Failure is a part of learning and finding your niche. Be proud of your accomplishments because they have brought you where you are today. Being happy within yourself will only highlight your soon to be success."

- Follow up each wedding with an evaluation.
- Get to know the wedding vendors—limousine services, florists, caterers, owners of reception halls, photographers, and others—in your region. Then share leads and encourage referrals among this working group.
- Packy Boukis offers this tip that she says she feels really helped her business: "I have found that my ability to articulate to my client the description of the various services that I offer affects the rate in which I book that service. I am very detailed in the particular service that most fits their needs. I know that all brides can benefit from having a wedding consultant's services and they can have that advice in their price range by tailoring the service that matches what they can afford."

For More Information

Associations

Association of Bridal Consultants
200 Chestnutland Road
New Milford, CT 06776
< www.bridalassn.com >

An international trade organization with more than 2,500 members in the United States and 28 foreign countries. Offers a professional development program, seminars, comprehensive home study courses, a hotline, and a newsletter.

Association of Certified Professional Wedding Consultants
7791 Prestwick Circle
San Jose, CA 95135
< www.acpwc.com >

Licensed by the state of California. Personalized and correspondence home study course.

Books

The Ultimate Wedding Idea Book: 1001 Creative Ideas to Make Your Wedding Fun, Romantic, and Memorable, by Cynthia C. Muchnic (Roseville, CA: Prima Communications, 2001).

The Ultimate Wedding Planner and Organizer, by Elizabeth Lluch and Alex Lluch (San Diego, CA: Wedding Solutions Publishing, 2002).

Publications

Modern Bride magazine <www.modernbride.com>. Industry magazine and wedding resource site.

Start-Up Guide

Entrepreneur's Start-Up Guide, *Wedding Consultant.* For pricing and ordering information, visit <www.smallbizbooks.com> or call (800) 421-2300.

Wedding Planning Software

EZ Wedding Planner <www.ezweddingplanner.com>. Free online software.

Web Sites

<www.discountbridalservice.com>

Discount Bridal Service—"A Personal Buying Service for Brides." Also offers dealerships.

<www.sellthebride.com>

Sell the Bride—"The premier site for wedding professionals," founded by Brian Lawrence, author of *The Wedding Expert's Guide to Sales & Marketing.*

<www.weddingchannel.com>

WeddingChannel.com—Resource site of wedding planning information.

Additional Business Ideas

- Expand into selling and/or creating wedding supplies and accessories.
- Design wedding invitations—refer to BizyMom's e-book *How to Make Money Designing Wedding Invitations,* by Kim Siebold <www.bizymoms.com>.

Home Services

9
CLEANING: BLINDS

Residences, shops, offices, companies, and corporations will always need their blinds cleaned. Because blinds are difficult and time-consuming to clean, demand for this service is high. You can purchase a special blind-cleaning machine from the S. Morantz company (see "For More Information," later in this section, for address) or find the best method and formula that works for you. You also may want to learn how to install and/or repair blinds as an extra service.

Start-Up Costs and Financing Sources

- $7,000 to $16,000+ if you purchase a specialized machine. To keep initial costs down, rent cleaning equipment until you can purchase your own.
- Personal savings, small business loans.

Marketing and Advertising Methods and Tips

- Place classified ads in local newspapers.
- Post flyers on community bulletin boards.
- Send direct mailings to businesses that have blinds.
- Purchase a business telephone directory ad.

Essential Equipment

Buckets, drop cloths, small stepladder, cleaning cloths, handheld vacuum cleaner, cleaning solution (one that demagnetizes the dirt so it is not just pushed around), tools for repair and installation, vehicle large enough to carry equipment.

Recommended Training, Experience, or Needed Skills

- Work in a cleaning business to learn tricks of the trade.
- Volunteer to clean relatives' and friends' blinds.
- Contact manufacturers of blinds to see if they have cleaning booklets or offer seminars or workshops on cleaning blinds.
- Need physical dexterity.

Income Potential

Average charge is $12 to $17 per blind. If you clean 60 blinds a day and charge $12 for each blind, you will make $750 per day.

Type of Business

One-fourth in-home for arranging appointments, record keeping, marketing; three-fourths out-of-the-home.

Target Market

Businesses; organizations' headquarters.

Success Tips

- Doing a "little extra" as well as being quick and efficient will result in referrals to other potential customers.
- Lisa Morantz, vice president of S. Morantz Inc., says, "In the blind cleaning business, the most important factor is *training*. Too many people think they can buy a machine, put a blind into the tank, and it will come out clean. While this may work some of the time, there are factors involved that affect the cleaning efficiency such as temperature, time, and drying techniques. Without this knowledge, the types of blinds that can be cleaned will be extremely limited, and the business owner will be missing out on making money. Check with the manufacturer. They should offer free training as we do."

For More Information

Books and Publications

Cleaning Up for a Living, by Don Aslet (Cincinnati, OH: F & W Publications, 1991).

Cleaning industry training and educational materials (books, manuals, magazine, software, and videos), seminars, and a product index. Cleaning Consultants Services, P.O. Box 1273, Seattle, WA 98111; <www.cleaningconsultants.com>. Visit the Web site for a listing and more information.

Start-Up Guide

Entrepreneur's Start-Up Guide, *How to Start a Cleaning Service.* For pricing and ordering information, visit <www.smallbiz-books.com> or call (800) 421-2300.

Equipment

S. Morantz Inc., 9984 Gantry Road, Philadelphia, PA 19115. For information on the Morantz Li'l Baby Blind Cleaning Machine, a portable, ultrasonic cleaning system, and other machines, visit the Web site <www.morantz.com> or contact via e-mail <stan@morantz.com> or phone (215) 969-0266.

Additional Business Ideas

Sell replacement blinds and custom window treatments.

10

CLEANING: CARPETS AND RUGS

Cleaning carpets and rugs is a competitive business. You have to aggressively market your service and be ready to tell potential customers why your service is better than another's.

Start-Up Costs and Financing Sources

- As low as $800 to $1,500 if you lease your equipment, as much as $15,000 to $22,000 if you buy equipment.
- Personal savings, credit card credit line, small business loans.

Pricing Guidelines

Charges may range from 15 to 20+ cents per square foot, up to 35 cents per square foot if you have to move furniture. Some business owners charge a flat rate per room, which may vary with room size. Collect payment on completion of each job.

Marketing and Advertising Methods and Tips

- Send direct mail to businesses.
- Purchase ads (with coupons for discounts) in co-op mailing services to homes.
- Take out an ad in the business telephone directory.
- Post and hand out flyers in your neighborhood.
- Contact real estate agents whose clients may need carpet cleaning before selling or after buying their homes.
- Look to register with a homeowners' referral network.

Essential Equipment

Business phone and/or cell phone with answering machine, service, or voice mail; carpet and drapery cleaning machine (can be leased); vehicle. Powerful vacuum cleaner, rug and carpet stain remover, shampoos.

Recommended Training, Experience, or Needed Skills

- Work in a carpet cleaning business, or rent a machine and clean your and your friends' carpets to get on-the-job training.
- Become knowledgeable on how to clean different kinds of carpets.

Income Potential

Some business owners who have cleaning crews earn into the six figures.

Type of Business

One-fourth in-home; three-fourths out-of-the-home doing the cleaning or supervising.

Target Market

You can target individuals who are apartment dwellers and homeowners; owners of small hotels, motels, offices, real estate offices; or institutions or organizations with buildings needing carpets cleaned.

Success Tips

- Pick a unique name for your business and buy uniforms for a recognized look.
- Establish a regular cleaning schedule with your customers—in a signed contract—to ensure a predictable and regular income.

Franchises, Distributorships, and Licenses (just one of many!)

Chem-Dry Carpet Cleaning (Harris Research)
1530 North 1000 West
Logan, UT 84321
< www.chemdry.com >

Specializes in the care of carpets, draperies, upholstery, and most fabrics. Sells a patented, nontoxic cleaner and specializes in the removal of red dyes, pet stains, and odors. This franchise can be run out of an office or your home, part-time or full-time.

For More Information

Books and Publications

Carpet cleaning books. Cleaning Consultant Services, P.O. Box 1273, Seattle, WA 98111; < www.cleaningconsultants.com >.

The Cleaning Encyclopedia: Your A to Z Illustrated Guide to Cleaning Like the Pros, illustrated ed., by Don Aslett (New York: Dell Books, 1999).

Start-Up Guide

Entrepreneur's Start-Up Guide, *How to Start a Cleaning Service*. For pricing and ordering information, visit <www.smallbizbooks.com> or call (800) 421-2300.

Web Site

<www.cmmonline.com>

Cleaning and Maintenance Management Online—Commercial cleaning news and information as well as carpet and floor cleaning news and articles.

Additional Business Ideas

Specialize in or also offer drapery cleaning, upholstery cleaning, carpet dyeing, or hardwood and noncarpeted floor cleaning.

11
CLEANING: HOMES AND APARTMENTS

With so many couples having full-time jobs today, the need for a high-quality cleaning service has grown. Many home and apartment cleaners are sole proprietors, but some hire a staff and then manage the business. It is difficult to find employees because so many can start their own cleaning service.

Cleaning is a physically demanding job, which is why an owner who does everything herself is somewhat limited in her income potential. Jobs vary from light duties to heavy tasks.

Arrange cleaning visits on a regular basis according to your customers' needs. It may be a good idea to have you or your workers bonded. Be aware that these businesses traditionally have a high turnover of employees.

Start-Up Costs and Financing Sources

- $2,000 to $14,000.

- Personal savings, small business loans, borrowing from friends or family.

Pricing Guidelines

$30 to $40 per hour for cleaning and organizing; charge extra for other requested duties such as window cleaning or labor-intensive chores. Have a rate and estimate sheet to give to prospective customers when you first meet them.

Marketing and Advertising Methods and Tips

- Encourage word-of-mouth referrals from satisfied customers.
- Post flyers on community bulletin boards.
- Place ads in weekly classified newspapers.
- Place magnetic signs on your vehicles.
- Print up brochures describing your cleaning services.
- Research the locations of white-collar neighborhoods through your chamber of commerce. Concentrate your advertising on reaching those residents.

Essential Equipment

Various kinds of cleaning equipment, telephone answering machine or service, filing and billing systems.

Recommended Training, Experience, or Needed Skills

- Work in a cleaning business to learn professional tips on how to clean quickly and efficiently.
- Be well organized; pay attention to detail.

Income Potential

In a sole proprietorship, you can average $20,000 annually, part-time, up to $50,000, full-time. Count on twice that amount if you hire staff. Some cleaning business owners report earnings of $600 to $900 per week.

Type of Business

One-fourth in-home for billing, scheduling, and organizational matters; three-fourths out-of-the-home for cleaning visits.

Target Market

Single professionals, married working couples with families, households earning $50,000 or more per year; mature adults who are no longer able to physically clean their homes; people who are moving in or out of an apartment or a house.

Success Tips

- Use a checklist to keep track of your customers' needs.
- Purchase liability insurance. Have a small business lawyer draw up a standard contract for you and your customer to sign as it relates to your charges, payment, and your specific duties.
- Offer "extras" or specialties with your service, such as carpet cleaning, cleaning out garages, organizing closets, and so forth, and bill accordingly.
- You will find that you will become more efficient in cleaning for your clients, which will cut down on the amount of time it takes you to complete a job, but make sure your contract states that you are paid for each full hour of work, even if you finish earlier than you expected.

Franchises, Distributorships, and Licenses

Check the newsstands for *Entrepreneur* <www.entrepreneur.com> and *Home Business* <www.homebusinessmag.com> magazines for their issues featuring various home-based cleaning franchises currently available, or visit their online sites for more information about these opportunities.

Consultant Services

Cleaning Consultant Services
3693 East Marginal Way South
Seattle, WA 98134

< www.cleaningconsultants.com >

Offers cleaning industry training and educational materials (books, magazines, software, and videos), seminars, and a product index. Provides information for custodial managers.

For More Information

Associations

Cleaning Management Institute
13 Century Drive
Latham, NY 12110
< www.facility-maintenance.com >

Books and Publications

Coming Clean: Dirty Little Secrets from a Professional Housecleaner, by Schar Ward (Minnetonka, MN: Book Peddlers, 2002).

How to Get Red Wine out of a White Carpet: And 2000 Other Household Hints, Tips and Formulas for Cleaning, Repairing and Organizing Your Home and Simplifying Your Life, by Erik A. Bruun (New York: Black Dog & Leventhal Publishers, 2001).

(See also "Cleaning: Blinds," page 88.)

Start-Up Guide

Entrepreneur's Start-Up Guide, *How to Start a Cleaning Service.* For pricing and ordering information, visit < www.smallbizbooks.com > or call (800) 421-2300.

Additional Business Ideas

Specialize in window washing; garage, ceiling, or attic cleaning; one-time cleaning (before and after) for parties or holidays; cleaning decks, pools or outdoor furniture, boats, and other particular items; or in a disaster, clean up and perform other specialized cleaning services. See *More 101 Best Home-Based Businesses for Women,* by Priscilla Y. Huff (Roseville, CA: Prima Communications, 1998).

12
ESTATE SALES

This business involves organizing and selling the entire contents of a house or property while striving to get your clients the best value for their items to be sold. Profits are made on a set percentage of the sales. An estate sales broker should have a network of collectors and buyers who can be trusted to make fair market value offers to purchase your clients' items. These persons are often invited to a private sale. The remaining items can then be sold at a sale open to the public and, after that, at a yard sale. Some estate sale specialists focus on types of properties or specify a minimum amount of money for the properties they will liquidate.

Start-Up Costs and Financing Sources

- $5,000 to $8,000.
- Personal savings, small business loans.

Pricing Guidelines

A contract should designate the percentage of profits or commission you expect. An average fee is 25 to 30 percent commission of total sales.

Marketing and Advertising Methods and Tips

- Encourage word-of-mouth referrals from satisfied clients and your expert appraisers' and collectors' network.
- Print up business cards.
- Charge clients for advertising their estate sale: send out flyers to antique merchants; place announcements in the local newspapers and buy ad time with local cable television and radio stations; post flyers on community bulletin boards.
- Have a Web site and develop an e-mail list for regular contact with your buyers and collectors.

Essential Equipment

Computer and software for keeping a database of current values for antiques and collectibles; business telephone line and fax; tables and linens to display items; tags, receipt books, or portable cash register; assorted bags and boxes for items sold.

Recommended Training, Experience, or Needed Skills

- Work for an auctioneer of estates, at an auction house specializing in the sale of antiques, or at an antique shop.
- Read antique trade publications and price guides to familiarize yourself with the current prices of objects.
- Attend estate sales to see how they are conducted.
- Volunteer to help at a relative's or friend's estate sale.
- Be well organized.

Income Potential

$3,500 + gross per sale (will vary with the number and quality of items).

Type of Business

One-eighth in-home for organizing and marketing the business; seven-eighths out-of-the-home for conducting sales.

Target Market

People who are moving into nursing homes or smaller homes; also homeowners, architects, accounting firms, builders, collectors, insurance businesses, probate and bankruptcy attorneys, real estate agents. Buyers include interior designers, antique dealers, and collectors.

Success Tips

- If you are not sure of an object's value, hire appraisers you trust so you can get the best price for your client's items.
- If possible, do not have the customer present during the sale.

- Clean, polish, and display the items to look their best.
- Hire helpers to keep things running smoothly and to help prevent theft.
- Build your business to have a reputation of being honest and professional.
- Check with the local authorities as to the legalities of holding estate and other sales.

For More Information

Books

How to Establish and Operate a Successful Estate/Tag Sale Business, by August R. Fetcko. Order from Past Glories Press, Suite 432-PYH, 29 Gibson Street, North East, PA 16428. ($45 plus $3 for shipping and handling (PA residents add $2.70 sales tax).

Kovels' Antiques and Collectibles Price List 2002, 34th ed. (New York: Ballantine Books, 2001).

Business Packages

Everything Goes Estate Liquidations, 973 Orchard Lake Road, Pontiac, MI 48341; e-mail: <egoes@aol.com>; Web site <www.everything-goes.com/main.htm>. Offers "Estate Sale Business Start-Up Package." Write or visit the Web site for more information.

Publication

Antiques & Auction News, Route 230 West, Mount Joy, PA 17552.

Seminars

Certified Estate Liquidator and Appraiser seminars are sponsored by Edinboro University of Pennsylvania, Continuing Education, 139 Meadville Street, Edinboro, PA 16444. Send an SASE for more information.

Additional Business Ideas

Antique sales; antiques restoration; selling items on Internet auctions.

13
GARAGE SALES

In this business, you sell the household goods and clothing of people who are too busy or do not want to go through the process of holding their own garage sale.

A garage sale—also called a yard, patio, basement, porch, or moving sale—may run one, two, or more days. They may be held by a single family, several families, an entire neighborhood block, or organizations and clubs.

A garage sale business, like all businesses, benefits from a well-thought-out business plan that lists start-up costs along with pricing, advertising, and marketing strategies.

Start-Up Costs and Financing Sources

- $600 to $1,500, depending on the size and length of the sale, or if you or the customers pay for advertising. Costs are more if you have to carry liability insurance or have a lawyer draw up a standard contract.
- Personal savings, small business loan, or use the profits from your own garage sales to launch your business.

Pricing Guidelines

Offer a free or a small-fee consultation. Draw up a contract stating your terms and services. Average commissions run from 20 percent to 35 percent of sales.

Marketing and Advertising Methods and Tips

For Your Business

- Run classified ads in the local newspapers.
- Place flyers on community bulletin boards; pass out flyers to residents in new developments.
- Send out direct mailings to real estate agents.
- Print up business cards to hand out at garage sales.
- Encourage referrals from customers.

- Send out a press release every spring to your local newspaper, giving tips on organizing a garage sale.
- Use word of mouth to talk about your business to friends, family, coworkers, and other people you know. For example, post a business flyer at your favorite hair salon or at senior centers where many mature adults may want to sell unwanted items but do not have the time to conduct a sale.

For the Sale

- Place ads in local daily and/or weekly newspapers.
- Put up posters where permissible.
- Post flyers on community bulletin boards.
- Purchase ads on local cable television stations.
- Encourage your customers to also use word of mouth to spread the news about the upcoming sale to their friends and neighbors.

Essential Equipment

Tags, receipt books, bags for purchases, signs for advertising and at the sale itself, portable cash register, telephone line with answering machine or service, record-keeping forms.

Recommended Training, Experience, or Needed Skills

- Visit other garage sales to familiarize yourself with the resale prices of most items. Used items are usually sold for 20 percent to 30 percent of their original price; clothing, 10 percent. Clothes with designer labels, special baby items, unique clothes like little girls' smocked dresses, and new or slightly used products can be priced higher.
- Hold a garage sale yourself or for your friends.
- Be well organized and people-friendly.
- Take courses in antiques and collectibles (often offered at adult evening schools), read books on current prices of collectibles in case you run across items that may be valuable. Urge your customers to consult with a professional appraiser if in doubt.

Income Potential

$60 to $250+ per sale. You may want to limit yourself to only large or multiple family sales to make it worth your time.

Type of Business

Primarily an out-of-the-home business.

Target Market

Busy families or couples, working couples who have just moved into a new home, people who are moving. Nonprofit organizations wishing to hold a community flea market, selling tables to raise money.

Success Tips

- Be honest about pricing and market value with your customers and with the people attending the sale.
- Decide on policies for people making offers on items—some items may have firm prices; others may be sold "as is."
- Start planning early. Have an alternative or rain date in case of unforeseen circumstances.
- Have professional-looking signs and tags printed.
- If it is a joint garage sale (neighbors, relatives), have color-coded labels to track each customer's sales.
- If possible, have everything marked and arranged the night before. Cover items that can be damaged by moisture or do not put them out until the day of the sale.
- Have items organized in categories, but have some pricier items mixed with inexpensive items to encourage people to look at all the tables.
- Hire an assistant to take the money while you keep items straightened up and oversee the sale.
- Make it fun and colorful. Attach balloons and streamers to tables and have some attention-getting item posted outside at the end of the driveway, like a huge stuffed animal or one of the neighborhood children dressed as a clown, waving to people as they drive by.

For More Information

Books

The Great Garage Sale Book: How to Run a Garage, Tag, Attic, Barn, or Yard Sale, by Sylvia Simmons (Campbell, CA: iUniverse, 2000).

Visit your local public library for out-of-print garage sale tips books.

Additional Business Ideas

- Specialize in tag sales for people who are moving. Items to be sold are tagged, and customers can walk through several rooms of the house to see what there is to buy.
- Specialize in cleaning garages.

14
INTERIOR DECORATING AND DESIGN

Home decorating and remodeling have grown in the past few years due to the rising real estate prices. People are more likely to change the look of their interiors than to go deeper into debt by buying a new house.

An interior decorator or designer has to have the knowledge, training, and/or on-the-job experience to be competitive in this market. Interior designers undertake comprehensive formal education and plan the layouts for interior decorators. Interior designers are required to be licensed by at least eighteen states. Interior decorators concentrate more on the material aspects of rooms and spaces.

Interior designers and decorators appraise, plan, and design interiors of homes, businesses, and institutions. They coordinate colors and materials in the spaces to be used, all within the clients' budgets. Many specialize according to their own training and preferences.

Start-Up Costs and Financing Sources

- $8,000 to $20,000.
- Personal savings, small business loans.

Pricing Guidelines

Your fee will vary according to your expertise and experience—whether you are certified or have completed a degree program.

Pricing options include the following:

- Flat fee.
- Hourly rate, which can range from $45 to $155 per hour.
- A service charge that is added on to the price of any items purchased for your client.
- Per-room charges.

Marketing and Advertising Methods and Tips

- Take out an ad in the business telephone directory.
- Encourage referrals from customers, home furnishing retailers, painting and wallpapering businesses, home decorating centers, builders, real estate agents, fabric centers, and floor covering retailers.
- Place classified ads in local and regional newspapers and magazines.
- Send out direct mailings to home furnishing retailers.
- Rent a booth at home furnishing trade shows.
- Assemble a portfolio of your designs and recommendations from satisfied clients.
- Establish a Web site with photos of your work.
- Gather samples from paint stores, upholsterers, and custom drapery and curtain businesses to show your prospective clients.

Essential Equipment

Drafting equipment, computer and graphic design software, copier, telephone with fax, answering machine or service, samples, swatches.

Recommended Training, Experience, or Needed Skills

- Work as an apprentice for an interior decorator.
- Become familiar with industry standards—join a professional association, read trade publications. Certification is required by some states.
- Work as a sales clerk in stores selling interior finishings.
- Work as a decorator's apprentice.
- Attend classes at professional schools that offer two- or three-year certificates or diplomas in interior design. (See "For More Information," later in this section.) Many architectural firms, design firms, stores, and so forth, hire only designers with formal training.
- Have a sense of color, balance, and proportion; keep abreast of current fashion trends.
- Communicate well with clients and understand their preferences.
- Need to be able to coordinate and work with suppliers—builders, remodeling contractors, and other professionals—of your decorating services, furnishings, and other items.

Income Potential

$35,000 to $100,000.

Type of Business

About one-half in-home, coordinating and planning; one-half out-of-the-home, consulting with suppliers, customers, and overseeing the work done.

Target Market

New homeowners, single or married professionals wishing to remodel new or old homes, clients in wealthy neighborhoods. Real estate brokers for housing developments, to decorate their model homes.

Success Tips

- Pay attention to detail.
- Check zoning and licensing requirements for your state.

✤ Draw up a contract that leaves no room for doubt as to what you will do and what the customer wants, and include surcharge information if a project should extend beyond what was originally contracted for.

Franchises, Distributorships, and Licenses

Decorating Den
19100 Montgomery Village Avenue
Montgomery Village, MD 20886
(800) DEC-DENS
< www.decoratingden.com >

Business opportunity information; also sells the book *Smart and Simple Decorating*, by Carol Donayre Bugg (New York: Time-Life Books, 1999).

For More Information

Associations

American Society of Interior Designers
608 Massachusetts Avenue, NE
Washington, DC 20002
< www.asid.org >

Membership requires six years of education and experience. Qualify for professional membership by passing the National Council for Interior Design Qualification (NCIDQ) exam. The Web site offers books, information, and tools to foster business success.

Books, Publications, and Videos

How to Start a Home-Based Interior Design Business, by Suzanne DeWalt. (Old Saybrook, CT: Globe Pequot Press, 1997).

Start Your Own Interior Design Business and Keep It Growing! Your Guide to Business Success, by Linda M. Ramsay, 1997. Touch of Design, 475 College Boulevard, Suite 6290, Oceanside, CA 92057; < www.touchofdesign.com >. Visit the Web site or send an LSASE for information on books, videos, links, and other interior design resources.

Magazine

Interior Design <www.interiordesignmag.com>. Trade publication that includes an annual buyers' guide and bonus issues of *Market,* a large-format publication issued twice a year that features popular products for the trade. The Web site has current and archived articles, a listing of industry trade shows, a listing of accredited schools, subscription details, and more industry-related information.

Home Study Courses

Distance Education and Training Council (DETC)
1601 18th Street, NW
Washington, DC 20009
<www.detc.org>

Write for a brochure of schools offering home study courses or visit the Web site. DETC home study courses are primarily for decorating instruction, not for interior design certification. For those schools, write to:

Interior Design Educators Council
9202 North Meridian Street, Suite 200
Indianapolis, IN 46260
<www.idec.org>

Write or visit the Web site for a listing of institutions that provide formal interior design education.

Additional Business Ideas

- Holiday decorating service—For homeowners and stores.
- Design interiors for persons with physical or mental disabilities.
- Design home offices.
- Design using furnishings people already have—help them rearrange and add different accents, and so forth. This is a much more affordable service for clients and thus is a popular alternative to complete redecoration. Potential income could reach $100,000 and more per year.

15
LAMPSHADES

Before the invention of the lightbulb, most shades for gas lamps were made of glass or pierced metal to prevent them from catching fire. After Thomas Edison invented the first commercial incandescent lightbulb in 1879, lampshades were made from various fabrics to cut down on the glare.

Early on, most shades were purely functional, but as the interest in interior design flourished, lampshade makers began to create shades to match a room's decor or to complement a uniquely designed lamp. Lampshade makers use a variety of materials. The shades that Dorothy, a lampshade maker for years, makes in her business are either "soft" shades or "hard" shades. She gets more than half of her business from making the soft, or more commonly called silk, shades (though few are made from pure silk). The silk or soft shade—always made of fabric—is stretched over a framework of wire ribs between the top and bottom rings. Most customers want their silk shades recovered because of damage or age or because a particular make of silk shade was discontinued by the manufacturer.

The other kind of shade that Dorothy makes is the hard shade. Dorothy uses watercolor paper that is stiff enough to separate and support the rings. Dorothy likes making this shade the best because she uses her artistic talents as she paints and cuts any number of designs on them.

Many women like Dorothy find that making lampshades can be a lucrative and creatively satisfying home-based business.

Start-Up Costs and Financing Sources

- $300 to $600 minimum for supplies, books, course fees, advertising, and so forth.
- Personal savings, small business loan and/or a line of credit from your local bank.

Pricing Guidelines

$75 for a simple shade to $600 for a more elaborate one; extra charges for fringes, hand-painted scenes, expensive material. Some lampshade makers charge by the inch, measuring the bottom circumference of the shade.

Marketing and Advertising Methods and Tips

- Encourage word-of-mouth referrals.
- Teach a course on making lampshades for an adult evening school.
- Take out an ad in the business telephone directory and local newspapers.
- Use a Web site to display photos of your work and your contact information.
- Print up business cards and flyers to post on community bulletin boards, or leave them at lamp shops, antique shops, and decorating centers.
- Send out direct mailings to interior decorators.
- Take time to build up a solid reputation for quality and beautiful work.
- Take samples of your work to antique shops, home furnishings stores, and Victorian specialty shops. They may not only buy your products and services outright, but they may also refer customers to you.

Essential Equipment

Sewing machine and notions, paint supplies, assorted fabrics and art paper for cutout or painted shades, craft knife and tracing paper, unusual frames (look for these at garage sales and flea markets), printed business cards and flyers.

Recommended Training, Experience, or Needed Skills

- Study how-to books and videos, and practice on your own shades or on those bought at flea markets or garage sales.

- Enroll in lampshade-making courses at craft centers or adult evening schools.
- It helps to have an artistic talent or a creative flair.

Income Potential

$600 to $700 per week. Some lampshade makers earn $20,000 to $35,000 per year.

Type of Business

Primarily an in-home business. Your customers can come to you for consultation and estimates.

Success Tips

- Dorothy says, "You should be able to make both hard and cloth shades as well as do basic repairs as an added service."
- Dorothy gives estimates to her customers at the consultation and tells them to give her a call if they want her to make the shades. This gives them time to consider spending money on a custom shade, which is more costly than a manufactured one.
- Keep a portfolio of your designs and photos of your custom shades to show to clients.
- Keep a file card for reference on each shade you make with the time it took to make it, the fabric and supplies used, and the price charged.

For More Information

Book

The Lamp Shade Book: 80 Traditional and Innovative Projects, by Dawn Cusick (New York: Sterling Publications, 1998).

Supplies

The Lamp Shade Shop
P.O. Box 3606
Department N
Concord, NH 03302
<www.lampshop.com>

Offers kits, books, papers, and other lampshade items, plus a catalog for $3 or downloadable free from the Web site.

Videos

How to Make Victorian Style Lamp Shades
How to Restore Traditional Style Lamp Shades
Advanced Techniques for Victorian Lampshades
Custom designs by Mary Maxwell. Order from Heart Enterprises, 101 Sharon Way, Roseville, CA 95678; <www.victorianlampshadesupply.com>; $48 each plus shipping and handling.

Additional Business Ideas

- Offer to repair and make lamps as an added service. Look in your local library for books on making and repairing lamps.
- Buy unusual vintage lamps, then rewire them, create new shades for them, and resell them. (Be sure that any rewiring is performed by a licensed electrician.)
- Make custom lamps out of a person's unique items (e.g., vases or trophies). Refer to *Making Great Lamps: 50 Illuminating Projects, Techniques, and Ideas,* by Deborah Morganthal (Ashville, NC: Lark Books, Asheville, 1998).
- Create stained-glass shades. Refer to *Shade Parade,* by Donna Babylon, and order how-to stained-glass design books from Papillion Publications, P.O. Box 47608, San Antonio, TX 78265; <http://papillon.home.texas.net>.

16
REFERRAL SERVICE

This service refers potential customers to businesses that offer various products or services to consumers. Clients might include small home remodeling contractors, hairdressers, special event and wedding planners, house- and pet-sitting services, and professional services offered by dentists, doctors, day care services, nannies, home health care experts, and tutors.

The owners of a referral service are paid by the business or sometimes by both the business and the customer. Fees can be charged at regular intervals or on commission, based on the number of customers a business receives through your referrals. Constant evaluating of the businesses you refer and searching for new ones to add are important elements in the success of this business.

Debra Cohen, president of Home Remedies, what Cohen calls a Homeowner Referral Network (HRN) business, started her business after the birth of her daughter. Her company represents home improvement contractors ranging from painters, plumbers, and carpenters to handymen, decorative painters, and floor refinishers. By placing a call to Cohen, homeowners are introduced to the most capable professionals in their respective fields. The contractors pay a commission to Cohen's business for any work secured through her network so her services are therefore free to the homeowner.

Start-Up Costs and Financing Sources

- $4,000 to $7,000.
- Personal savings; small business loan.

Pricing Guidelines

A percentage of what the businesses you recommend charge their customers.

Marketing and Advertising Methods and Tips

- Put up flyers.
- Send out direct mailings to the businesses in which your referral business will specialize.
- Make appointments to interview prospective businesses.
- Get names of businesses recommended by people you know. Ask prospective clients for references from satisfied customers.
- Send out press releases to business section editors of the local newspapers or the business supplements of regional newspapers.

- Rent a booth at a local home show.
- Make sure your local chamber of commerce knows your referral service is in business.
- Cohen says, "In a referral business like mine, the art of networking is everything. I never hesitate to talk about my business with people in my community (at school, running errands, at the post office) and it inevitably generates a lead of some kind. Don't be hesitant to tell people about your service . . . word of mouth is a powerful and inexpensive promotional tool."

Essential Equipment

Filing system (computer is best) and business and database software; business telephone line with fax, an answering service or voice mail; a modem if you offer online computer referrals; promotional materials (business cards, brochures, flyers for a professional look); a standard contract (consult with your lawyer).

Recommended Training, Experience, or Needed Skills

- Work in the business or businesses in which your service specializes so you are knowledgeable about the industry.
- Make customer service your number one priority.
- Be confident and handle business matters and any problems with a professional and confident manner.
- Enjoy working with people.

Income Potential

$30,000 to $80,000 or more.

Type of Business

About one-half in-home for general business matters, making new contacts, and calling customers who use your service; the other half is spent out-of-the-home interviewing new businesses.

Target Market

Newcomers to your community, new businesses in your community, homeowners in affluent neighborhoods with dual incomes.

Success Tips

- Your goal is to make people happy with the businesses in your referral service and to help good-quality businesses get the customers they need.
- Evaluate the businesses through interviews with customers—only keep those that are the best!
- Check with local chambers of commerce, consumer offices, and your local Better Business Bureau to ensure the businesses you refer are reputable.

For More Information

Business Opportunity/Manual

Homeowner Referral Network (HRN) Business, "An Ideal Work From Home Solution." For business package prices call (516) 374-8504; e-mail: <homremdies@aol.com>; Web site: <www.homereferralbiz.com>. Also available for purchase, by itself or with her business packages, *The Complete Guide To Owning And Operating A Successful Homeowner Referral Network* by Debra Cohen. Write for current price: Debra Cohen, Home Remedies of NY, Inc., 1539 Hewlett, NY 11557.

Additional Business Ideas

Call your county's consumer bureau and ask what types of service businesses consumers file complaints against most often. Then start a referral business specializing in that occupation or business.

17
WALLPAPERING AND PAINTING

Women of all ages and former occupations are finding painting and wallpapering to be a creative and lucrative home-based business and one that will be in demand as long as people want to remodel or redecorate their homes. JoAnn Kaiser, a home decorating store clerk, started Wall Works after a customer asked if Kaiser would paper her walls after she had bought some wallpaper. Kaiser did the job and the customer, the dean of a woman's college, urged Kaiser to go into wallpapering and painting as a business.

After enrolling in a series of small business start-up seminars, Kaiser began to look for wallpapering jobs part-time while she held another job in home health care. She says, "I gained confidence and perfected my skills when I did papering part-time and had the opportunity to figure out a pricing guide." When it became too much to do both jobs, Kaiser decided to go full-time into wallpapering and has been doing it ever since.

Start-Up Costs and Financing Sources

- About $8,000 for basic supplies and office equipment.
- Personal savings, loans from friends or family, small business loans.

Pricing Guidelines

- Wallpaper hangers and painters charge by the roll, by the hour, and according to the difficulty of the job. Find out what other paperhangers in your area charge.
- Painting is priced according to the square foot and the kind of paint used.
- Stenciling is priced from per linear foot with extra charges for multicolor stenciling.
- Never give an estimate over the phone. Your pricing will be determined by the size of the job (the size and number of

rooms to be painted, or wallpapered); the type of wallpaper to be used (some papers are more difficult to apply than others); your estimated time to complete the job; and any supplies needed other than the paper or paint, which will be charged to your customer.
- Search for paper and painting stores that give discounts to regular contractors.

Marketing and Advertising Methods and Tips

- Encourage word-of-mouth referrals from satisfied customers.
- Hand out flyers and business cards.
- Place classified ads in local newspapers.
- Buy ad time on local cable television channels.
- Offer a wallpapering workshop at a local decorator's shop.
- Send out direct mailings to retirement homes, schools, businesses, and interior decorators.
- Pamela White, author of the *Bizy's Guide to Starting a Painting and Wallpapering Service,* provides these marketing and success tips: "Never underestimate the power of word-of-mouth advertising and tell friends, neighbors, and relatives to tell as many others as they can about your new venture. Remember not to disappoint your customers or the referrals will dry up and encourage satisfied customers to make referrals to their friends. I wish I could say 'Then just sit back and let the business roll in,' but it takes consistency and dedication to your work to keep your excellent reputation."

Essential Equipment

Ladders, assorted paint brushes and rollers, papering brushes and rollers, knives, razor blades for cutting paper, drop cloths, vehicle for carrying your supplies.

Your home office would require a telephone line with answering machine, answering service, or voice mail, filing system (manual or computer for billing, customer and supplier database, and so forth).

Recommended Training, Experience, or Needed Skills

- Work with a professional paperhanger. Joann Kaiser says, "I would have learned the tips and methods faster if I had worked for a paperhanger before I started doing it on my own."
- Volunteer with friends and family to help them wallpaper or paint, or try it in your own home.
- Take a course at a school or local decorating, hardware, or paint center. (See "For More Information," later in this section.)
- Need physical dexterity, a working knowledge of math, familiarity with color, and an ability to communicate well with your customers.

Income Potential

$18,000 to $50,000 + average annual earnings; $300 to $800 per week. If you hire assistants you have a potential to earn more.

Type of Business

Primarily an out-of-the-home business for consultations and for doing the work.

Success Tips

- Kaiser says after you and your customer agree on the estimated cost, "Always get a signed contract to ensure payment."
- Pay attention to detail, protect the furniture and belongings of your customers, and do quality work, which will lead to referrals to other potential customers.
- Kaiser says, "Don't think of this being only a man's business. Many women tell me they feel more comfortable having a woman come to their house. They say they can relax more, and often when they change their minds—like one of my customers who changed her mind three times after I had begun papering—they know I'll understand."

For More Information

Association

National Guild of Professional Paperhangers
136 South Keowee Street
Dayton, OH 45402
<www.ngpp.org>

Provides a directory, a certified program, educational videotapes, and the bimonthly publication *NGPP Wallcovering Installer.* Send a business-size SASE for more information, or visit the Web site.

Books

The Complete Book of Painting Techniques for the Home: The Definitive Step-by-Step Guide to Paint Finishes and Interior Decoration Techniques, by Annie Sloan and Kate Gwyn (Cincinnati, OH: F & W Publications, 1999).

Painting and Wallpapering for Dummies, by Gene Hamilton, Katie Hamilton, and Roy Barnhart (Foster City, CA: IDG Books Worldwide, 2002).

Stenciling: Ideas and Decorating Techniques, by Better Homes and Gardens (Des Moines, IA: Meredith Books, 2001).

E-Book

Bizy's Guide to Starting a Painting and Wallpapering Service, by Pamela White. Visit <www.bizymoms.com> for ordering information.

Magazine

PWC (Painting & Wallcovering Contractor), Finan Publishing, 107 West Pacific Avenue, St. Louis, MO 63119; <www.paintstore.com>. "The official publication of the Painting and Decorating Contractors of America" <www.pdca.org>, a 3,500-member national trade association headquartered in Fairfax, Virginia.

Additional Business Ideas

- Paint store windows for holidays.

- Paint custom floorcloths and floors of homes. Refer to *Floor Style: Decorating Techniques for Beautiful Floors and Floorcloths*, by Susan Goans Driggers (New York: Sterling Publishing Company, 2001).

18
WELCOMING SERVICE

In this service you welcome new homeowners to your community by introducing them to banks, stores, medical services, day care facilities, private schools, recreational facilities, and other community businesses. You can visit these newcomers and bring them an attractive welcoming package containing coupons and/or samples from local retailers and restaurants, complimentary copies of local newspapers, directories of local organizations, schools, and other institutions. You are paid a monthly fee by the business owners and establishments that provide introductory items to promote their products and services.

Start-Up Costs and Financing Sources
- $1,000 to $5,000.
- Personal savings, bank line of credit, sponsorship by businesses you promote.

Pricing Guidelines
Businesses may pay you monthly or based on the number of responses they receive from the people you visit. Track this through the coupons or inquiries the business receives as a result of your visits.

Marketing and Advertising Methods and Tips
- Place ads in free real estate booklets and classified newspapers.
- Send out direct mailings to real estate agencies whose agents can refer you to people who have just moved into the community.

- Advertise on your local radio or cable television.
- Schedule appointments with prospective sponsors and your local chamber of commerce. Give them a brochure describing how your service works and how it can help increase their business and sales.

Essential Equipment

Standard home office supplies, including a copier, computer with billing software, business telephone line with answering machine or service, professional wardrobe, dependable and attractive vehicle, a pager. Consult with a lawyer to draw up your contracts.

Recommended Training, Experience, or Needed Skills

- Work part-time for a welcoming service in a nearby (but not competing) community.
- Make a good impression: have poise and professionalism and be well spoken, congenial, enthusiastic, and knowledgeable about your community.

Income Potential

$15,000 to $18,000.

Type of Business

One-third in-home for general business matters and to schedule appointments with businesses and newcomers; one-third out-of-the-home introducing yourself to businesses that will be paying you to sell their services; one-third out-of-the-home visiting newcomers.

Target Market

New and established businesses, newcomers. Other customers most likely to use this service would be working couples, the elderly, or persons with disabilities.

Success Tips

- ✤ Entice newcomers to use your clients' services with gift or welcome baskets filled with free samples or coupons.
- ✤ Be professional in dealing with the businesses and show them that you can increase their sales.
- ✤ Do follow-up evaluations with your newcomers: how did they like the businesses and services you recommended? You can pass this information on to the businesses to help them improve.
- ✤ Try different methods of advertising to see which type gets you the best response.
- ✤ Check with your insurance agent to find out if you need liability insurance or whether you should be bonded.

Franchises, Distributorships, and Licenses

See the regular issues of such print publications as *Entrepreneur* <www.entrepreneur.com> and *Home Business* <www.homebusinessmag.com> magazines and their Web sites for listings of business opportunities and franchises.

For More Information

E-Book

Bizy's Guide to Starting Your Own Welcoming Service by Joan Curtis. Visit <www.bizymoms.com> for ordering information.

Additional Business Ideas

- ✤ Start an unpacking service that helps new homeowners or apartment dwellers unpack and organize their household goods and personal belongings in their new residence. Either unpack alone (with a detailed diagram from the customer) or work alongside your customer.
- ✤ Special services like washing windows or general cleaning could be offered for homeowners and apartment dwellers moving in or moving out. You could charge an hourly rate, a per-job rate, or a fee according to the square footage of the residence.

Personal Services

19
CHILD CARE

With millions of preschool children in need of day care and a shortage of spaces in day care centers and preschools, the need for in-home (at-home) private child care businesses is great and will continue to be so for some time to come. Most home-based child care businesses care for four to six children, who may come full-time, part-time, or as drop-ins. Some businesses specify the age range of the children they feel most comfortable with and can handle.

Before starting a home-based child care service, check your state's regulations and licensing requirements. Many states require a background check for those who teach or work with children.

Start-Up Costs and Financing Sources

- Can be as low as $700 to as high as $20,000, depending on the equipment you buy and use. If you need to remodel a room or play area, the upper estimate applies.
- Personal savings, SBA loan, line of credit at your bank, government funding (in some states, government funds are available to sponsor children of low-income families who attend your day care).

Pricing Guidelines

$130 to $255 per week per child; $35 to $50 per day for infant care; $35 for a half-day and $45 for a full day. (Prices vary for different parts of the country.)

Marketing and Advertising Methods and Tips

- Encourage word-of-mouth referrals.
- Place a listing with a child care referral service.

Essential Equipment

Good furniture (can be bought used), learning toys (checked for safety), cribs, high chairs, playpens, first aid supplies, craft supplies, business telephone line.

Recommended Training, Experience, or Needed Skills

- Patricia C. Gallagher, author of *Start Your Own At-Home Child Care Business* and *So You Want to Open a Profitable Day Care Center,* says, "If your background includes baby-sitting, teaching, nursing, mothering, or any position that has included working with children, you are probably highly qualified to start a child care business; but of course, the most important credential is a love of children."
- Work in a day care center and see if you would like to do this kind of work every day.
- Take courses in child care or early childhood education at local community colleges.
- Use your experience with children from infancy to six years old as a mother (if you are one) or a caretaker.
- Have a love of children and enjoy teaching and working with them!
- Have patience, be well organized, and think like a child in the way you plan activities for them.

Income Potential

$125 to $250 per child per week; $25,000 to $45,000 + per year.

Type of Business
An in-home business.

Target Market
Parents who work, parents who want to go shopping or to an appointment.

Success Tips
✤ Begin by looking into the licensing, zoning, and insurance regulations in your community and state. Regulations vary from state to state and from town to town. Visit both the offices of your local authorities and state congresspersons for the codes you are required to meet. They will also inform you about personnel background checks and procedures.
✤ Talk to child care center directors, owners of in-home child care businesses (in noncompeting areas), parents of children who attend day care; and/or work or volunteer in a child care setting yourself to get firsthand experience and an idea of the programs, schedules, and so forth, that such a business involves.
✤ Prepare a business plan to help you organize and prepare your business start-up, as well as to assist you in obtaining funding should you need it. You may need to do some remodeling to conform to safety, health, and security codes.
✤ Consulting with a lawyer familiar with child care laws and liability is very important to fully understand your legal options and ramifications. Have your lawyer draw up a contract so both you and the parents are sure about the terms of the day care arrangement (especially payment and when parents should pick up their children).
✤ Have a trial period for newcomers.
✤ Have a back-up worker ready in the event you should become ill.
✤ Know emergency and first aid procedures.
✤ Be sure you can handle five days a week, 10 hours a day.
✤ "Caring and interacting with children can be one of the most rewarding (but exhausting!) experiences in one's life," says

Gallagher. "Opening an in-home child care or a child care center takes months of careful planning and organizing, but one that brings many intangible benefits."

Franchises, Distributorships, and Licenses

See the regular issues of such print publications as *Entrepreneur* <www.entrepreneur.com> and *Home Business* <www.homebusinessmag.com> magazines and their Web sites for listings of related business opportunities and other franchises.

For More Information

Associations

Send an LSASE to any of the following for information on membership, accreditation, and legislation affecting child care issues and news:

Child Care Action Campaign
330 Seventh Avenue, 14th Floor
New York, NY 10001
<www.childcareaction.org>

Child care advocacy organization.

National Association for Family Child Care
5202 Pinemont Drive
Salt Lake City, UT 84123
<www.nafcc.org>

National Association for the Education of Young Children
1509 16th Street, NW
Washington, DC 20036
<www.naeyc.org>

Books

How to Own and Operate Your Home Day Care Business Successfully Without Going Nuts!: The Day Care Survival Handbook and Guide for Aspiring Home Day Care, by Terri Simmons (Phoenix, AZ: Amber Books, 1999).

Start Your Own At-Home Child Care Business, rev. ed., by Patricia Gallagher (St. Louis, MO:, Mosby-Year Book, 1995).

E-Book

Bizy's Guide to Starting Your Own Child Care Service by Karen Potter. Visit <www.bizymoms.com> for ordering information.

Home Study Course

Distance Education and Training Council
1601 18th Street, NW
Washington, DC 20009
<www.detc.org>

Professional Career Development Institute (PCDI)
430 Technology Parkway
Norcross, GA 30092
<www.pcdi.com>

Start-Up Guides

Entrepreneur's Start-Up Guide, *How to Start a Child Care Service.* For pricing and ordering information, visit <www.smallbiz books.com> or call (800) 421-2300.

Additional Business Ideas

- Nanny, child care referral service. Find baby-sitters, then check their qualifications and references and refer them to people needing reliable child care services. You are paid by the persons looking for baby-sitters.
- Start a nanny referral or placement service to help parents find professional in-home nannies for their children. Contact: The International Nanny Association, Station House #438, 900 Haddon Avenue, Collingswood, NY 08108; <www.nanny .org> A nonprofit organization for nanny professionals, nanny placement agencies, and others involved with in-home child care. Send an LSASE for information.
- Child care consulting service. Help businesses start a day care center for their employees' children. Charge $5,000 to $15,000 for a consulting fee.

- Child transportation service.
- Child care for sick children.
- Play group.
- Drop-in child care services for stay-at-home parents (home-based business owners need uninterrupted time to conduct business), for part-time workers, for parents who are students, are traveling, or are going through crises, or for some other temporary situation creating a child care need. Staying open longer hours on Fridays or Saturdays can give working parents a few hours for leisure activities.
- Special-needs, preschool children who are not enrolled in special programs or for parents who need respite care.
- Children with minor illnesses or in need of temporary medical care for whom other child care services are not capable of handling.
- After-school care is in great demand as many children are alone in the afternoons with a potential risk of getting into trouble. It is not uncommon for such programs to make from $65,000 to $125,000 a year! School districts often contract these services out to businesses to run.

20
CREDIT CONSULTING

According to the Federal Reserve, together consumers owe $7.3 trillion—double the amount they carried into the last recession. Anyone can be faced with high credit card debt and/or personal bankruptcy due to periodic slow economic times leading to lay-offs or unexpected illnesses and personal crises. Even worse is when your credit suffers due to an identity theft or an unresolved credit dispute. A credit consultant is a financial expert who can assist her clients in taking the steps needed to restore their credit and become solvent again.

In this service you offer credit counseling and take steps to restore the credit of your customers. Requirements for credit repair agencies fall under the Credit Organization Act. Not all states have this law, however, and legislation differs state by state.

Deborah McNaughton, nationally known credit and financial coach, offers two programs: the Credit Consulting business, which shows individuals how to set up a credit consulting business, and a distributorship, the Credit and Financial Strategies seminars, which sells books, manuals, audio- and videotapes. (Contact information is given at the end of this section.)

Start-Up Costs

$3,000 to $12,000.

Pricing Guidelines

Prices can vary when operating a credit consulting business. To assist clients with their credit reports, you can charge a flat fee, such as $350 to $650, to cover your entire service, or charge a certain amount for each credit report you handle, perhaps $100+ per credit report. There are three major credit reporting agencies. A married couple has separate, individual reports, which would total six reports. It is advisable to give a discount to a married couple and charge $450+, for example.

Marketing and Advertising Methods and Tips

- Place ads in newspapers, in community publications or other inexpensive weeklies, and on local radio and cable television stations.
- Send flyers to individual businesses that qualify individuals for lines of credit.
- Arrange referrals from mortgage companies, car dealers, and real estate companies.
- Offer seminars to various community groups to educate individuals on how to establish credit, how to deal with credit problems, and how to repair credit.

Essential Equipment

Business phone line with voice mail or answering machine, typewriter, computer and modem, insurance, pager, cellular phone, pager, stationery, copier.

Recommended Training, Experience, or Needed Skills

- Study manuals, take seminars.
- Gain experience by working in credit offices. This is helpful but not necessary.
- Degree in related field. You must have the necessary certification and financial education (credit consultants are certified and in some states regulated) to be this type of consultant.
- Knowledge of banking industry and online research tools.

Income Potential

$30,000 to $65,000 and more, depending on the number of clients you have.

Type of Business

Can be in-home or out-of-the-home in an office.

Target Market

Any individual who needs guidance or assistance with credit issues: establishing credit, dealing with credit problems, credit repair. Get referrals from financial institutions, credit unions, and satisfied clients.

Success Tips

- Being nonjudgmental is important as you assist and educate your clients in getting and staying out of debt.
- McNaughton says, "There is an answer to every situation regarding financial hurdles. Faith, hope and a plan. Faith you can do it, hope there is an answer, and a plan to make it happen."

Franchises, Distributorships, and Licenses

Distributorship

Deborah McNaughton
1100 Irvine Boulevard, #541
Tustin, CA 92780
(714) 541-2637

Offers Credit and Financial Strategies seminars, videos, and a workbook and "Yes, You Can" distributorships.

For More Information

Foundation

National Foundation for Credit Counseling
801 Roeder Road, Suite 900
Silver Spring, MD 20920
<www.nfcc.org>

Books and Publications

Credit Card Debt Management, by Scott Bilker (Barnegat, NJ: Press One Publications, 1996).

Credit Card Nation: The Consequences of America's Addiction to Credit, by Robert D. Manning (New York: Basic Books, 2000). The Web site <www.creditcardnation.com> offers "opportunities for financial education regarding how most effectively to use credit cards and to understand the role that credit cards play in people's everyday lives."

Financially Secure: An Easy-to-Follow Money Program for Women, by Deborah McNaughton (Nashville, TN: Thomas Nelson, 2002).

The Get Out of Debt Kit, by Deborah McNaughton (Chicago, IL: Dearborn Financial Publishing, 2002).

The Insiders Guide to Managing Your Credit, by Deborah McNaughton (Chicago, IL: Dearborn Financial Publishing, 1998).

Solving Credit Problems and Your Credit: A Complete Guide, booklet from the Federal Consumer Information Catalog, P.O. Box 100, Pueblo, CO 81002; <www.pueblo.gsa.gov>.

The Ultimate Credit Handbook, new ed., by Gerri Detweiler (New York: Penguin, 1997).

Publications

Financial Victory <www.financialvictory.com> is a free monthly newsletter by Deborah McNaughton, author and founder of Professional Credit Counselors, 1100 Irvine Boulevard, #541, Tustin, CA 92780.

Web Site

<www.debtsmart.com>

DebtSmart—Credit card debt and information; statistics; related books and other important information.

21
DATING SERVICE

Because nearly one out of every two marriages ends in divorce, and more than 76 million single adults live in our country (U.S. Census Bureau), there is an increased need and demand for legitimate and reliable dating services. The Internet has seen an explosion in the number of online matchmaking services. If you are interested in starting this personal service business, you first have to determine if there is a large enough population of singles in your area. Check with the Census Bureau or local county seat for population statistics.

Some of the most popular dating services cater to specialized populations: the physically challenged; ethnic groups; religious affiliations; or people with similar hobbies, education, or interests. Survey single people in your area to find out if they have ever used a dating service. If so, what did they like or not like about it? Maybe you will come up with a dating service unique to your area.

You must have a reliable way to verify the identification of each client and suggest a public place for the first meeting of your matched couples. One dating service in Philadelphia has the matched couple meet at a city restaurant for lunch. Each person pays for his or her lunch. It is a fun and safe way to meet new people.

You should also urge your clients to think of blind dating as a way to meet other persons with related likes and dislikes—not as a potential marital partner. Matchmaking experts say this helps to promote realistic expectations of your clients and less anxiety in using a matchmaking service.

You can match your clients using a computer, videos, questionnaires, or all three methods. Follow-up calls and evaluations are important to improve and update your service.

Start-Up Costs and Financing Sources

- $15,000 to $50,000. Most money will be spent on advertising in the beginning.
- Personal savings, small business loan, investors.

Pricing Guidelines

Charge a monthly or retainer fee or an annual fee. (Call other dating services in your area or research online to see what the going rates are and charge accordingly.) You want to charge enough to make sure your clients are serious about finding suitable dates. Arrange for a bonus fee if the client marries.

Marketing and Advertising Methods and Tips

- Market and advertise constantly. Turnover of clients is high—some (happily) get married, others move, and some may try other services.
- Target your advertising, if specializing your service, to the proper magazines and newspapers.
- Send out press releases to newspapers, magazines, and local television and radio stations, which may result in articles or stories that will help increase your service's visibility.
- Advertise your successful matches—marriages and number of babies.
- Encourage word-of-mouth referrals from satisfied clients.
- A Web site is a must to keep up with the competition and to attract more customers.

Essential Equipment

A business telephone line with an answering service or voice mail; computer with software for matching clients, for billing, and with database capabilities; video equipment if you tape your clients; business cards; stationery; brochures.

Recommended Training, Experience, or Needed Skills

- Work in a dating service as an interviewer or investigate other services in noncompeting geographical regions or areas of interest. See what appeals (or does not) to you about them.
- Make people feel at ease if you interview them personally.
- Having an educational background in psychology and counseling is helpful.

Income Potential

$40,000 to $100,000 or more, depending on the number of clients and your initial registration and ongoing fees.

Type of Business

An in-house business. You should have a home office with a conference area or room for interviewing or taping clients. Be sure zoning laws permit such an office along with parking space.

Target Market

Singles who are interested in meeting new people.

Success Tips

- The competition is fierce, so stay updated in the latest trends and the latest technology to run this type of business.
- Have a public meeting place for the first date that is interesting and impressive (a prestigious restaurant, a lecture, a musical event) and arrange occasional private gatherings of your clients so they can see and meet more than one person at a time.

- Have all clients screened to protect one another. Make sure they are single and have no criminal history.
- Have the finances to advertise and sustain your business. Dating service owners say it takes a couple of years to get established.
- Check with your lawyer and insurance agents concerning privacy laws and liability insurance.

Franchises, Distributorships, and Licenses

See the regular issues of such print publications as *Entrepreneur* <www.entrepreneur.com> and *Home Business* <www.homebusinessmag.com> magazines (find at newsstands and bookstores) and their Web sites for listings of related business opportunities and franchises.

For More Information

Books

Dating for Dummies, by J. Browne (Foster City, CA: IDG Books, 1997).

The Everything Dating Book: How to Meet New People, Where to Go and What to Say—Make the Most of Every Date!, by Leah Furman and Elina Furman (Holbrook, MA: Adams Media, 1999).

Additional Business Ideas

Start a member newspaper, a newsletter, or an online e-zine profiling registered clients in your service.

22
ELDER CARE SERVICES

The U.S. Census Bureau estimates that by the year 2030, more than 70 million people will be elderly. With the costs of nursing homes and private care escalating every year, every month, the demand for high-quality, affordable in-home or day care services for the elderly is also growing. Many adults cannot take care of their elderly parents: They may have moved out of the area or maybe both husband and wife work and have demanding schedules due to children.

Elder care services can encompass a range of needs to include transportation to stores and medical appointments; running errands and shopping; daily monitoring of those who live at home; handling security checks, arranging visits by nurses and other professionals, and providing respite care workers when families go on vacation.

A free consultation is offered to evaluate and assess what services are needed. Each service is priced accordingly. Contacts are made with referral agencies if home professional care is needed. You coordinate the services and supply the needs of each of your clients.

Start-Up Costs

$6,000 to $15,000 for office equipment, advertising, and publicity materials for marketing and advertising.

Pricing Guidelines

Charge weekly, monthly, and per service. You may also be paid a fee by any referral agencies that get business through you.

Marketing and Advertising Methods and Tips

- Contact social service and home health care agencies as well as senior centers with direct mail, and then schedule an appointment with them for a presentation. Contact, too, the religious centers in your neighborhood because they regularly visit elderly members in their residences.
- Encourage word-of-mouth referrals from adult children.
- Purchase radio and local cable television and newspaper ads. Free classified newspapers are good avenues because they reach most households in their circulation areas and usually have a faithful readership.
- Put together professional-looking promotional materials describing your services.
- A basic Web site and a listing in your local telephone directory is also a good way to describe your services.

Essential Equipment

Home office equipment: computer; record-keeping and billing software; business telephone line and answering machine, service, or voice mail; fax machine and copier; cellular phone; insurance; suitable furniture if you have clients and workers come to your office to be interviewed or for consultations; dependable vehicle.

Recommended Training, Experience, or Needed Skills

- Work in your county's home services agency to familiarize yourself with seniors' needs.
- Enroll in courses in geriatrics.
- Work as a nursing assistant in a nursing or group home.
- Need to be patient yet persistent in finding persons who provide the best quality services your clients need.
- Be well organized.

Income Potential

$30,000 to $65,000 and more, depending on the number of clients you have and if you hire employees.

Type of Business

Primarily an in-home business, except to interview referrals and clients.

Target Market

Seniors who are relatively independent but need some at-home support and monitoring.

Success Tips

- Treat every client as an individual and provide the best services possible for each one's needs.
- Check with your insurance agent and lawyer as to what insurance or contracts you should have to protect you and your business.

- Paula Kay, owner and president of Ageless Placements, a business that hires mobile seniors to assist other seniors in their homes (not health care), says, "As elderly family members age, their well being typically falls upon caregivers within the family unit, especially those living the closest. Statistics show that there are more than twenty-two million Americans who are responsible for an aging family member. Three-quarters of them are working women with school-aged children still living at home. Also, an average of eighteen hours per week is spent caring for a parent with needs."
- It is important to consider everyone's needs and feelings in order for the aging process to occur as stress-free as possible.

Franchises, Distributorships, and Licenses

Franchises

Home Instead Senior Care
604 North 109th Court
Omaha, NE 68154
<www.homeinstead.com>

Business Opportunities

Ageless Placements, Inc.
8130 66th Street North, Suite 4
Pinellas Park, FL 33781
(727) 547-4337

Owner Paula Kay says, "As a service provider for elderly people, our focus is not only on our older client, but for the entire family. We are there when the caregivers, with busy careers and demanding schedules, cannot be . . . offering peace of mind."

For More Information

Association

National Association for Home Care (NAHC)
228 Seventh Street, SE
Washington, DC 20003
<www.nahc.org>

"Committed to representing the interests of the home care and hospice community." Send an LSASE or visit the Web site for information.

Books

The Complete Eldercare Planner: Where to Start, Questions to Ask, and How to Help, rev. ed., by Joy Loverde (New York: Crown Publishing Group, 2000).

How to Care for Aging Parents: A Complete Guide, by Virginia Morris. (New York: Workman Publishing Company, 1996).

LeBoeuf's Home Health Care Handbook: All You Need to Become a Caregiver in Your Home, by Gene LeBoeuf (Taunton, MA: LeBoeuf & Associates, 1997).

Additional Business Ideas

Monitoring service or specialized meal-delivery service.

23
ERRAND SERVICE

This business is as varied as the many errands individuals or businesses need to run almost every day. Trips to and from day care centers, pharmacies, grocery stores, post offices and mailing centers, bill payment centers, and libraries are just a few of the errand-running possibilities.

You can specialize in picking up and delivering forms and documents for businesses, or go food shopping for individuals. Or you can diversify and perform any number of tasks for people who cannot get away from their jobs or homes to run errands themselves. Conduct market research surveys in your community to see which errands are most in demand. Once you start, you may find other errands need to be run, which you did not even know existed until you received requests for them.

Rob Spina, author of *How to Start and Operate an Errand Service,* says, "As long as there are businesses in need (such as local printers, real estate firms, ad agencies, lawyers and accountants, and large corporations) and consumers in need (such as senior citizens, new moms, and most importantly, dual income households), this service will always have a supply of paying customers."

Start-Up Costs and Financing Sources

- From $1,000 for basic ads and the printing and copying of flyers and business cards to $8,000 for a computer and cellular phone and/or pager, a PDA, and other supplies.
- Personal savings, small business loan, personal line of credit with your bank.

Pricing Guidelines

$18 to $35 per hour ($100+ per hour in large metropolitan areas or for some corporate clients). You can charge weekly or monthly fees for an agreed number of errands within a certain mile radius (charge more for mileage if outside that radius). You can also charge by the hour for more complex jobs and per errand if it is an easy and fast one like a dry cleaning pickup.

Marketing and Advertising Methods and Tips

- As with any business idea you are contemplating, make sure you conduct research in your community to see what types of errands are most in demand and how much potential customers are willing to pay. One young mother who tried to start an errand service in her community found out that while there was a need in her area for her business, the potential customers were conservative spenders and were not willing to pay even her basic rates. Instead of giving up, she researched the need in a nearby town where there were working couples who *were* willing to pay for the time she gave them and ran her business there.
- Place classified ads in the local newspapers.
- Post flyers on community bulletin boards and leave at individual residences and businesses.

- Send a press release to your local paper to prompt a follow-up article on your business.
- Purchase local radio and cable television ads.
- Offer free hours of errand running at a community benefit auction.

Essential Equipment

Reliable vehicle for use in all kinds of weather that gets good gas mileage; record-keeping and billing files or software; business telephone line with answering machine, answering service, or voice mail, cellular phone and/or pager; organizer.

Recommended Training, Experience, or Needed Skills

- Work for a messenger or errand service.
- Volunteer to do your relatives' errands for a time to see if it will be profitable.
- Know your area and the location of services, businesses, and stores.
- Be well organized and prompt, and use your time as efficiently as possible.

Income Potential

$15,000, part-time; $60,000+, full-time. Earnings can be more if you hire others to run the errands.

Type of Business

One-fourth in-home, running the business and scheduling runs; three-fourths out-of-the home, running the errands.

Target Market

New mothers, persons recuperating from illnesses or injuries, shut-ins, persons with certain disabilities or serious illnesses, people on business trips or vacations, seasonal customers who do not have time to shop for gifts or fill out and send tax forms, working couples.

Spina, who ran a successful errand service with his wife for a number of years, says his customers came from both upper- and middle-income families. He says that generally people are working more weekly hours and would rather spend their "off hours" relaxing or being involved in other pastimes than doing tedious chores. "It's one of those perfect little businesses you can easily start up on your own, with low overhead and investment . . . out of your home," says Spina.

Success Tips

- Check licensing requirements and tax laws.
- Check with your insurance agent for liability coverage. See if you need to be bonded.
- Consult with your lawyer on contracts you should have.
- Have the option to turn down a job if the distance is too far (unless the client is willing to pay for your extra time and mileage) or if the job is not one you want to do.
- Be dependable, timely, and trustworthy. Your faithful customers will come to depend on you and you do not want to let them down. If possible, have a backup plan in the event you cannot carry out an errand or a task.

Franchises, Distributorships, and Licenses

See the regular issues of such print publications as *Entrepreneur* <www.entrepreneur.com> and *Home Business* <www.homebusinessmag.com> magazines (find at newsstands and bookstores) and their Web sites for listings of related business opportunities and franchises.

For More Information

Association

International Concierge and Errand Association
4932 Castor Avenue
Philadelphia, PA 19124
<www.iceaweb.org>

Networking association whose member benefits include listing in an online directory, a newsletter, and other various resources. For membership information, send an LSASE or visit the Web site.

Book

How to Start and Operate an Errand Service, rev. ed., by Rob Spina (Laurel Springs, NJ: Legacy Marketing, 2001).

Web Site

<www.legacymarketing.net>

Legacy Marketing—The site is dedicated to those who want to start and operate a small business headquartered from home.

24

FINANCIAL CONSULTANT

A financial consultant service helps people manage their money, borrow money for college or business, and plan for a financially sound future through wise investments, a well-constructed budget, and money-management strategies to prepare for their retirement years.

Start-Up Costs and Financing Sources

- $10,000 to $20,000. You will need to have a fully equipped, professional in-home office that is suitable to receive clients. This start-up estimate also includes advertising and promotional costs.
- Personal savings, small business loan.

Pricing Guidelines

- By the hour—from $50 to $200.
- A one-time fee for a sample and for financial aid and scholarship searches.

- Charge one flat fee per financial plan.
- A one-time fee and a monthly retainer.

Marketing and Advertising Methods and Tips

- Take out an ad in the business telephone directory.
- You can educate and attract potential clients by presenting talks and/or conducting workshops or seminars on financial planning.
- Produce a quarterly newsletter or an e-zine and send it out to prospective clients.
- Most financial consultants or planners get client leads from the referrals of friends, family, and acquaintances, but you must be proactive in your marketing of your services in order to achieve success.

Essential Equipment

Home office equipment, including computer, fax machine, and financial management software and report-writing software to put all your information into organized reports for your clients. For financial aid consulting, you will need access to related industry databases.

Recommended Training, Experience, or Needed Skills

- Have formal training or education—a bachelor's degree and more, if you are planning to be a certified public accountant (CPA) or certified financial planner (CFP). Licenses and certifications are needed to sell stocks, insurance, or real estate, so check your state and the federal regulations that regulate the activities of financial consultants, financial planners, and other financial advisers. Other professionals who also provide financial consulting services can be certified financial planners: accredited estate planners, certified investment management consultants, financial analysts, and other professionals specializing in certain areas of finance.

- With financial aid services, you need to be familiar with the forms and procedures involved in getting loans and scholarships and have access to computerized databases on college and private schools. You are paid by the college student or his or her family for the information you find.

Income Potential

For a financial planner: $20,000 and more (part-time) to six-figure incomes if assisting wealthier clients. For a financial aid adviser: $7,000 to $80,000, depending on the number of students you assist. Obviously, your income will be based on your experience, training, and credentials and the clients you serve.

Type of Business

One-third out-of-the-home, meeting with clients; two-thirds in-home, meeting with clients, plus researching and planning.

Target Market

People who have money to spend and invest, professional working couples, college-bound students (any age, these days). Baby boomers planning for their retirement, people recently laid off from their jobs, people needing credit counseling, and elder adults who need assistance in managing their money (especially if the spouse who handled the couple's finances has died).

Success Tips

- Understand what the client wants and hopes to achieve financially.
- Keep current with financial information and trends that deal directly with your clients' needs.
- With financial aid services, use computer databases to keep current on what money is available as well as changing regulations.
- Keep current with college and university scholarship and student funding programs.

Franchises, Distributorships, and Licenses

See the regular issues of such print publications as *Entrepreneur* <www.entrepreneur.com> and *Home Business* <www.homebusinessmag.com> magazines (find at newsstands and bookstores) and their Web sites for listings of related business opportunities and franchises.

For More Information

Associations

National Association of Student Financial Aid Administrators
1129 20th Street, NW, Suite 400
Washington, DC 20036
<www.nasfaa.org>

Books

Getting Started in Financial Consulting, by Edward J. Stone (New York: John Wiley & Sons, 2000).

The Scholarship Book: The Complete Guide to Private Sector Scholarships, Fellowships, Grants, and Loans for the Undergraduate (with CD-ROM), by Daniel J. Cassidy and Michael J. Alves (New York: Prentice-Hall Press, 2001).

Magazine

Family Money magazine, published by *Better Homes and Gardens.* <www.familymoney.com> A bimonthly finance magazine that provides good information for planning family finances.

Additional Business Ideas

- Financial services for seniors. Help take care of seniors' personal financial matters.
- The Financial Planning Association (FPA), 1615 L Street, NW, Suite 650, Washington, DC 20036; <www.fpanet.org>. Certification, bookstore, conferences, educational programs, and other membership benefits.
- Tax preparation for individuals and small and home-based businesses. (See Tax Preparation Service, page 438.)

25

IMAGE CONSULTING SERVICE

In this business you assist individuals and corporate employees in improving their overall appearances, speech, and manners, thereby enabling clients to project the images they need to achieve their personal or professional goals. Some of the reasons professional image consultants are hired include the following: job promotions, interviews for jobs or admittance to programs, appearances on television, public speaking, competitions, adult rehabilitation programs, companies wanting to upgrade their employees' images, entertainers wanting to improve their public image.

In this business an image consultant can specialize in makeup or wardrobe, for example, or might advise clients in several areas in which they wish to improve.

Another area some image consultants pursue is improving the business or professional image of businesses and how they present their companies to customers when they advertise at trade shows, and/or how they project themselves to potential customers and the business community as a whole.

Start-Up Costs

From $6,000 to $16,000 and up for a home office equipped to receive customers for consultation.

Pricing Guidelines

$50 to $250 per hour (up to $300 an hour for corporate clients). You might also charge a flat fee per day or workshop session—$700 to $4,000 and up.

Marketing and Advertising Methods and Tips

- Research your target market well to know what advertising will attract customers.
- Network with professionals and let them know of your service.

- Have professional-looking, well-designed promotional materials ready to hand out or present at meetings, conventions, seminars, and business trade shows.
- Give talks or hold workshops for companies.
- Contact the chamber of commerce and other local and civic groups for individual clients. Join those that provide the best networking opportunities and potential leads.
- Have a Web site with customer comments and photos.

Essential Equipment

A good personal wardrobe and accessories; standard PC with software and e-mail; business telephone line with an answering machine, answering service, or voice mail; cell phone; copier; fax machine; comfortable chairs and a small conference table for talking with clients; audio and visual aids if you are giving talks or conducting workshops; portfolio of before and after photos of clients; a 35mm camera and/or a digital camera for loading photos onto the Internet.

Recommended Training, Experience, or Needed Skills

- Talk with personal image consultants for tips.
- Decide if you will specialize or generalize.
- Enroll in image and marketing courses.
- Try to apprentice or work with experienced image consultants in the industry you wish to specialize.
- Need expertise in your area or areas. Many image consultants have had training or experience in fashion design, cosmetology, clothing merchandising, business marketing, makeup techniques, public relations, and speech and grammar education.
- Need to be positive and self-assured, which will help instill confidence in your advice to your clients.

Income Potential

$25,000 to $100,000 or more.

Type of Business

One-fourth in-home for initial consultations, running the business, gathering information, and planning; three-fourths out-of-the-home for making presentations, giving instructions, shopping with the client for wardrobe, and so forth.

Target Market

Professionals or executives who want to enhance their images to help them in their careers, new college graduates, women who are returning to the workforce, people who want to prepare for job interviews. Small businesses that want to improve, focus, or change their business's message and impression.

Success Tips

- ✤ According to the Academy of Fashion and Image, you can be a successful image consultant if you have at least two of the following:
    1. A natural sense of style or color.
    2. Background in the retail, fashion, or cosmetic industry.
    3. An ability to structure your time and set your own hours.
    4. A genuine desire to help others look and be their best.
- ✤ Encourage word-of-mouth referrals from satisfied clients.
- ✤ Develop different sidelines to your business, such as conducting workshops or seminars; helping people who are physically or mentally challenged; assisting adults who are returning to work after a long layoff or period of unemployment to find professional-looking clothes for their jobs; writing articles or columns on how to put together a wardrobe when on a budget, for example.

For More Information

Association

Association of Image Consultants International
12300 Ford Road, Suite 135
Dallas, TX 75234
<www.aici.org>

Nonprofit, professional organization offering members various benefits, including resources (home study sources, conferences), mentoring, and other networking opportunities. Send an LSASE for more information or visit the Web site.

Book

The Perfect Fit: How to Start an Image Consulting Business, by Lynne Henderson Marks and Dominique Isbecque (Orlando, FL: First Publish, 2001).

Home Study Courses and Schools

Distance Education and Training Council
1601 18th Street, NW
Washington, DC 20009
< www.detc.org >

Write for a brochure of schools offering home study courses on this topic or visit the Web site.

Additional Business Ideas

- Hold self-improvement seminars. Refer to *Getting Started in Speaking, Training, or Seminar Consulting,* by Robert Bly (New York: John Wiley & Sons, 2002).
- Sell cosmetics and fashion accessories.

26
INVENTORY SERVICE

This service business involves taking a one-time or periodic inventory of an individual's possessions or a business's stock of merchandise that involves counting and cataloging merchandise and analyzing and computing the figures into reports. For homeowners, you could offer to engrave their items for identification purposes.

Inventories are important for insurance purposes and help businesses know what products they have on hand. You can run this business by yourself or hire others to work together part-time on large projects.

Start-Up Costs and Financing Sources

- $4,000 to $8,000 and up.
- Personal savings, line of credit from a bank, small business loan for home office equipment and/or vehicle.

Pricing Guidelines

$75 to $100+ per hour or a flat fee for a project; $2 to $4 per thousand dollars of merchandise.

Marketing and Advertising Methods and Tips

- Send out direct mailings to stores, institutions, and warehouse clubs.
- Make presentations on the value of inventories in crime prevention to neighborhood watch groups, local law enforcement officials, and insurance agents for business referrals.
- Rent a booth at home trade shows.
- Print brochures and business cards. Collect letters from satisfied customers.
- Advertise on radio and local cable television.
- Give talks to local chamber of commerce groups.

Essential Equipment

Home office supplies: handheld or laptop computer and a PC with inventory features (report capabilities, billing software) and other technology such as data collection software with bar coding, radio frequency identification tracking (RFID), voice recognition, digitization, imaging and weighing scale and handheld portable equipment for data recording, scanning, and printing; video recorder, instant and/or digital photo camera; engraving tool; cellular phone and pager, business line and answering devices or service; dependable vehicle.

Recommended Training, Experience, or Needed Skills

- Work in a department store doing their annual inventories.
- Background in retail business and/or businesses in which you may target your inventory service.

- Work in an insurance company and take courses about protecting home valuables and assets.
- Be familiar with insurance and law enforcement rules and procedures.
- Be efficient, well organized, and professional.

Income Potential

$35,000 to $60,000 or more, depending on your clients and the number of inventories you do per year.

Type of Business

One-fourth in-home for running the business and preparing reports; three-fourths out-of-the-home for the inventories.

Target Market

Homeowners or apartment dwellers who own valuables; institutions; general merchandise department stores; businesses that want their equipment and inventory protected; schools, hospitals, or other institutions that need inventory reports to write their annual budgets.

Success Tips

- Consult with your insurance agent about liability coverage and being bonded.
- Check with your lawyer about drawing up contracts and assessing your liability needs.
- Know how insurance agents and law enforcement officers want items to be inventoried in the event of theft.
- Provide detailed reports and inventories to your clients and keep their records confidential.

For More Information

Book

Basics of Inventory Management: From Warehouse to Distribution Center, by J. David Viale and Christopher Carrigan (editor) (Menlo Park, CA: Crisp Publications, 1997).

Additional Business Ideas

- Offer your inventory services to estate sale holders, auction houses, or nonprofit organizations.
- Create home or business inventory kits to sell.

27
PERSONAL CONCIERGE

This is a relatively new personal service and one that is growing in demand. A personal concierge service differs from an errand service in that, with this personal business, you work as a personal assistant for individuals—executives, busy professionals, wealthy individuals—and shop, plan meetings, make travel arrangements, and perform other tasks that they are too busy to do. You can either generalize or specialize your services to shop for items such as gifts, clothes, groceries, or other everyday goods that busy people do not have the time to get for themselves. Of course, you must like to shop, know the best stores (or the stores your customers prefer), recognize a good's quality, know current prices, and have a good network of contacts in order to arrange or get the items or services your clients need.

Start-Up Costs and Financing Sources

- $3,000 to $5,000 average for advertising and basic home office supplies and equipment (not including a dependable vehicle).
- Personal savings, credit line from your local bank.

Pricing Guidelines

Concierges usually charge by the hour or by the service, and those who have corporate clients also charge a retainer fee. Factor in your time, expertise, overhead, and wear and tear on your vehicle: You might include a minimum charge, then so many cents per mile and an additional charge per stop of $3 to $5 + . Or you can simply charge by the hour.

Marketing and Advertising Methods and Tips

- Send out attention-getting direct mailings to corporations and media to encourage responses and possibly feature articles about your service. Also contact high-end stores for referrals.
- Post flyers on community bulletin boards.
- Print up business cards.
- Offer seminars and talks to groups you know are your target customers.
- Place ads in publications and newspapers that your target customers read.
- Write articles in business publications and magazines.

Essential Equipment

Publicity and marketing materials; business telephone line with answering machine, answering service, or voice mail; computer with database software to track your clients' assignments and favorite stores and their layouts, contact persons (retailers and wholesalers); printer; promotional materials; business telephones (cell phone and ground line); pager and other equipment (not including a dependable vehicle). You will also need to be covered by such insurances as auto, general liability, employee crime, property coverage, and any others that may apply to your business (check with your insurance agent).

Recommended Training, Experience, or Needed Skills

- Have experience, knowledge, and expertise either from personal or work experience or from training and study in the area of shopping in which you plan to specialize.
- Be efficient, dependable, and honest and know what kind of purchases best please each of your customers.
- Have a Web site and an option enabling potential customers to reach you.
- Be persistent in finding out the information and accomplishing the tasks your client asks.
- Being flexible, resourceful, creative, and a problem solver are good characteristics to have.
- Be a good online researcher.

Income Potential

Depending on your clientele, you can earn anywhere from $20,000 per year to a six-figure income, if you have higher-income and corporate clients.

Type of Business

One-fourth in-home, marketing and running the business; three-fourths out-of-the-home, shopping, making presentations, and meeting with clients.

Target Market

Professional working couples, business executives, wealthy individuals.

Success Tips

- Prove to your customers that they can trust you to get the best quality items for their money and that you are dependable.
- Know the clients you want to target, their tastes, and the stores they like best.
- Consult regularly with contact people at the stores you visit for the latest tips on sales, trends, and so forth.
- Be able to shop and perform tasks for more than one customer at a time.
- Urban areas offer more potential for clients.

For More Information

Associations

International Concierge and Errand Association
1139 Cantrell Street
Philadelphia, PA 19148
< www.iceaweb.org >

Networking association whose member benefits include listing in an online directory, a newsletter, and other various resources. For membership information, send an LSASE or visit the Web site.

National Concierge Association
P.O. Box 4371
Scottsdale, AZ 85261
<http://conciergeassoc.org>

Nonprofit organization offering educational and promotional opportunities to concierges throughout the world.

Start-Up Guide

Entrepreneur's Start-Up Guide, *How to Start a Personal Concierge Service.* For pricing and ordering information, visit <www.smallbizbooks.com> or call (800) 421-2300.

Additional Business Ideas

- Hotel Concierge. Refer to: <http://hollyspeaks.com>. Articles, book about being a hotel concierge. (Does not have start-up information for being a personal concierge.)
- Mystery shopping service (you evaluate employees' customer service for employers). Refer to e-booklet: *Mystery Shopping Earns You Perks* by Alyice Edrich. Visit the Web site of The Dabbling Mum.com <http://thedabblingmum.com> for more information.

28
PERSONAL SALON SERVICES

One of the earliest home-based businesses run by women were home beauty salons. Today, home salons offer varied beauty treatments such as facials, cosmetic consulting, pedicures, nail treatments, and massage therapy sessions, in addition to offering haircuts to the entire family.

Sue Marx has run her home salon for more than 20 years. After discovering she would no longer receive a commission for part-time work at the beauty shop where she was employed, she promptly quit and began to do hairdressing in her apartment.

She and her husband saved to build their first home, which included a salon they designed. When a stone quarry purchased their home for the land, Sue and her husband built a second home, with an expanded waiting area and access for persons with disabilities.

Marx went from just cutting women's hair to cutting the hair of entire families. "It makes it more convenient for families to all come together for their haircuts these days," says Marx, "because families' lifestyles are so hectic with work, school sports and other activities."

Marx has to renew her cosmetologist license each year, and her salon is inspected every year by a state inspector. She has never had to advertise—all her customers come from word-of-mouth referrals. She has steady work and prefers to work only from Wednesday afternoons to Saturdays at noon, leaving time for her family. Her salon has its own business telephone line and electrical line, separate from her house.

Marx was able to start with good used equipment and had her chairs reupholstered when she wanted to remodel her shop. Her husband built cabinets, installed shelves, and finished the decor to Marx's specifications. "It's been a good business for my family. The customers have been great in scheduling appointments whenever I have wanted to take a scheduled or impromptu day or week off."

Start-Up Costs and Financing Sources

- $10,000 to $40,000 or more for equipment and furnishings. Costs vary for the services you offer, the new or good used equipment you buy, the costs of your products, and so forth. This does not include the cost of your training and licenses or permits to operate from your home.
- Personal savings, small business loan.

Pricing Guidelines

Check with the going rate of hair, skin, pedicure, and nail care services and make your prices competitive. If you have a home salon, you can offer lower prices because you will not have to pay rent, but you still have to figure in your overhead and expenses to run your business.

If you do not have the training to offer additional services, you can have specialists offer their services on certain days of the week at your salon. They pay you a percentage of their take, pay rent for the space used, or pay a commission for each customer you schedule for them.

Marketing and Advertising Methods and Tips

- Have a grand opening and possibly an open house for customers to visit your salon and meet you and any other beauty professionals who will be working with you. Announce it with a press release.
- Encourage word-of-mouth referrals from satisfied customers.
- Offer special deals for the entire family.
- Offer coupons in advertising mail services for a free facial or nail treatment.
- Donate your services to help your community and garner good PR for your business. Some examples: have a "cut-a-thon" once a year to raise money for a local nonprofit organization and/or provide free coupons to women's shelters or offer free hairstyling to women in nursing homes to celebrate Mother's Day.
- Join a local women's business organization for networking purposes.

Essential Equipment

Home office business supplies, standard equipment and supplies, business line and answering machine, service, or voice mail. Also, commercial supplies such as hair dryers, chemicals, linens, and fixtures.

Recommended Training, Experience, or Needed Skills

- Attend cosmetology or beautician schools.
- Work in a commercial salon for the experience and to develop a following.
- Enjoy working with people.

Income Potential

$25,000 to $55,000 or more, depending on your clients, the kinds of personal care services you offer, commissions from other beauty specialists, and the sale of related beauty products and other beauty care items.

Type of Business

In-home.

Target Market

You can cater to entire families or certain groups such as seniors, teens, children, men, or individuals with special needs.

Success Tips

- Listen to what your customers want and try to make those services available.
- Keep up-to-date on the latest trends and products through trade shows and publications.
- Use bookkeeping software like QuickBooks to track your inventory and product sales to help you manage your cash flow.
- Know what licensing and training requirements you need.
- Check the local and state government regulations regarding home salons.
- Visit a number of home salons and talk to their owners to see the layout of their salons and to get some practical tips from them for designing and operating your salon efficiently and profitably. Plan your salon to be as friendly and relaxing as possible for your customers.

Franchises, Distributorships, and Licenses

There are a number of commercial hair, skin, and nail franchise opportunities. See the regular issues of such print publications as *Entrepreneur* <www.entrepreneur.com> and *Home Business* <www.homebusinessmag.com> magazines (find at newsstands and bookstores) and their Web sites for listings of related business opportunities and franchises.

For More Information

Associations

Association of Cosmetologists and Hairdressers (ACH)
1811 Monroe
Dearborn, MI 48124

Send an LSASE for membership information.

National Cosmetology Association
< www.salonprofessionals.org >

Offers members newsletter and other benefits.

Web Sites

< www.beautytech.com >

BeautyTech—Comprehensive site for hairdressers, nail technicians, cosmetologists, and salon owners. Directory of links for suppliers, books, tapes, videos, and so forth.

< www.hair-news.com >

Hair News magazine—"Dedicated to the Art and Science of Hair."

Books

How to Start and Manage a Hair Styling Salon Business: Step by Step Guide to Starting and Managing Your Own Business, by Jerre G. Lewis and Leslie D. Renn (Interlochen, MI: Lewis & Renn Associates, 1999).

The Transition: How to Become a Salon Professional, by Louise Cotter and Frances London Dubose (Stamford, CT: Thomson Learning, 1996).

Publications

Contact industry associations that provide their members with related publications.

Software

HARMS Software, 50 Galesi Drive, Wayne, NJ 07470; < www.salon-solutions.com >. Software to enable beauty salons and spas to manage daily operations.

Additional Business Ideas

- ✤ Home-based nail salon. To keep up with the latest nail care methods, trends, products, and licensing, nail technicians recommend attending trade shows and seminars. See notices in *NAILS* magazine and information from the Nails Industry Association (NIA), 2512 Artesia Boulevard, Redondo Beach, CA 90278. Check state regulations regarding licenses for a nail salon. Also refer to: *Milady's Art & Science of Nail Technology,* 2nd ed. (Milady Publishing Corporation, 1997) and *Salonovations' Nail Q and a Book,* by Vicki Peters (Stamford, CT: Thomson Learning, 1996).
- ✤ Facialist or cosmetician. You need a state license.
- ✤ Mobile hair dresser. Do hair for recovering hospital patients, nursing home residents, shut-ins, special-needs persons residing in group homes; go to brides' homes or churches to do their hair on their wedding days; do special hair braiding in customers' homes.
- ✤ Independent makeup artist for brides, models, and others needing expert makeup application.

29
PROFESSIONAL ORGANIZER

Carole J. Manna of Skokie, Illinois, has always been an organized person. Even when she was three years old, she would arrange her toys in order. She quit her teaching job and went to work in broadcasting in California. While there, she realized she had a talent for organizing, which she applied while working on different assignments and projects in her company's office.

Manna decided to go out on her own, and for the past 20 years, her business, Organization Unlimited, has served both residential and corporate clients in setting up library and filing systems in addition to general time and space management. She also produced a video on organizational tips that was sponsored by Stanley Hardware and Rubbermaid.

Manna says, "Eighty percent of clutter is not due to insufficient space, but disorganization. I help people regain control of their surroundings once again, which gives them peace of mind in their otherwise hectic schedules."

Professional organizers assist clients in their homes and offices manage their time, papers, space, clutter, and other aspects of their personal and work lives that need order. This can range from organizing kitchens, closets, home libraries, home offices, computer files, and anything else that has gotten out of hand as far as clutter and disorganization is concerned. Many items once thought permanently lost often turn up when a professional organizer is at work, such as money, airline tickets, and other "buried" items.

Start-Up Costs and Financing Sources

- $5,000 to $7,000.
- Personal savings, small business loans, credit line from your bank.

Pricing Guidelines

- $35 to $150+ per hour, depending on your clients (individuals, corporations); have at least a four-hour per day minimum.
- Options include setting up a one-time service or a regular, periodic service.
- More can usually be charged in urban areas than rural.
- Charge more according to your experience and expertise.

Marketing and Advertising Methods and Tips

- Develop a marketing program and modify it to fit the customers you are targeting. You need different marketing methods for corporate clients and residential clients.
- Send out press releases and follow up with phone calls when you are ready for business.
- Volunteer to give speeches on organizing.

- Offer one free hour of consultation to benefit auctions.
- Advertise on local radio and cable television.
- Put together a portfolio to give to prospective clients. Manna's portfolio includes copies of letters from satisfied customers, copies of articles written about her in newspapers and magazines, and a business card and brochure of her services. Also include before and after pictures.
- Advertise in the business telephone directory.
- Leave promotional materials at closet organizing stores.

Essential Equipment

Filing system (manual or computerized); cell phone, business telephone line (ground line) with answering machine, answering service, or voice mail; dependable vehicle; space containers; organizing supplies based on customer needs.

Recommended Training, Experience, or Needed Skills

- Volunteer to organize others' residential rooms or offices to see if you like this business and if you have a talent for it.
- Read books on organizing.
- Have a talent for organizing and be able to visualize (almost like an artist) what needs to be done to a room or space, according to Manna.
- Have good people skills and be able to deal with individual styles and tastes.
- Attend organizing seminars.

Income Potential

$30,000 to $57,000. It will take some time to build a client base.

Type of Business

One-fourth in-home for running the business and planning; three-fourths out-of-the-home for organizing and giving talks.

Target Market

Professionals with business or home offices; people who work full-time and are involved in community projects at the same time; people with extensive private libraries; people who work from their homes, such as writers, researchers, college students, professional practitioners; business executives.

Success Tips

- Teach your clients how to stay organized through effective and easy-to-follow methods.
- Customize your knowledge to your customer's needs.
- Always put your customer's needs first. Be flexible.
- Market your business continually to keep the customers coming.
- Have a variety of options from which your clients can choose—a one-time visit or an ongoing service.
- Debbie Williams, an organizing strategist and the author of *Home Management 101: A Guide for Busy Parents* (Vancouver, WA: Champion Press, 2001) says, "The biggest tip I can share with anyone interested in pursuing a career as a professional organizer is to find a niche or specialty and stick with it—being a 'generalist' and offering all services to home and residential clients will spread you so thin that you may give up before you even get a good start! Choose a specialty like working with seniors or medical offices, and service that niche to the best of your ability."

For More Information

Association

National Association of Professional Organizers
P.O. Box 140647
Austin, TX 78714
<www.napo.net>

Conference, newsletter, certification; LSASE for membership information or visit the Web site.

Books

For Packrats Only: How to Clean Up, Clear Out and Dejunk Your Life Forever!, by Don Aslett (Pocatello, ID: Marsh Creek Press, 2002).

Organizing from the Inside Out: The Foolproof System for Organizing Your Home, Your Office, and Your Life, by Julie Morgenstern (New York: Henry Holt & Co., 1998).

Web Sites, Education and Support

< www.organizedu.com >

OrganizedUniversity—Offers training for all your organized needs; and site also offers listing of professional organizers.

< http://organizedtimes.com >

OrganizedTimes—Presents organizing solutions and a weekly e-zine, plus an annual online expo.

Web Site, Organizing Tips and Free Planners

< www.organizetips.com >

Organizetips.com.

Additional Business Ideas

- Conduct research studies for specific businesses on how to make the most efficient use of their space and time.
- Specialize in organizing closets and installing closet kits.

30
RÉSUMÉ WRITING SERVICE

No matter what shape the economy is in, résumés are always needed by job seekers—in a slow economy, people downsized or laid off need a résumé to look for new employment; and in a good economy, people need a résumé to find a better job within or outside of their companies. A well-written and well-presented résumé is an important asset in helping a person land a job: It creates a first impression that can make a difference between a person getting hired or not, especially if there are many applicants. The goal of a résumé writing service is to promote your client's abilities, training, and work experience in concise language that emphasizes the strengths of your client and targets what an employer is looking for.

Résumé writers can offer to type a résumé, edit those written by clients, or interview a client and write it. The standard formats are chronological, functional, and a combination of the two, and they should project the image that the customer wishes to project to a prospective employer. Résumés run from one page to several, depending on the employer who will be doing the screening. Styles and formats change somewhat, so it is important to keep up with the latest industry standards through trade publications and associations.

Résumé professionals often add extra services—career testing, job coaching, follow-up letters, résumé disk storage, and other related services—to persons seeking a new job or position.

Start-Up Costs and Financing Sources

- $5,000 to $15,000 for a home office setup to receive customers.
- Personal savings, line of credit from a bank. Start with only typing résumés and put aside the money you earn to purchase the furnishings and equipment you need.

Pricing Guidelines

$100 to $300+ for résumé packages; $95 for student, first-time job search; $140 to $200 for customers with several years of job history; up to $350 or more for executives. Also check industry standards (see Professional Association of Résumé Writers and Career Coaches entry, later in this section).

Marketing and Advertising Methods and Tips

- Advertise in the business telephone directory.
- Encourage word-of-mouth referrals from satisfied customers.

- Post flyers on college bulletin boards.
- Place classified ads in newspapers and on local cable television stations.
- Give résumé writing tips seminars or talks to companies or government agencies that are downsizing or laying off employees. Leave your brochures and business cards on completion of your talk.
- Keep a database of customers and send them a periodic newsletter or e-newsletter via the Internet, with job search tips and highlighting new services you may be offering.

Essential Equipment

Computer and word processing software (store your client's résumé on a computer disk and sell them the disk as part of the package); office and résumé software and good graphics software programs such as Adobe InDesign or QuarkXPress; laser printer for professional quality print-outs; copier and inexpensive copy paper for rough drafts; standard (8½"×11") white bond paper (20 or 25 lb. weight) for final version; envelopes for mailing; other presentation folders.

Recommended Training, Experience, or Needed Skills

- Volunteer to write the résumés of friends, coworkers, and relatives.
- Take résumé courses and seminars; study examples of the different types of résumés.
- Work for a résumé writing service.
- Research the trade language for a particular position.
- Write concisely, accurately, factually, creatively, quickly, and in an easy-to-read style that accentuates your client's attributes and strengths.
- Become certified as a professional résumé writer.
- Take writing, grammar, and copyediting courses so you will not make any mistakes in writing the résumé.

Income Potential

$35,000 to $150,000 or more.

Type of Business

An in-home business, unless you interview your clients in some other location.

Success Tips

- ✤ Produce professional-looking (no typos and no spelling or grammatical errors), creative résumés in a relatively short time, which will produce referrals from satisfied customers.
- ✤ Do your market research to find out who are the best customers in your area.
- ✤ Learn the professional standards in this business and practice them before you open for business.
- ✤ Translate former military positions into civilian jobs and skills so that prospective employers can understand what duties or functions the client did in military service.
- ✤ Take time to create a solid business plan that sets your goals and plans for your business's growth.
- ✤ Teena Rose, author of *Bizy's Guide to How to Start a Résumé Service,* offers these tips:

  Have the following:

  A master plan . . .

  Aggressively market a résumé business by devising a daily and weekly list of public relations and marketing strategies.

  No-charge exposure . . .

  Whether operating locally, online, or both, items could include a quote to the local media, link exchange requests, press releases, and business alliance e-mails, letters, or phone calls. Taking advantage of free advertising is "smart business," since most home-based start-ups possess limited funds.

  Paid advertising . . .

  Résumé writers tend to add a "cocktail" of paid—yellow page listing, newspaper ad, business memberships, and networking groups—advertising to the overall plan. Each is designed to bring in new business, while a referral bonus and an informative newsletter will encourage repeat and referral clients.

For More Information

Association

Professional Association of Résumé Writers and Career Coaches
1388 Brightwaters Boulevard, NE
St. Petersburg, FL 33704
< www.parw.com >

Offers courses, holds seminars, and provides certification.

Books and Publications

Cover Letters for Dummies, 2nd ed., by Joyce Lain Kennedy (Foster City, CA: IDG Books Worldwide, 2000).

How to Start a Home-Based Résumé Business, 2nd ed., by Jan Melnick (Old Saybrook, CT: Globe Pequot Press, 1997).

Job Interviews for Dummies, 2nd ed., by Joyce Lain Kennedy (Foster City, CA: IDG Books Worldwide, 2000).

Resumes for Dummies, 3rd ed., by Joyce Lain Kennedy (Foster City, CA: IDG Books Worldwide, 2000).

E-Book

Bizy's Guide to How to Start a Résumé Service, by Teena Rose. See < www.bizymoms.com > for ordering information.

Software

Resume Deluxe, 9.0, by WinWay < www.winway.com > .

Additional Business Ideas

- ✤ Offer additional writing services: cover letters, brochures, reports, editing, proofreading.
- ✤ Offer job counseling, referrals, interview coaching.

31
TUTORING SERVICE

With cutbacks in funding for education, crowded classrooms, and rising numbers of students dropping out of school every year, tutoring and remedial education services are needed in almost every area of the country. People who need help with their educational skills include the following: college-bound students (or students *in* college), adults wanting to brush up on their basic skills or to prepare to go or return to college, people in physical or drug rehabilitation programs, and new citizens wanting to get a better grasp of the English language.

Deborah and a friend, both former teachers who had stopped teaching to have children, decided to start their own tutoring business after receiving many requests to tutor their friends' children. Deborah and her friend consulted with a lawyer about starting their own tutoring business and then registered with local and state authorities. Next, they established accounts with educational publishers so they could get next-day delivery of materials when needed.

Deborah even had an addition built onto her home to accommodate her home business, and business grew with referrals from parents and schools. Deborah and her friend contacted local schoolteachers and invited them to come to Deborah's home to review their materials and credentials. "We work closely with a student's teacher and have a checklist for the teacher to fill out and then give periodic reports to keep the communication going between teacher, student, the parents, and us."

Today, Deborah's friend has returned to teaching, and Deborah has gone on to expand her business, called Teach Me Tutoring, to include preparing for the SATs, helping honor students apply for scholarships, consulting for homeschooling lessons, and teaching homebound students who are recuperating from illnesses. Deborah also tutors youths at a drug rehabilitation center and goes to a local hospital every week to help head trauma victims with their cognitive skills.

Companies also ask her to review English and grammar skills with executives and to help Hispanic employees learn English.

Often parents of students will request tutoring for themselves in subjects they feel they never really grasped while in school.

In order to accommodate her growing business, Deborah purchased a nearby older, three-story home, which she says involved adhering to a number of state and local regulations. She has had to hire teachers to tutor her growing list of students. "I hire teachers who really care about my students, and it gives us all the satisfaction of having the time to help those who really need it."

Start-Up Costs

$5,000 to $10,000 for home office supplies and equipment, educational materials, tables, desks, and lamps. Your costs will involve equipping your tutoring area with desks, computers, texts, and other supplies, as well as the standard legalizing of any business that is required. With education, you will also want to contact your state department of education to see what other requirements you may need to fulfill.

Pricing Guidelines

$35 to $50+ per hour; $600 to $900 for an SAT preparation course. If you hire tutors to work for you, you can take 30 percent of their pay. Thus you will be able to charge by the hour—what the going rate is for teachers of your qualifications—or by the course if you are conducting an SAT preparation class series, for example. The two women tutors also added a sideline to their business by offering a summer reading enrichment program. With the growing number of states requiring students to meet certain standards in order to be promoted to the next grade or to graduate, there will no doubt be an increased need for summer tutoring and educational programs.

Marketing and Advertising Methods and Tips

- Encourage word-of-mouth referrals from parents of students.
- Arrange for referrals from local schools. Most professional tutors get their students through word-of-mouth referrals and

from the institutions they work with. You can also place ads in local parenting newspapers or offer presentations to school parents' groups about various educational issues.

- Place classified ads in local newspapers about special summer reading camps, SAT test preparation courses (class and independent study with a computer and software program), and special study groups.
- Call to offer your service to social service agencies that help prepare and train low-income adults for a job or career.
- Place flyers on community and/or campus bulletin boards.
- Advertise from a Web site.

Essential Equipment

Educational materials and supplies for ages K–adult, computer(s) and educational software, copier, study areas, desks, tables, business line with answering machine or service, brochures, business cards.

Recommended Training, Experience, or Needed Skills

- It will depend on the type of tutoring you are doing, but many institutions as well as state and/or federal programs require a tutor to be certified in the area(s) in which they teach. Of course, you must have enthusiasm for the subject you are teaching and be able to relate and communicate well with the age and level of your students.
- Work at a tutoring center or volunteer in local programs that teach adults to read to see if you like this type of business.
- Check with your state's department of education for regulations and licensing requirements.
- Enjoy helping others to learn. Have patience and a good sense of humor.

Income Potential

$20,000 to $25,000, part-time; $30,000 to $50,000, full-time; more if you have other tutors working for you.

Type of Business

At first it may be both in-home and out-of-the-home because you (or your tutors) may tutor at the students' homes. Deborah put on an addition to her home to serve many students at once.

Target Market

- Honors students who are competing for scholarships and SATs.
- Parents of homeschooling groups, which are growing rapidly throughout the nation.
- Youth rehabilitation centers.
- Homebound students with permanent or temporary disabilities due to accidents or illnesses.
- Cognitive therapy programs for brain trauma victims.
- Community mental health programs and day centers serving developmentally delayed children and adults.
- Adult literacy programs.
- Businesses that want (1) grammar refresher skills for promoted executives or (2) English language tutoring for employees who speak a foreign language.
- College students—traditional and nontraditional (older adults going to college for the first time or returning to complete their studies).

Success Tips

- Work with the child's teacher and parents to establish good communication.
- Check licensing regulations.
- Expand your tutorial service to include all ages, in addition to community businesses and programs.
- Care about your students and accentuate the positive.
- Teach your students good study habits and good organizational skills to help them from falling behind in their subjects.
- One professional tutor says, "I would advise those starting a tutoring business to be patient at first. Signing up your first students takes time, so don't get discouraged if you don't fill up your schedule right away. If you stick with it, though, you'll

build your business to the point that you won't have to advertise anymore; word-of-mouth referrals will keep you busy!"

- Another tutor says, in her opinion, the biggest problem between school students and teachers is "the lack of communication between the teacher, student, and parent." She bridges this communication gap by providing a checklist for each teacher to fill out concerning the academic requirements the student is to satisfy (which is reviewed each time she meets with that student); plus she encourages positive support from parents and family members.
- You might also want to work at a tutoring center or volunteer in adult literacy programs to see if you like this type of work.
- In summary, the personal tutor who cares about each student—and is willing to be flexible to adapt her service to fit a range of students—will help keep her tutoring business profitable while enjoying the challenges of teaching a diversity of students.

Franchises, Distributorships, and Licenses

HOPE (Helping Others Pursue Education) Career Centers
4274 Lakeview Drive
Ogden, UT 84403
< www.hopecareercenter.com >

Provides educational information and financial aid services for high school graduates, workers who have lost their jobs, people wishing to change careers, and businesses that offer partial reimbursement programs for their employees. Send an LSASE for more information or visit the Web site.

For More Information

Association

National Association of Tutoring
Jacksonville State University
Ramona Wood Building #105
700 Belham Road North
Jacksonville, AL 36265

Send an LSASE for membership information.

Books

Becoming an Effective Tutor, by Lynda Myers (Menlo Park, CA: Crisp Publications, 1990).

The Master Tutor: A Guidebook for More Effective Tutoring, by Ross B. MacDonald (Cambridge England: Stratford, Ltd., 1994).

Tutoring for Pay: Earn While You Help Others Learn, by Betty O. Carpenter (Springfield IL: Charles C. Thomas Publisher, 1991).

Tutoring Matters: Everything You Always Wanted to Know About How to Tutor, by Jerome Rabow, Tiffani Chin, and Nima Fahimian (Philadelphia, PA: Temple University Press, 1999).

Web Sites

< www.cleverapple.com >

Clever Apple—Kim Clapp's tutoring program (manual and video).

< www.tutor2000.com >

Tutor2000—Tutor referrals.

Books, Games, Supplies.

Homeschool Basics (formerly The Education Connection)
P.O. Box 910367
St. George, UT 84791
< www.educationconnection.com >

Additional Business Ideas

- Homeschooling consultant. Refer to: *Homeschooling Almanac, 2000-2001: How to Start, What to Do, Who to Call, Resources, Products, Teaching Supplies, Support Groups, Conferences, and More!*, by Mary and Michael Leppert (Roseville, CA: Prima Communications, 1999). Another resource is *Home Education Magazine,* P.O. Box 1083, Tonasket, WA 98855; < www.home-ed-magazine.com >. Send an LSASE for subscription information.
- Classes (not tutoring). Teach your expertise to others at adult evening school classes, in colleges, seminars, and so forth.

Health Services

32
HOME HEALTH CARE

The research department of the National Association for Home Care reported in 2001 more than 20,000 providers delivered home care services to some 7.6 million individuals who required services because of acute illness, long-term health conditions, permanent disability, or terminal illness, and the Health Care Financing Administration, Office of the Actuary stated (March 2001) that annual expenditures for home health care would be about $41.3 billion in 2001.

With the dramatic rising cost of medical care and lack of facilities to handle our health needs, home health care businesses are in demand. This service coordinates and provides caring health services to people at home for a fraction of the price of hospitalization or institutional care, while enabling persons to stay in the comfort and familiarity of their own homes.

Some health care agencies specialize in medical and follow-up care, some specialize in "comfort" or palliative care, while others add extra services in their businesses. At present, it is difficult and time-consuming to get funding from government agencies for any of your services. Many home health care agencies work with the local, state, and federal agencies and fill in with services that the governmental agencies do not cover for their clients, or they may bypass the government altogether and are paid by the clients, their families, or their private insurance carriers, depending on the financial resources of their patients.

This is a good business for those who enjoy helping people and their families and are skilled at coordinating and organizing services.

Start-Up Costs and Financing Sources

- $20,000 to $100,000, depending on whether you want to start small and build up your client base and services later, or start large right away. Small business loan or line of credit from your local bank.

Pricing Guidelines

Check with trade associations for industry standards. Interview a number of agencies to see what services they offer and how much they charge, what contracts they have, how often they make visits.

Marketing and Advertising Methods and Tips

- Place an ad in the business telephone directory.
- Send out direct mailings to developments or homes where older adults live.
- Make presentations to health care professionals, networking groups, institutions, senior citizen centers, adult day care centers, child care centers (for sick-children care), social service agencies, nonprofit associations and groups serving mentally and physically challenged persons, hospice programs.
- Advertise on radio and local cable television.

Essential Equipment

Home office supplies and equipment: computer with billing, mailing, and management software; cell phone and business telephone (ground) line with answering machine or service and fax; pagers for employees; comfortable furniture if you receive clients in your office for consultation; copier. Promotional materials: brochures, videos (if you can afford to send tapes to prospective clients).

Recommended Training, Experience, or Needed Skills

- Work for a home health care agency or have experience and/or health care training with older adults or nonambulatory persons.
- Be able to hire workers who care and are knowledgeable about their jobs.
- Have a caring and positive attitude.
- Should have a professional degree in the health field, and medical management experience.

Income Potential

$50,000 to $100,000 and up, depending on the number of clients and employees you have.

Type of Business

About one-half in-home and one-half out-of-the-home when you start the business. Full-time in-home for running the business, scheduling, hiring and recruiting personnel if you hire employees to be the caregivers.

Target Market

Older adults, families with special-needs children, persons with terminal illnesses, individuals with disabilities, or anyone who needs some assistance in his or her home.

Success Tips

- Find caring and capable employees to provide services as soon as you begin operating.
- Obviously, consult with insurance experts about the types of coverage you will need.

- ✤ Research thoroughly all the aspects of this business before you open. Take the time to learn all you can.
- ✤ Stay current with the regulations and changes in this industry.

For More Information

Association

National Association for Home Care (NAHC)
228 Seventh Street, SE
Washington, DC 20003
<www.nahc.org>

The NAHC is the nation's largest trade association representing the interests and concerns of home care agencies, hospices, home care aide organizations, and medical equipment suppliers. It offers a section online called "Resources for Starting a Home Care Agency," as well as related publications and products.

Book

How to Start and Manage a Home Health Care Business: Step by Step Guide to Business Success, by Jerre G. Lewis and Leslie D. Renn. Order from Lewis and Renn Associates, 10315 Harmony Drive, Interlochen, MI 49643.

Publications

HomeCare magazine <www.homecaremag.com>. Visit the Web site for subscription information.

Additional Business Ideas

- ✤ Services other than health care: cleaning, shopping, running errands, preparing meals, assisting with personal needs, providing transportation, being a day companion, providing respite care while caregivers are away.
- ✤ Start in-home foster care houses for elderly adults.
- ✤ Check-in service for the elderly. For more information, contact Paula Kay, Ageless Placements, 8130 66th Street North,

Suite 4, Pinellas Park, FL 33781; (727) 547-4337. "Providing Safeguard Visits for Seniors."

- Nursing businesses, nurse entrepreneurs. Contact National Nurses in Business Association (NNBA), P.O. Box 561081, Rockledge, FL 32956; <www.nnba.net>. Networking, conference, support for nurse entrepreneurs. Offers members tapes, e-books, and books like *How to Start Your Own $100,000 Nursing Agency* (home based).

33
MEDICAL BILLING

The health insurance industry is an ever-growing and bureaucratic segment of the economy, and it seems the complexity of paperwork for both patients and medical professionals regarding their health insurance and other claims is only getting worse! Many people—or their health care professionals—have to file medical billing claims accurately and quickly. The owner of a medical billing business assists clients in completing and filing claims or disputing those claims rejected by Medicare or private insurance companies.

Merlin B. Coslick, executive director of the Electronic Medical Billing Network of America, says, "I typically begin my seminars by explaining exactly what medical billing is all about. Medical billing is not a medical function—it is a bookkeeping or accounting function. Medical billing involves bills, accounts receivable, posting payment, patient statements—the kind of terms an accountant or bookkeeper would use. It has nothing to do with medicine . . . you are a home-based data entry clerk, entering data into a special software program that sends claims to insurance carriers. But your function is in no way medical. You need to know how to operate a software program."

However, Coslick cautions that to be a successful *home-based* medical claims biller, you have to know how to find clients who need your services and you must market your business. "Education and training in marketing skills is far more necessary than buying software," says Coslick.

Start-Up Costs and Financing Sources

- $7,000 to $15,000.
- Personal savings, loans from family or friends, small business loans, lines of credit from your local bank.

Marketing and Advertising Methods and Tips

- Send direct mail to physicians' offices and medical insurance companies.
- Coslick says that the software sellers only help you run your software, not market your business. He recommends . . . "So the key is to find that 1 percent of the marketplace that is dissatisfied with their current billing system and to discover and find them, and you do that through direct mail marketing and it's nothing fancy—just the matter of putting out some postcards to a large population. You can't do this in the hills of Montana. There has to be a population of at least 1,000 providers within 10 square miles."

  He continues, "You market to all 1,000 of them on a very simplistic basis by postcards, every month, to find the 1 percent that need your services. Within those 1,000, there are 10, so maybe most of them don't like the way you look when you go in to visit them. That's alright because you only need one to get started. So for a response, you're looking for one-tenth of 1 percent, and that is a pretty good average. That gets you up and running and you are on your way. And then you get referrals from there. This is going to be difficult work, but there is a way to do it, to accomplish it. You need three months of persistent marketing, and out will come clients."
- Place ads in local newspapers.
- Attend hospital seminars.
- Place an ad in the business telephone directory.
- Print business cards and brochures.

Essential Equipment

Updated computer with a tape backup system; claims processing, billing, and spreadsheet software; fast modem for transmitting and receiving claims; photocopier; fax and separate telephone line with answering machine or answering service.

Coslick says, "When buying software, the general rule of thumb we recommend is to buy software priced between $500 and $1,000. That is the average amount spent by the majority of professional billers. Anything less is junk. Anything more is highly questionable."

Merry Schiff, founder of the National Electronic Billers Alliance, agrees with Coslick when she says, "The software you see advertised—whether $299 or $10,000—will not make you a medical biller. I think people should understand these are scams and they've been designated scams by the Federal Trade Commission (FTC)." (See "Software," later in this section.)

Recommended Training, Experience, or Needed Skills

- Enroll in courses offered by medical insurance companies and local business schools and organizations like the Electronic Medical Billing Network and the National Electronic Billers Alliance. (These two organizations are reputable and the major ones existing in this industry.)
- Work in a medical or insurance claims office.
- Be familiar with sending and receiving information over the Internet.
- Be familiar with insurance and Medicare policies and procedures.
- Know medical terminology.

Income Potential

$10,000 to $20,000 part-time. It takes time to build up a client base.

Type of Business

Primarily an in-home business.

Target Market

Doctors and other medical professionals who need to file claims to insurance companies or Medicare. Coslick says that good prospective clients are the smaller offices, where often the doctors tend to overwork their staff, and as a result, their billing falls into disarray.

For More Information

Associations

The following two medical billing organizations are recognized by the medical billing profession as being reputable and important networking and information resources.

Electronic Medical Billing Network (EMBN) of America
51 Eton Court
Bedminster, NJ 07921
< www.medicalbillingnetwork.com >

This respected trade organization is the oldest and largest trade association and school for independent medical billers in America. The Electronic Medical Billing Network of America offers seminars, certification membership support, vendor (including software) referrals, and publications and books like *Medical Billing Secrets: Building Your Successful Home-Based Business,* by Merlin B. Coslick (executive director). For information about membership, seminars, and ordering of publications, send an LSASE or visit the Web site.

National Electronic Billers Alliance (NEBA)
2226-A Westborough Boulevard, #504 S
San Francisco, CA 94080
< www.nebazone.com >

NEBA was founded by Merry Schiff, the first person to do electronic claims in the state of California. This professional billers' association offers members a current home study medical billing course, a newsletter, and discounts on some recommended medical billing software.

Books

Medical Billing Secrets: Building Your Successful Home-Based Business, by Merlin B. Coslick, 2002 (order through EMBN; see "Associations," earlier in this section).

Setting Up Your Medical Billing Business: Step-by-Step Procedures for Starting and Managing a Computer-Based Electronic Medical Billing Business, by Merlin B. Coslick, 1999 (order through EMBN; see "Associations," earlier in this section).

Software

With so many medical billing scams, it is best to order from vendors trusted by other professional medical billers and follow the recommendations of the two organizations already discussed, EMBN and NEBA. The Federal Trade Commission has charged a number of companies for presenting false information about promised earnings. See the FTC Web site <www.ftc.gov> for more information.

Start-Up Guide

Entrepreneur's Start-Up Guide, *How to Start a Medical Claims Billing Service.* For pricing and ordering information, visit <www.smallbizbooks.com> or call (800) 421-2300.

34

PERSONAL FITNESS TRAINER

As each decade passes, more technological advances are taking over physical chores for us, and statistics are revealing that more Americans—both adults and children—lack even basic physical fitness. Statistics show that even though we spend billions of dollars on fitness equipment and exercise tapes, the majority of us remain unfit. Many start an exercise routine or regimen, but few maintain it over time. Family and job demands make it difficult to find even a few minutes to exercise. Lack of motivation and boredom with a fitness plan also diminish the desire to exercise.

Being physically fit is more than just a fad. It increases both mental and physical health and helps prevent a myriad health problems, including heart disease. A personal fitness trainer designs custom fitness plans for individuals in such a way to keep clients motivated to stay fit. With a personal fitness trainer guiding clients through their workouts on a regular basis, the probability of their getting bored and abandoning exercise is reduced.

If you have the experience and expertise necessary, you can train athletes for the sports in which they compete. You can go to clients' homes, to gyms, to recreation facilities, or to businesses that have workout areas and equipment for their employees. You can plan individual training sessions or hold classes for groups or go to schools and day care centers on a contract basis to give exercise classes. Market research will show you what age groups or people would be most likely to use your services.

Start-Up Costs

About $3,000 to $6,000.

Pricing Guidelines

Some trainers charge from $50 to $200+ per session. Others charge $20 to $50 per hour for classes. One option is to charge $400 for a six-week, twice-a-week program that teaches basic exercise principles and techniques (stretching, cross training, prevention of athletic injuries) plus instructs on the proper way to use fitness equipment.

Marketing and Advertising Methods and Tips

- Encourage personal referrals. Arrange for referrals from the gym you belong to. (You may even hold classes or training for members at the gym.)
- Give talks, presentations, and demonstrations to community groups, workers at businesses that promote employee fitness, and at hospital wellness fairs; or teach classes at adult evening schools.
- Advertise on local cable television. See if you can host a daily or weekly exercise program.

- Give workshops for coaches.
- Write a weekly column on fitness for your local newspapers.
- Be fit yourself! Run in benefit races to garner good PR for your business and keep in shape.
- Put together a portfolio of "before" and "after" photos of clients.
- Send direct mail to nursery schools, day care centers, and senior citizen centers offering fun fitness sessions.

Essential Equipment

Video player, portable tape player, portable fitness equipment (small weights, jump ropes, mats, boxes for step-ups, and other related equipment). Balls, hoops, and so forth, if teaching children. Exercise outfits; audio- and videotapes; reference books on physical fitness, weight training, nutrition, games, and exercises; separate telephone (ground) line and answering machine or service; cell phone and pager; business cards; brochures.

Recommended Training, Experience, or Needed Skills

- Know fitness and exercise basics and sensible nutrition, either through your own sports experiences, training, and/or education or from taking community college courses on exercise, nutrition, sports psychology, and athletic training.
- Have a basic knowledge of human or child psychology, which helps you understand what motivates people; some colleges and universities have sports psychology courses.
- Enjoy working and teaching the age group(s) with which you are working.
- Become certified by the American Council on Exercise or the American College of Sports Medicine (see addresses later in this section).

Income Potential

$20,000 to $80,000, depending on your credentials, your clients, and what other classes or groups you teach or give talks to.

Type of Business

Most of your time is spent out-of-the-home for training and teaching. Some time is spent in-home managing your business and planning workouts.

Target Market

Professionals who do not have the time or motivation to exercise by themselves, schools or centers that do not have the funds to hire a full-time exercise specialist, athletes who want specialized training for a competition, individuals who just want to look and feel better or are told by their physician to get into shape for their health (e.g., heart, prevention of diabetes).

Success Tips

- Be able to design fitness programs that your clients will continue to do on their own. Educate them on the correct way to exercise and how to plan their own exercise programs that are both challenging and fun.
- Have your clients' doctors' permission to start an exercise program if they have not been exercising previously.
- Partner with a licensed nutritionist and/or dietitian to help plan a total fitness and wellness plan for each client.
- Check with your lawyer and insurance agent about liability coverage and any waivers your clients should sign.
- If your zoning permits it, you might consider setting up a fitness room in your home—a remodeled garage or an outbuilding is ideal.

Franchises, Distributorships, and Licenses

See the regular issues of such print publications as *Entrepreneur* <www.entrepreneur.com> and *Home Business* <www.homebusinessmag.com> magazines (find at newsstands and bookstores) and their Web sites for listings of related business opportunities and franchises.

For More Information

Associations

American College of Sports Medicine
Certification and Career Center
401 West Michigan Street
Indianapolis, IN 46202
(317) 637-9200
<www.acsm.org>

For sports medicine and health and fitness professionals. Offers certification programs, journals, books, videos, and other membership benefits.

American Council on Exercise (ACE)
4851 Paramount Drive
San Diego, CA 92123
(800) 825-3636
<www.acefitness.org>

ACE is a nonprofit organization that sets certification and education standards for fitness instructors and through ongoing public education about the importance of exercise. Provides information on certification exams and study materials. Publishes personal trainer manuals and home study program.

Books and Publications

Booklets and online articles, such as *Fitness and Exercise I* and *Walking for Exercise and Pleasure*, from the Consumer Information Catalog, Consumer Information Center, P.O. Box 100, Pueblo, CO 81002; <www.pueblo.gsa.gov>. Contact or check online for the current informational booklets on fitness, exercise, and nutrition.

Personal Trainer's Handbook, by Teri S. O'Brien (Champaign, IL: Human Kinetics Publishers, 1998).

E-Book

Bizy's Guide to Exercising for Profit, by Adrian Terrell. Visit <www.bizymoms.com> for ordering information.

Home Study Courses

Distance Education and Training Council
1601 18th Street, NW
Washington, DC 20009
<www.detc.org>

Write for a brochure of schools offering home study courses for approved certification programs or visit the Web site.

Web Sites

<www.afpafitness.com>

American Fitness Professionals and Associates (AFPA)—Offers the health and fitness professional a variety of certification programs, continuing education courses, home correspondence courses, and regional conventions.

<www.netsweat.com>

Netsweat.com—Fitness sources and links.

Additional Business Ideas

Aerobics instructor. Contact Aerobics and Fitness Association of America, 15250 Ventura Boulevard, Suite 200, Sherman Oaks, CA 91403; <www.afaa.com>. Workshops and health and fitness information for fitness professionals. The organization offers certification and home study courses.

35

PERSONAL WEIGHT MANAGEMENT CONSULTANT

The American Obesity Association states on its Web site <www.obesity.org> that an estimated 120 million adults in the United States are overweight or obese. Obesity is a health hazard because it can increase an individual's risk of illness from about 30 serious medical conditions. The diet industry is making millions of dollars on people desperate to lose weight. People's obsessions about weight have led to anorexia, bulimia, and other eating disorders. What diet and health professionals advise are sensible, individual weight-loss plans that use a combination of exercise, nutritional education, and behavior modification methods. These plans encourage clients to change their bad habits by creating an individualized diet and exercise plan they can follow the rest of their lives.

As a personal weight management consultant, you can help overweight people shed those unwanted pounds. You may start small, using an extra room in your home to meet clients as individuals or in small groups, or you can visit your clients at their homes or work to guide and advise them on methods to lose weight. You may want to partner with a personal trainer, dietitian, and/or nutritionist to create a healthier, new lifestyle for your clients.

Start-Up Costs and Financing Sources

- $4,000 to $20,000 for advertising and home office supplies. Costs will be more if you purchase a franchise.
- Personal savings, loan from family or friends.

Pricing Guidelines

Charge per session (call local weight-loss centers for the going rates). Some consultants charge $600 to $1,000 for a 12-week program of periodic weigh-ins and counseling.

Marketing and Advertising Methods and Tips

- Attend health fair shows.
- Send direct mailings to hospitals, health care professionals, and businesses that promote health and exercise programs for their employees.
- Give talks or write a column in the local newspaper on personal weight management, fitness, or nutrition.
- Advertise in the business telephone directory and on local radio and cable television.

- Print promotional materials: business cards, portfolio of "before" and "after" pictures, and testimonials.
- Publish a print or online newsletter that provides ongoing healthy tips and items like low-fat recipes, as well as profiles of clients whose lifestyles have improved because of the weight loss and who are in better health as a result of enrolling in your program.

Essential Equipment

Business telephone line and answering machine or service; computer and diet software; contracts; home library of nutrition and fitness books; accurate weight scale; comfortable, attractive furniture if you meet clients in your home office.

Recommended Training, Experience, or Needed Skills

- Have an educational background, training, and/or experience in the health, nutrition, or fitness professions.
- Work as a weight-loss counselor in a franchise program.
- Try one of the popular weight-loss programs if you need to lose weight yourself to see what you liked or disliked about their methods.
- Take nutrition and fitness courses at local colleges.
- Take home study courses on weight loss and fitness.
- Check with state regulations about licensing requirements.
- Be an encouraging, positive person with good communication skills.
- Pat Barone <www.patbarone.com>, of Catalyst Weight Management, describes herself as a "weight-loss coach." She offers this tip: "Hone your assessment skills so you can assess potential clients' deepest intentions as well as their current state of mind. Some 99 out of 100 people will tell you they want to lose weight but most of them aren't ready to do the hard work it takes to really solve their problems with food and change their lifestyles. Unless you have the skills to de-

tect a client's readiness to make a commitment, the door to your business will be a revolving one!"

Income Potential

$18,000 to $80,000 or more, depending on your location and number of clients.

Type of Business

This depends on if you meet your clients in-home or out-of-the-home.

Success Tips

- Rent a community room in a church or library to have your meetings if you don't have adequate space in your home.
- Check with your local and state regulatory agencies on certification and licensing requirements.
- Concentrate on advertising and promotions to get your first clients. If they successfully lose weight, their referrals will be your best source of new customers.
- Try to help each client achieve some success. Concentrate on personal attention to each client, giving more than they would get at the larger franchise operations.
- Urge all clients to have a physical by their physician before they embark on any weight-loss and/or exercise program.
- Be honest and set realistic and achievable goals for each client.
- Require that all clients have approval from a physician before they enroll in a diet or exercise program.

Franchises, Distributorships, and Licenses

See the regular issues of such print publications as *Entrepreneur* <www.entrepreneur.com> and *Home Business* <www.homebusinessmag.com> magazines (find at newsstands and bookstores) and their Web sites for listings of related business opportunities and franchises.

For More Information

Association

American Dietetic Association (ADA)
216 West Jackson Boulevard
Chicago, IL 60606
<www.eatright.org>

The ADA is the world's largest organization of food and nutrition professionals, with nearly 70,000 members. The Web site features links to nutrition and health resources.

Books and Publications

Booklets, such as *Ways to Win at Weight Loss: Finding a Weight Loss Program that Works for You,* from the Consumer Information Center, P.O. Box 100, Pueblo, CO 81002; <www.pueblo.gsa.gov>. Order the booklets in print or read them on the Web site.

The American Dietetic Association's Complete Food & Nutrition Guide, by Roberta Larson Duyff (New York: John Wiley & Sons, 2002).

Home Study Course

Distance Education and Training Council
1601 18th Street, NW
Washington, DC 20009
<www.detc.org>

Write for a brochure of schools offering home study courses in fitness or nutrition or visit the Web site.

Other

American Council on Exercise (ACE) <www.acefitness.org>. Provides health and fitness articles and additional related information in free monthly e-newsletter.

Software

Weight Commander (for Windows), by Weight Commander, 220 East Walton, #4W, Chicago, IL 60611; <www.weight

commander.com >. Software for weight loss. Send an LSASE or visit the Web site for information.

Additional Business Ideas

- Nutritional and exercise counseling for children and teenagers. Cooperate with physicians to find out what is appropriate for a certain age group and body type. Help instill good eating and exercise habits to improve self-esteem and overall health.
- Sell natural nutritional products (no drugs) as an independent consultant.

36
REFLEXOLOGIST

Reflexology works on the principle that reflexes in the feet, hands, head, and other parts of the body are related to each and every organ and other part of the body. Foot and hand reflexology is the type most often practiced. Reflexology should not be confused with massage, although some reflexologists may add massages to their services.

According to the International Institute of Reflexology, the Original Ingham Method of Reflexology is used primarily for releasing tension. It helps normalize body functions but is not intended to replace conventional medical treatment. Reflexologists and their clients say that reflexology also helps increase the circulation of the blood, thereby spreading nutrients more completely throughout the body while also speeding the process of elimination of waste products. And as one regular reflexologist client says, "It just feels so good!!"

Claudette, a single mother of two, studied a year with a certified reflexologist and then went on to receive her certification. She has been a reflexologist for almost 30 years. Today she works 25 to 40 hours a week, offering appointments of 30 minutes for reflexology alone or 45 minutes for reflexology plus massage, in which she is also certified. Claudette started her business in her home but moved to a former machine shed that she remodeled, which is only a short walk from her house. Working close to home gives Claudette the flexibility to adjust her schedule around her children's needs. She also likes having a separate area to meet clients.

Start-Up Costs and Financing Sources

- $500 to $6,000. Costs are at the higher end if you plan to remodel a room into your office. Training by a reflexologist or enrolling in courses costs $500 to $1,000.
- Personal finances. Buy more equipment as your client list grows.

Pricing Guidelines

$25 to $35 per 30-minute reflexology session; $45 to $50 for 45 minutes of reflexology and massage.

Marketing and Advertising Methods and Tips

- Advertise in the business telephone directory.
- Place a sign in a place visible to drivers.
- Encourage word-of-mouth referrals.
- Write some articles about the benefits of reflexology.
- Write a press release when you are ready for clients. Send along a photo of you working on a client's foot. (Photos increase your chances of getting the press release published and may lead to a profile article in your local newspaper.)

Essential Equipment

Lounge chair, business telephone line and answering machine or service, scheduling book, record-keeping system, books on reflexology.

Recommended Training, Experience, or Needed Skills

- Generally, you do not have to be licensed. Claudette took weekly instructions for a year from both a reflexologist and a masseuse.
- It helps to get certified by a reflexology institute or through a seminar.
- You can take reflexology courses at some community colleges.

Income Potential

$500 to $800 or more per week. Claudette has clients she sees weekly, every other week, or monthly, or she schedules sessions as needed. If a client is sick or in the hospital, Claudette will go to them for a session.

Type of Business

Primarily an in-home business, except if you go to the client's home or to a hospital.

Target Market

Men and women of all ages who need to reduce their stress and tension.

Success Tips

- Treat each client, each day, as if he or she were your first client. Do not get complacent or bored with your work.
- Treat your profession as a business and keep accurate records and report your earnings honestly.
- Charge enough for your services, but reasonably.
- Study, study, study! Keep up to date on the information and issues concerning reflexology.
- Offer off-hours appointments. Many clients can only come to you in the evening, after work.
- Approach some local personal salons that offer a variety of personal services to work some part-time hours and meet prospective clients.

For More Information

Association

International Institute of Reflexology
Ingham Publishing
5650 First Avenue, N
P.O. Box 12642
St. Petersburg, FL 33733
< www.reflexology-usa.net >

Send an LSASE or visit the Web site for information on seminars, workshops, certification, books, charts, and how to contact a certified reflexologist near you.

Books

Body Reflexology: Healing at Your Fingertips, rev. ed., by Mildred Carter and Tammy Weber (West Nyack, NY: Parker Publishing, 1994).

Reflexology: Complete Illustrated Guide, by Inge Dougans (Canada: HarperCollins, 2002).

Reflexology for Beginners: Healing Through Foot Massage of Pressure Points, by David F. Vennells. (St. Paul, MN: Llewellyn Publications, 2001).

Reflexology: The Definitive Practitioners Manual, by Beryl Crane (Rockport, MA: Element Publishing, 1997).

Stories the Feet Can Tell Through Reflexology and *Stories the Feet Have Told Through Reflexology,* both by Eunice D. Ingham (St. Petersburg, FL: Ingham Publishing, 1984).

Additional Business Ideas

Massage therapy. Refer to: *Marketing Massage,* by Monica Roseberry (Albany, NY: Milady Publishing Company, 2001). See also *More 101 Best Home-Based Businesses,* by Priscilla Y. Huff (Roseville, CA: Prima Communications, 1998).

Sewing Services

Sewing Resources

Sewing at home is a popular leisure-time activity. The American Home Sewing and Craft Association estimates that more than 21 million people sew from their homes. Many sew designer clothes from patterns at a fraction of the cost of buying them ready-made, as well as making decorations, quilts, crafts, and countless other items using their sewing machines.

Correct pricing of products will determine how profitable your business will be. Ellen Rittenhouse, whose company Snugglewool < www.snugglewool.com > creates baby blankets, mattress pads, baby buntings, and other products out of natural wool, says, "Home-based sewing businesses can be profitable, in addition to fulfilling our service and creative needs, when we value and price our skills appropriately. If we underprice our service and skills they will be undervalued by the customer."

Rittenhouse adds, "When I purchased my business, the previous owner had maintained his prices by increasing shipping and handling costs. It was easy to see why he was out of business when his costs were barely covered. As I raised the prices to better represent the value of the products, I did not lose the good customers, and in fact, seemed to gain new and better customers."

Many women have turned their sewing skills from hobbies into profitable businesses. This chapter presents a few of the many ways women are making money by sewing. These examples may give you the impetus to start your own business.

Note: Because in the previous centuries, people who did home sewing were exploited by some businesses, some types of home sewing is unlawful. Check with the office of the U.S. Department of Labor <www.dol.gov> to learn about the latest regulations.

Here are some helpful resources to start you on your way:

Associations

Home Sewing Association
1350 Broadway, Suite 1601
New York, NY 10018
(212) 714-1633
<www.sewing.org>

A not-for-profit organization representing members from every facet of the sewing industry. The organization's goal is to "Get People Sewing." A must for all home sewers! Offers a sewing guild network, educational materials, sewing expos, sewing tips, and other member benefits.

Professional Association of Custom Clothiers (PACC)
494 Eighth Avenue, Suite 802
New York, NY 10001
<www.paccprofessionals.org>

PACC is a "nationwide nonprofit organization for custom clothiers in both home-based and commercial settings," as well as those in other sewing-related fields and allied professionals.

American Needlepoint Guild (ANG)
P.O. Box 1027
Cordova, TN 38088
<www.needlepoint.org>

National seminar, correspondence classes, community service projects, e-newsletter, and other membership benefits.

The Embroiderers' Guild of America, Inc.
335 West Broadway, Suite 100
Louisville, KY 40202
<www.egausa.org>

"The purpose of this organization shall be to foster the highest standards of excellence in the practice of the art of embroidery through an active program of education and study and to preserve the heritage of the art of embroidery."

Books and Publications

The Business of Sewing, by Barbara Wright Sykes (Chino Hills, CA: Collins Publications, 1992).

Creative Cash: How to Sell Your Crafts, Needlework, Designs and Know-How, 6th ed., by Barbara Brabec (Roseville, CA: Prima Communications, 1998).

Creative Machine Arts series and the *Know Your Machine* series. Chilton Book Company, 1 Chilton Way, Radnor, PA 19089.

Pricing Without Fear: A Sewing Entrepreneur's Guide, by Barbara Wright Sykes (Chino Hills, CA: Collins Publications, 1999).

Sew to Success: How to Make Money in a Home-Based Sewing Business, by Kathleen Spike (Portland, OR: Palmer/Pletsch Associates, 1995).

Sew Up a Storm: All the Way to the Bank!, by Karen L. Maslowski (Cincinnati, OH: Sewstorm Publishing, 1997). May be purchased through Clotilde (catalog or <www.clotilde.com>).

Directory

Designer Source Listing, by Maryanne Burgess, 1999. Carikean Publishing, 846 West Ainslie Street, Suite R1, Chicago, IL 60640. Comprehensive listing of sources—beads, blanks, books, buttons, fabrics, millinery supplies, notions, patterns, videos, and more! Write for ordering information.

Magazines and Catalogs

Sew News magazine, Sew News, Box 56907, Boulder, CO 80322. <www.sewnews.com>

SewWHAT? magazine, Professional Drapery Seminars, 180 Buckeye Access Road, Swannanoa, NC 28778; <www.professionaldrapery.com>. For drapery professionals.

Threads magazine, The Taunton Press, 63 South Main Street, P.O. Box 5506, Newtown, CT 06470; <www.taunton.com/threads/

index.asp >. Print publication covering a wide arrange of creative sewing techniques.

Notions Catalogs (also books, patterns, supplies, videos)

Clotilde
B3000
Louisiana, MO 63353
< www.clotilde.com >

Nancy's Notions
333 Beichl Avenue
P.O. Box 683
Beaver Dam, WI 53916
< www.nancysnotions.com >

Publishers of Sewing and Sewing Business Books

See also "Notions Catalogs."

Chilton Books
1 Chilton Way
Radnor, PA 19809

Collins Publications
3233 Grand Avenue, Suite N-294C
Chino Hills, CA 91709
< www.collinspub.com >

Palmer/Pletsch
P.O. Box 12046
Portland, OR 97212
< www.palmerpletsch.com >

Sewing Machines and Parts

Hayes Sewing Machine Company, 9 East Baltimore Pike, Clifton Heights, PA 19018; (610) 259-5959; < www.trevhayes.com >. Parts for old sewing machines; Berina, Singer, serger dealer; also out-of-print books. Call or write for information or visit the Web site.

Correspondence Course

Fashion Tuition Services, Suite 33, 10 Barley Mow Passage, Chiswick, London W4 4PH; <www.justsew.mistral.co.uk>. Sewing, dressmaking, and overlocking courses.

Software, Sewing

Wild Ginger Software, 630 Fogg Street, Nashville, TN 37203; <www.wildginger.com>. Software for sewing enthusiasts, sewing retailers, independent pattern makers, and custom clothiers and costumers.

Web Sites

<www.kayewood.com>

Kaye Wood—Quilting, sewing, and craft links.

<www.sewingconnection.com>

Shirley Adams, Sewing Connection.

Additional Business Ideas

Check your local public library for more current and/or out-of-print sewing books on the following topics:

- Children's cloth books.
- Doll clothes. Refer to *A Closetful of Doll Clothes,* by Rosemarie Lonker (New York: Portfolio Press, 2000).
- Hats. Contact the Wonderful World of Hats, 897 Wade Road, Siletz, OR 97380; <www.worldofhats.com>. Offers videos and hat-making home study courses and published the *Hat Lover's Dictionary.* See also *Classic Millinery Techniques: A Complete Guide to Making and Designing Today's Hats,* by Ann Albrizio (Asheville, NC: Lark Books, 1998).
- Sewing classes. *The Business of Teaching Sewing* (Portland, OR: Palmer/Pletsch Associates, 1996).
- Windsocks. *Soft Kites & Windsocks,* by Jim Rowlands and John Crooks (New York: St. Martin's Press, 1993).
- Banners. (See also Flags entry that follows.) *Making Beautiful Banners: More Than 70 Festive Designs to Decorate Your Home,*

by Barbara D. Webster (New York: Sterling Publishing Company, 1998).

✤ Flags. Contact Bob's Flags, 10726 Pineville Road, Pineville, NC 28134; < www.bobsflags.com >. Catalog costs $2 or view it online. Bob's Flags is one of the largest retailers of banners, flags, and windsocks. President Bob Burke also buys banners to carry in his catalog. Designs must be original and copyrighted to be considered. Send an LSASE for details.

37
ALTERATIONS

Today, many people don't have the time to make alterations to their favorite or used clothing. Tracy, a young mother of three, opened a consignment shop in the first floor of her home and soon found customers asking if she would make alterations to the used clothing they bought.

Tracy started out replacing zippers and sewing hems, but as news of her alterations spread, customers began requesting other kinds of modifications. To find out how much she should charge for various alterations, Tracy called cleaners and tailors and then came up with her own prices. With her alterations and home consignment shop, Tracy's business is steadily growing due to word-of-mouth referrals and her convenient location.

Start-Up Costs

$1,000 to $5,000, depending on whether you own a sewing machine.

Pricing Guidelines

$6 to $18 per garment, depending on the complexity of the job. You can add a 25 to 35 + percent charge for a rush job.

Marketing and Advertising Methods and Tips

✤ Encourage word-of-mouth referrals.

- Place seasonal sales ads in newspapers.
- Put up flyers on community bulletin boards.
- Place classified ads in weekly shopper papers.
- Send direct mailings to cleaners and clothing stores that do not offer alterations.
- Join a local women's business and professional club. Working women executives have little time to spend on altering their clothes so are good potential customers.

Essential Equipment

Heavy-duty sewing machine (contact sewing machine repair persons for used commercial machines for sale), sewing notions and threads, iron and ironing board, sewing reference books. PC and sewing software.

Recommended Training, Experience, or Needed Skills

- Take sewing courses on tailoring and alterations (contact your local sewing center or fabric outlet).
- Work in a clothing alteration or tailor shop.
- Volunteer to do alterations or mending for your family, your friends, or a thrift shop.
- Have professional-quality alteration skills.

Income Potential

$15,000 to $37,000 or more, depending on your location and number of customers.

Type of Business

An in-home business; unless you go to clients' homes or with your clients to their events (e.g., weddings, fashion shows, dance recitals) for last-minute alterations.

Target Market

Single men, working women with expensive wardrobes.

Success Tips

- Be confident when you talk with your customers so they, in turn, will have the confidence in you to do their alterations. Be honest if you feel you do not have the expertise to do the modification they ask.
- Do fast and expert work.
- Have a home-based location convenient to other shopping areas, so customers can drop off their clothing to be altered. Or offer to pick-up and return their altered clothing for an extra fee.

For More Information

See also "Sewing Resources," page 209.

Association

Professional Association of Custom Clothiers (PACC)
494 Eighth Avenue, Suite 802
New York, NY 10001
< www.paccprofessionals.org >

Books

Fast Fit: Easy Pattern Alterations for Every Figure, by Sandra Betzina (Newtown, CT: Taunton Press, 2001).

Every Sewer's Guide to the Perfect Fit: Customizing Your Patterns for a Sensational Look, by Mary Morris and Sally McCann (Ashville, NC: Lark Books, 1997).

Easy, Easier, Easiest Tailoring, rev. ed., by Pati Palmer with Susan Pletsch (Portland, OR: Palmer/Pletsch Associates, 1998).

Videos

Review the catalogs of Clotilde < www.clotilde.com > and Nancy's Notions < www.nancysnotions.com > for a current listing of their sewing videos, as well as the other resources listed in "Sewing Resources."

Additional Business Idea

Start a clothing (and used toy) consignment shop in your home. Refer to: *The Consignment Workbook,* by Sue Harris. For current pricing and ordering information, send an LSASE to Scandia International, 133 Olney's Road, Petersburgh, NY 12138; or visit the Web site <www.consignment.org>.

38
COSTUMES

Costumes are worn at dances, ceremonies, and parades and to celebrate holidays and special events. Many school, community, and college theater groups need costumes for their plays and musicals but do not have the funds to purchase costumes outright.

If you are skilled in sewing and talented in design, you may want to open your own costume sales, consulting, and rental business. You may start out of your garage or basement (with a separate outside entrance and zoning approval) and have customers come to you, or you can go to them.

Start-Up Costs and Financing Sources

- $6,000 to $30,000 and up.
- Personal savings, credit at fabric stores, line of credit from a bank, small business loans.

Pricing Guidelines

$45 to $100 per day or week (depending on availability) for rental. Period costumes can sell for $1,500 or more, depending on the complexity of design, fabric used, sewing details, and other special details. A consultant for a large cosmopolitan theater group may charge $50 to $100 per hour.

Marketing and Advertising Methods and Tips

- Send direct mailings to schools, theater and musical groups, and churches.
- Advertise in the business telephone directory and dance, hobby, and theater magazines.

- Have a Web site or advertise on one that lists costume makers.
- Participate in community parades.
- Encourage word-of-mouth referrals from satisfied customers.
- Write a special seasonal column in your local newspaper on costume-making tips for mothers.
- Print promotional materials: business cards, brochures.
- Purchase ads on local radio and cable television.
- Hold community workshops or courses (at schools or fabric centers) on how to make children's costumes.

Essential Equipment

Heavy-duty sewing machine, assorted fabrics, costume boxes, storage space, changing space, sewing forms and notions, business telephone and answering machine or service, record and billing system (manual or software), computer with design capabilities if you design costumes, personal library of period and present-day costume books.

Recommended Training, Experience, or Needed Skills

- Take sewing classes. Gain work experience in garment sewing.
- Work or volunteer in creating and constructing costumes for local theater groups or plays.
- Have a talent for designing and enjoy creative challenges.
- Know the history of clothing from different periods.
- Having background, experience, or training in theater is a plus.

Income Potential

$40,000 to $65,000 for a small business; up to $250,000 for a large costume rental business in an urban area. $100 to $440 for solo dance costumes.

Type of Business

An in-home business except for fittings or consulting.

Target Market

Theater groups, schools or college drama clubs or societies, filmmakers, individuals who need costumes for a holiday or special event, civic groups sponsoring special events, parades, historical groups, museums, entertainers (clowns, magicians, mascots, balloon delivery businesses).

Other potential customers are those wanting costumes for roller- and ice-skating, school dance and cheerleading teams, baton twirlists, dance clubs (country-western, folk), ballroom competitors, belly dancers, Irish dancers, ethnic groups, and large church groups holding religious pageants. People in this industry state that there is a demand for dance recital costumers and also for solo dancers.

Success Tips

- ✤ Be creative in your marketing—appear at special community functions, fairs, parades, and holiday celebrations dressed in your costumes appropriate for the occasion. Have plenty of business cards to hand out.
- ✤ Be willing to design and create a costume to the customer's specifications even if you have never made one before.
- ✤ Be able to bring in business during slow periods and keep up with business in hectic periods.

For More Information

Association

The United States Institute for Theater Technology (USITT)
6443 Ridings Road
Syracuse, NY 13206
<www.usitt.org>

The Association of Design, Production, and Technology Professionals in the Performing Arts and Entertainment Industry. Twenty percent of USITT members are costumers. Offers projects and resources. Holds conventions and conferences.

Books

The Fantastic Costume Book, by Michelle Lipson and Friends (New York: Sterling Publishing, 1992).

A History of Costume: With Over 600 Patterns and Illustrations, by Carl Kohler and Emma Von Schart (editor) (Mineola, NY: Dover Pulications, 1972).

The Illustrated Encyclopedia of Costume and Fashion, revised ed., by J. Cassin Scott and Run Green (London: Studio Vista Books, 1994).

Medieval Costume and Fashion, by Herbert Norris (Mineola NY: Dover Publications, 1999).

Patterns for Theatrical Costumes: Garments, Trims, and Accessories from Ancient Egypt to 1915, reprint, by Katherin Strand Holkeboer (Hollywood, CA: Quite Specific Media Group, 1993).

Software

Wild Ginger Software, 630 Fogg Street, Nashville, TN 37203; <www.wildginger.com>. Software for sewing enthusiasts, sewing retailers, independent pattern makers, and custom clothiers and costumers.

Supplies

Amazon Drygoods
411 Brady Street
Davenport, IA 52801
<www.amazondrygoods.com>

"The Pattern Catalog" contains more than 1,000 patterns for men, women, and children. Medieval through 1950s clothing, with an emphasis on the Victorian era. $7.00.

Web Site

<www.fabrics.net>

Fabrics.net—Excellent resource site about fabrics and related resources and information.

Additional Business Ideas

- Specialize in costumes for theater, television, or film.

- Specialize in different countries' costumes for celebrations of their cultural-awareness days, museums, and so forth.
- Make costumes for pets and sell wholesale to pet stores and distributors.
- Make costumes for historic dolls.
- Make costumes and/or puppets for puppet theaters.

39

CURTAINS, DRAPERIES, AND SHADES

Sewing custom curtains, draperies, and shades is a profitable home-based business for many women. Some began by using their sewing skills to decorate their own homes and then expanded to doing window treatments for friends, relatives, and eventually customers. Others have worked in curtain and drapery workrooms and discovered they could make more money in their own businesses.

If you think a window treatment business is one you would like, try sewing for yourself, family, or friends. Check with your local sewing center to see if it offers special classes on making curtains, draperies, and shades. Start off your business part-time before you invest in expensive equipment.

Start-Up Costs

$5,000 if you own a sewing machine.

Pricing Guidelines

$400 to $1,200+ per window treatment, depending on the style, size, and material chosen. Consult trade publications for pricing guidelines.

Marketing and Advertising Methods and Tips

- Place classified ads in local publications.
- Encourage word-of-mouth referrals.

- ✤ Contact local interior decorators for referrals.
- ✤ Put together a portfolio of windows you have done.
- ✤ Leave business cards and flyers at sewing centers, on community bulletin boards, and in drapery hardware stores.
- ✤ Send direct mailings to owners in new housing developments.
- ✤ Exhibit at home shows.
- ✤ Offer to do the windows of local restaurants, sample or historic homes, or homes participating in holiday open house tours.

Essential Equipment

Professional sewing machine(s), workspace and table, sewing notions and supplies, samples of materials.

Recommended Training, Experience, or Needed Skills

- ✤ Take sewing courses or workshops, attend seminars.
- ✤ Sew your own curtains, draperies, and shades.
- ✤ Work for a drapery company.

Income Potential

$30,000 to $50,000.

Type of Business

In-home for sewing; out-of-the-home to meet with customers.

Target Market

Owners of newly built homes, people remodeling their homes, middle- to upper-income couples, interior decorators.

Success Tips

- ✤ Charge a fee to give an in-home estimate, which is refundable and can be used toward the purchase of curtains, draperies, or shades.
- ✤ Keep up to date with others in the industry.

For More Information

Books

Creative Window Treatments: Curtains, Shades, Top Treatments and No-Sew Styles, by the editors of Creative Publishing International (Minnetonka, MN: Creative Publishing International, 2000).

Make Custom Draperies, Yes You Can!, by Claira Dobry (Pasadena, MD: Dobry Enterprises, 1988).

The Shade Book, by Judy Landahl (Portland, OR: Palmer/Pletsch Associates, 1996).

The Ultimate Curtain Book: A Comprehensive Guide to Creating Your Own Window Treatments, by Isabella Forbes (Pleasantville, NY: Reader's Digest Association, 2002).

Window Treatments, by Karla J. Nielson (New York: John Wiley & Sons, 1997).

Equipment

S. Morantz Inc., 9984 Gantry Road, Philadelphia, PA 19115; (215) 969-0266; <www.morantz.com>. Drapery workroom equipment.

Patterns

Amazon Drygoods, 411 Brady Street, Davenport, IA 52801; <www.amazondrygoods.com>. Window treatment catalog of a few dozen full-sized valance, drapery, and shade patterns. $3.

Publications

SewWHAT? magazine, Professional Drapery Seminars, 180 Buckeye Access Road, Swannanoa, NC 28778; <www.professionaldrapery.com>. For drapery professionals.

Additional Business Ideas

Make custom window treatments for nonresidential or commercial offices. Note, though, that these have to meet specific safety codes and requirements.

40
CUSTOM APPAREL

If you are talented with a needle and thread, then consider the three examples of custom apparel businesses that follow: wedding gowns, accessories, and headpieces; christening gowns and prom gowns; and clothing for people with special needs.

Start-Up Costs and Financing Sources

- Wedding gowns and accessories: $5,000 to $15,000.
- Christening gowns and prom gowns: $4,000.
- Clothing for those with special needs: $5,000 to $8,000, which includes advertising and protecting designs.
- Financing sources for all three: personal loans, lines of credit from your bank, credit at fabric stores, small business loans.

Pricing Guidelines

Wedding Gowns
Charge according to the complexity and detail of the job and the fabrics used. You can charge more for an original design as opposed to one with a pattern. Accessories: compare prices at bridal shows and see how your work and designs compare. (Make sure the designs are your originals and not a copyrighted design.) Bridal veils and headpieces: $45 and more.

Christening Gowns
$65 to $90 for a gown from a pattern, $175 for an original design.

Prom Gowns
$110 and up.

Special-Needs Clothing
Clients include nursing mothers, people in wheelchairs, women with mastectomies.

Per hour price =
cost of materials + time + overhead percentage

See "Sewing Resources" for sewing business books that give recommendations on pricing for custom sewing. Network with other clothing professionals in your area about pricing.

Marketing and Advertising Methods and Tips

Wedding Gowns, Accessories, Headpieces

- Encourage word-of-mouth referrals.
- Place ads in local newspapers' bridal sections or supplements.
- Attend bridals shows and craft shows at malls (for accessories).
- Leave your business cards and brochures at fabric shops.
- Have a Web site with photos of your work.

Christening Gowns, Prom Gowns

- Encourage word-of-mouth referrals.
- Place ads in local newspapers.
- Post flyers or business cards on community and hospital bulletin boards.
- Place ads in school programs.
- Attend teen fashion shows.

Special-Needs Clothing

- Send direct mailing to rehabilitation centers and organizations that sponsor group homes and support groups.
- Rent a booth at health fairs and expos for persons with disabilities.
- Advertise in seniors' publications and nonprofit group newsletters.
- Send out press releases to newspapers and magazines.
- Attend fashion shows.
- Advertise on Web sites featuring products for persons with disabilities, such as The Boulevard <www.blvd.com>.

Essential Equipment (for all three)

Industrial sewing machine, overlock machine to finish seams, serger, cutting table, sewing notions, a mannequin, storage for patterns, fabric, source of fine fabrics, design and reference sewing books.

Recommended Training, Experience, or Needed Skills

Wedding Gowns

- Apprentice at a bridal shop.
- Work in a fabric shop that has a wedding department to learn about fabrics and laces.
- Have a design and/or a fashion degree as well as taking ongoing workshops and courses.

Christening and Prom Gowns

- Read books on sewing for infants and children, take courses at fabric centers.
- Take dressmaking courses.

Special-Needs Clothing

- Take courses on design and sewing at community colleges, vo-tech schools, or other schools of design.
- Work with physical and occupational therapists and rehabilitative specialists to customize clothing for each client.

Income Potential

Wedding Gowns

Hundreds to thousands of dollars per gown. Network with other dressmakers and members of the Professional Association of Custom Clothiers (address is listed later in this section).

Christening and Prom Gowns

$65 to $90 per christening gown. For prom gowns, check with retailers for average prices and network with other dressmakers.

Special-Needs Clothing
$30 to $50 + per garment, depending on time spent and materials used.

Type of Business
An in-home business except if you go to a person's home for fittings.

Target Market
Newly engaged women; new parents and grandparents; high school and college students; people with permanent or temporary physical disabilities in nursing homes, group homes, or institutions.

Success Tips
- When sewing wedding gowns, be able to work under pressure and to understand what the bride and/or mother of the bride wants.
- With prom gowns, you have to be able to please both the young woman and the person who is buying it as far as taste, expense, and the embellishments they want. Keep up to date on the latest fashions.
- With christening gowns, embroider your name and date on the gown.
- With special-needs clothing, talk with people who have disabilities to find out what kind of modifications to clothing would best suit them. Make the clothing comfortable, washable, and easy to put on and take off.

For More Information

Association

Professional Association of Custom Clothiers (PACC)
494 Eighth Avenue, Suite 802
New York, NY 10001
< www.paccprofessionals.org >

See "Sewing Resources" for additional information.

American Cancer Society Information Center
(800) ACS-2345
< www.cancer.org >

Provides special patterns for mastectomy patients.

Books

Bridal Couture: Fine Sewing Techniques for Wedding Gowns and Evening Wear, by Susan Khalye (Iola, WI: Krause Publications, 1997).

Bridal Gowns: The Basics of Designing, Fitting and Sewing Your Wedding Dress, by Susan E. Andrils (Portland, OR: Palmer/Pletsch Associates, 1999).

Couture Sewing: Techniques, by Claire B. Shaeffer (Newton, CT: Taunton Press, 2001).

Sewing for Special Occasions: Bridal, Prom, and Evening Dresses (Minnetonka, MN: Cowles Creative Publishers, 1994).

Fabrics, Patterns

Baltazor Fabrics & Laces for the Creative, 3406 Hessmer Avenue, Metairie, LA 70002; (504) 889-0333; < www.baltazor.com >. Christening gown patterns; bridal fabrics; also sewing books on smocking, children's sewing, others.

Home Study Courses, Schools, Seminars

Couture Sewing School
Box 51
Long Green, MD 21092
(410) 592-5711; (410) 592-6913 fax
< www.susankhalje.com >

Offers weeklong instruction in the fine art of couture bridal sewing taught by Susan Khalje.

Lifetime Career Schools
101 Harrison Street
Archbald, PA 18403
< www.lifetime-career.com >

Offers dressmaking courses.

Supplies

Bridals International
45 Albany Street
Cazenovia, NY 13035

Bridal fabrics and laces. Send an LSASE for information and the cost of their current catalog.

Software

Wild Ginger Software, 630 Fogg Street, Nashville, TN 37203; < www.wildginger.com >. Software for sewing enthusiasts, sewing retailers, independent pattern makers, and custom clothiers and costumers.

Additional Business Ideas

- Children's custom clothing. Design your own line or specialize in baby clothes. Online course: The Business of Sewing for Children by Lori McGuire.
- Sportswear. Design and sew your own styles to sell at craft shows and sports fairs.
- Make special blankets. E-book *Bizy's Guide to Making Sugglies!: A Step-by-Step Guide to Making and Starting Your Own Fleece Blanket Business* by Cinda Louden. Visit <www.bizy moms.com> for ordering information.
- Embroidery (by hand or machine). Start with monogramming and progress to other designs. Can purchase an embroidery attachment for your sewing machine or purchase an embroidery machine. Contact Sew-Knit Distributors, 9789 Florida Street, Baton Rouge, LA 70815. Send an LSASE for information and prices about an embroidery or monogramming machine. Also contact the Embroiderers' Guild of America, 335 West Broadway, Suite 100, Louisville, KY 40202; <www.egausa .org>. EGA publishes *Needle Arts,* offers correspondence courses, and holds seminars. The following books are good resources for embroidery information: *Donna Kooler's Encyclopedia of Needlework: Needlepoint, Embroidery, Counted Thread,* by Donna Kooler (Little Rock, AR: Leisure Arts, 2000); and

Embroidery Machine Essentials: How to Stabilize, Hoop and Stitch Decorative Designs, by Jeanine Twigg and Lindee Goodall (Iola, WI: Krause Publications, 2001).

41
CUSTOM CUSHIONS AND PILLOWS

In this business, you make custom cushions of all sizes and shapes for the following: dining room chairs, Adirondack chairs, boat seats, window seats, patio furniture, rocking chairs, and benches, to name a few. You can also make pillows to match your clients' furniture.

Karen began her business, Karen's Cushions, by selling her pillows at craft shows and flea markets. She had simple business cards printed up, which attracted the attention of an interior decorator. The decorator asked Karen to make samples, which the decorator's customers loved.

Karen worked for several decorators and perfected her sewing skills so that her pillows did not have a homemade look. Karen says, "I was frustrated that I never had the opportunity to talk directly to the decorators' customers, so I decided to advertise for customers myself." Her husband, a draftsman, helped her work out a price guide, and she steadily began to attract customers.

Today she has a steady business and makes one-of-a-kind pillows sewn from antique materials, beyond-repair old garments, and quilts. These pillows sell for as much as $100+ apiece.

Start-Up Costs and Financing Sources

- ✤ $3,000 to $6,000, which includes the cost of a good industrial sewing machine.
- ✤ Personal savings, small business loans.

Pricing Guidelines

Depends on the fabric used and the complexity of the design, and so forth. A handmade quilted pillow can start at $55; pillows made from antique materials can sell for $100+ apiece and up.

For custom-made cushions, factor in the time and materials used to come up with a price.

Marketing and Advertising Methods and Tips

- Rent a booth at craft shows and flea markets.
- Show samples of your work to interior decorators.
- Leave your business card and brochures at antique shops and furniture stores.
- Place ads in your local newspaper and in home or craft magazines.
- Attend home decorating shows and gift shows.

Essential Equipment

Industrial sewing machines—straight sewer and serger, button machine, electric knife for cutting foam, worktable, contracts for customers to sign, estimate sheets, filing system.

Recommended Training, Experience, or Needed Skills

- Enroll in sewing courses at local schools or fabric centers.
- Make cushions and pillows for your own home or friends' and relatives' homes.
- Work for an interior decorator.
- Need advance sewing skills to produce professional-quality pillows and cushions.

Income Potential

$20,000 to $30,000 or more. $400 or more each for pillows made with antique materials.

Type of Business

One-third out-of-the-home, visiting customers' homes for measuring and buying materials; two-thirds in-home for sewing.

Target Market

Homeowners, decorators, owners of furniture shops and antique shops.

Success Tips

- Start by buying a used sewing machine and put your first profits into buying a new one.
- Have the self-confidence and patience to learn new techniques and skills as your business requires them.

For More Information

Books

Country Living Handmade Pillows: Decorative Accents Throughout Your Home, by Arlene Hamilton Stewart (New York: Hearst Books, 1998).

Making Cushions and Covers, by Dorothy Wood (New York: Anness Publishing, 2001).

Additional Business Ideas

- Antique pillows. Hunt antique shops, sales, flea markets, and auctions for vintage materials and patterns. Sell to interior decorators, antique shops, furniture stores. Offer to make pillows from people's heirloom fabrics (old quilts, embroidery and other vintage needlework).
- Quilted and decorative frames made from fabric.
- Custom pillows from customers' finished needlework.
- Fabric photo pillows. Turn photos into pillows with a photocopy-transfer process that does not harm photos. See *Fabric Photos,* by Marjorie Croner (Loveland, CO: Interweave Press, 1989).

42
PATTERNS

In this business, you design and sell sewing patterns to fabric shops and quilting supply stores and to individual customers through the mail. Designs may be for stuffed toys, children's play items, dolls, clothes and accessories, jewelry and lingerie holders, or decorative items for the home.

Check sewing magazines and sewing industry shows to see what kinds of patterns are available and note current trends and styles.

Start-Up Costs and Financing Sources

- $400 to $4,000 for supplies, printing, and advertising.
- Personal savings, line of credit from your local bank, loans from family and friends.

Pricing Guidelines

$9 and up per pattern, depending on complexity of design.

Marketing and Advertising Methods and Tips

- Place ads in sewing, doll, quilting, children's, and home decorating magazines.
- Attend trade shows.
- Have friends and family wear clothing made from your patterns.
- Show your finished products to shops.
- Sell patterns wholesale through sales representatives.
- Give courses and workshops on how to make an item using your pattern and sell additional patterns.

Essential Equipment

Sewing machine, notions, design and worktable, computer with design capabilities, telephone, fax machine, answering machine, copier.

Recommended Training, Experience, or Needed Skills

- Take design and pattern-making courses at local technical schools or colleges.
- Buy and study patterns to gauge their quality and to see what is offered.
- Know your product, how to design it, and how to write easy-to-follow instructions.

Income Potential

$6,000 to $50,000, depending on your range of advertising and the number of stores that carry your patterns.

Type of Business

In-home, except for traveling to shows and shops to increase sales.

Target Market

People who sew as a hobby.

Success Tips

- ✤ Teach courses using your patterns. This will help you better understand what people need to successfully put together your product.
- ✤ Develop a line of unique patterns that will appeal to loyal and repeat customers.
- ✤ Offer your customers the most for their money: an assortment of designs in one pattern package; clear, typeset instructions.
- ✤ Find out who your best customers are and then focus your advertising on them.

For More Information

Books

Customize Your Sewing Patterns for a Perfect Fit, by Mary Morris and Sally McCann (New York: Sterling Publishing Company, 2002).

Patternmaking for Fashion Design, 3rd ed., by Helen Joseph Armstrong (Old Tappan, NJ: Prentice-Hall, 1999).

Software

Pattern Maker Software, P.O. Box 70306, Bellevue, WA 98005; < www.patternmaker.com > . Make, alter, and adjust flat patterns on your desktop. Write for more information or visit the Web site.

Wild Ginger Software, Inc. < www.wildginger.com > .

43
UPHOLSTERY

A good upholsterer is always in demand because many people have a favorite piece of furniture they do not want to throw away. Your customers can include individuals as well as small businesses. One mother homeschooled her two sons and also had a steady home-based upholstery business.

Ken Bowles, of Vista Enterprises/VUE and Upholster Magazine Online <www.upholster.com>, says, "Upholstery is one of the few trades a person can learn at home. And earn at the same time since a customer never has to see your work until it's done right."

Start-Up Costs
$300 to $6,000 if you start out with a good used commercial sewing machine and have a vehicle to transport furniture.

Pricing Guidelines
Call other upholstery businesses to find out what they charge per project. Have customers sign a written estimate.

Marketing and Advertising Methods and Tips
- Advertise in newspapers and on cable television.
- Place signs on your vehicle, your lawn, or your house where permitted by zoning laws.
- Encourage word-of-mouth referrals.
- Place an ad in the business telephone directory.
- Buy ads in coupon books.
- For publicity, offer to upholster some of the furniture featured in local historic homes or buildings.

Essential Equipment
Industrial sewing machine (contact sewing machine repair persons for good, used machines), air compressor, upholstery staple guns, hand tools, fabrics, vehicle for furniture pickups.

Recommended Training, Experience, or Needed Skills

- Enroll in upholstery courses at technical schools or through home study.
- Work in an upholstery shop. Work or apprentice for an upholstery business.
- Practice on used furniture of your own, of your friends, or at thrift shops.

Income Potential

$700 to $800 per week; $35,000 to $45,000 per year.

Type of Business

Primarily an in-home business, except for when you go to customers' homes or businesses for estimates and pickups.

Target Market

Homeowners, professional offices with waiting rooms, hair salons, motels.

Success Tips

- Check with local zoning laws about a home-based operation.
- Check with state agencies on requirements for stuffing used in furniture.
- Develop a good relationship with your upholstery suppliers.
- You will have to educate prospective customers as to the reason your prices may be the same or higher as purchasing a new piece of furniture. Emphasize it is the quality work you are doing as opposed to the mass-produced pieces of upholstered furniture.
- For an ongoing, online discussion of upholstery business tips, visit the Web site <www.upholster.com/business>.

For More Information

Books

Upholstery Basics (Minnetonka, MN: Cowles Creative Publishing, 1997).

Upholstery Tips and Hints, by David James (New York: Sterling Publishing Company, 2001).

Home Study Course

Foley-Belsaw Institute
6301 Equitable Road
Kansas City, MO 64120
<www.foley-belsaw.com>

Upholstery repair training.

Videos, Supplies

VUE
Box 128X
El Verano, CA 95433
<www.upholster.com>

Videos on furniture upholstery, one on making furniture slipcovers, and one on auto and marine seating. A business manual on running an upholstery shop, books, tool and supply information, and an online discussion board for questions. Write for current listing of products or visit the Web site.

Web Site

<www.upholster.com>

Upholster Magazine Online.

Additional Business Ideas

- Custom-made furniture slipcovers.
- Auto and marine seating.

Pet Services

The American Pet Association <www.apapets.com> states that as of March 1999, there were 43,143,849 dog owners in the United States, who owned a total of 61,542,900 dogs, and there were 74,894,580 cats, for a total of 136,437,480 pets. Of the 102.8 million households in the United States, 31.2 million have at least one cat as a pet. Of course, people all over the world have many other different kinds of pets besides dogs and cats: birds, fish, rabbits, potbelly pigs, rodents, reptiles, ferrets, and many other creatures. All this translates into services and products the pets' owners need to keep their pets of all sizes and types happy and healthy. If you love animals and have experience or expertise, a pet or animal business may be ideal for you.

44
PET GROOMING

Pet grooming is a service needed by people who want their pets to look their best yet do not have the time or expertise to regularly bathe, clip, and trim their pets. Grooming and care requires physical stamina, skill, and a love of animals.

One woman, Pam, a mother and teacher, started out by clipping her own poodles to save money. She then moved on to the pets of friends and family. When she began to make more money grooming pets than by substitute teaching, Pam decided to turn her garage into a grooming shop and started a full-time business.

Today, she has moved to a larger home and converted a former dentist's office into a thriving dog grooming business. She also hand-raises birds and sells supplies and various kinds of pet foods. Many pet groomers sell supplies and/or also offer boarding services for dogs, cats, and even exotic animals.

Start-Up Costs and Financing Sources

- $18,000 to $25,000 to set up your shop, workspace, sinks, or tubs; construct runs and cages; and purchase supplies. Your costs will be more if you will purchase a van to pick up and deliver your clients' pets.
- Small business loan, home equity loan.

Pricing Guidelines (all relative to your area)

$30 to $60 per grooming visit. Charges vary according to the size and breed and the animal's temperament. Cats bathed, brushed, nails clipped, $25 to $30. Boarding dogs overnight, $9.50 to $14 per pet; $8.50 for day care. (Charges depend on the size and weight of the dog.) $8.50 per pet to board cats overnight; $7.50 for day care. Charges for exotic animals depend on the type and care needed for the animal.

Marketing and Advertising Methods and Tips

- Encourage word-of-mouth referrals. The best referrals come from the best quality work and care of your customers' pets.
- Place an ad in the business telephone directory.
- Advertise in local newspapers and pet publications.
- Post flyers on community bulletin boards, in veterinarians' offices that do not offer boarding or grooming, at pet shops, and at animal feed and supply centers.
- Teach basic care and grooming classes at your place for people with new puppies.
- Offer to groom an animal shelter's "pet of the week," and announce that in a press release.

Essential Equipment

Stainless steel crates and cages; grooming table(s) and related equipment; bathing facilities; scheduling, filing, and billing methods (manual or software); bowls, brushes, food, and leashes; business telephone line (ground line), cell phone, and answering machine and/or service. PC with accounting and retail software.

Recommended Training, Experience, or Needed Skills

- Enroll in grooming classes.
- Work with a professional groomer.
- Groom friends' and relatives' pets.
- Study professional manuals.
- Attend dog and cat shows to see the latest grooming equipment.
- Subscribe to trade and/or breed publications.

Income Potential

$30,000 to $40,000 for a sole owner. $50,000 and up with an assistant.

Type of Business

An in-home business if you have a shop and/or kennels on your property. Check with zoning officials and neighbors before you open for business. With boarding, it helps to be in a more isolated location because of possible noise complaints.

Target Market

Pet owners of animal breeds with coats that need regular grooming or clipping, owners of exotic pets.

Success Tips

- Keep your facilities spotlessly clean and odor-free.
- Have a veterinarian on call for any emergencies. Know what shots animals must have before they can be boarded.
- Check with your insurance agent and lawyer about liability coverage.
- Treat each pet as if it were your own and give it the best possible care.

For More Information

Associations

American Pet Boarding Association
P.O. Box 931
Wheeling, IL 60096

Send a LSASE for information.

National Dog Groomers Association of America
Box 101
Clark, PA 16113

Newsletter, seminars, workshops, and certifications. Send an LSASE for information and a list of grooming schools.

Publication

Pet Age magazine, Subscription Department, 200 South Michigan Avenue, Suite 840, Chicago, IL 60604.

Books

From Problems to Profits: The Madison Management System for Pet Grooming Businesses, by Madeline Bright Olge (New York: The Madison Group, 1997).

The Stone Guide to Dog Grooming for All Breeds, by Ben and Pearl Stone (New York: Howell Books, 1981).

Supplies: Grooming Videos, Dog Bath

Peticures.com <http://peticures.com>. Grooming videos, dog bath, clipper sets, book.

Web Site

<www.petgroomer.com>

PetGroomer.com—Huge resource site with links for pet grooming and other products, guides, schools and home study courses, and more.

Additional Business Ideas

✤ Special tub for dog washing. Install a large, waist-high tub for owners to wash and dry their dogs. Charge $7 to $10 for small dogs, $11 to $13 for medium dogs, $15 and up for larger dogs.

Have the owner bring the towel and shampoo, and you provide the tub, table, and dryer. Include 15 minutes of free drying time. Charge extra for additional dryer time. Installation cost may be about $3,000 or more or you could purchase one of the portable dog baths and take it to your clients.

- Mobile pet groomer. Contact Professional Mobile Groomers International, 784 Morris Turnpike, No. 195, Short Hills, New Jersey 07078; <www.petgroomer.com/pmgi.htm>.
- Dog training. Contact the Association of Pet Dog Trainers, 17000 Commerce Parkway, Suite C, Mount Laurel, NJ 08054; <www.apdt.com>.

45
PET SITTING

This business generally involves visits to clients' homes to feed and exercise their pets. Some qualified persons may also offer in-home medical care (insulin shots, caring for wounds) while the owners are away. Your services may also include a home security check, watering plants, or collecting mail or newspapers. Most owners of pet sitting services are bonded.

You will need to set up appointments with your clients in their homes to go over the services requested and to give them cost estimates, as well as to observe how the people handle and treat their animals and for you to become acquainted with them.

Start-Up Costs and Financing Sources

- $5,000 to $11,000.
- Personal savings, small business loan.

Pricing Guidelines

$15 per day for one pet, one visit per day. Add $5 for each additional pet and visit. Offer a free visit and evaluation.

Marketing and Advertising Methods and Tips

- Place an ad in the business telephone directory.
- Post flyers on bulletin boards at veterinarian offices, grooming centers, pet stores, and animal food stores.
- Send direct mailings to local travel agencies, pet and animal associations and clubs.
- Advertise on local cable television, in newspapers, and in pet newsletters, especially in the spring and summer months.
- Rent a booth at pet and animal shows.
- Have a Web site presenting your prices and details of your services.

Essential Equipment

Animal supplies (food, crates, leashes, travel carriers in case you have to take the animal for medical care), dependable vehicle to transport animals in case of an emergency, billing and record-keeping systems, business telephone line and answering machine, pager or cellular phone, scheduling book.

Recommended Training, Experience, or Needed Skills

- Have experience and/or training with the kinds of animals you will care for.
- Work in a veterinarian's office or a pet store or volunteer at an animal shelter.
- Need a love of animals and a basic understanding of their needs and behavior.
- Enroll in animal care and first-aid courses.

Income Potential

$25,000 to $40,000, depending on the number of clients you have and the services you offer.

Type of Business

An out-of-the-home business.

Target Market

Retired or professional working couples or individuals who travel frequently and do not want their pets in a boarding facility, owners of exotic animals who cannot find boarding for their pets, owners of animals who for some reason are not able to have their animals boarded.

Success Tips

- Offer to sit for friends' or relatives' pets to get the experience.
- Instill trust in your owners that you will take the best possible care of their pets and homes. Treat each pet and home as if it were your own. If your business develops a good reputation for quality care, your business will increase from word-of-mouth referrals.
- Have a list of available, on-call professionals for both pet and home emergencies, 24 hours a day.
- Know how to reach your clients while they are away.
- Have a backup assistant in the event you cannot visit the pet's home.
- Have your lawyer draw up a standard contract.
- Check with your insurance agent about the best kinds of insurance to protect you and your business.

Franchises, Distributorships, and Licenses

Pets Are Inn
7723 Tanglewood Court, Suite 150
Edina, MN 55439
< www.petsareinn.com >

Boards pets in private homes.

For More Information

Association

National Association of Professional Pet Sitters
17000 Commerce Parkway, Suite C
Mt. Laurel, NJ 08054
< www.petsitters.org >

Certification, insurance, conferences.

Pet Sitters International
Patti Moran, Coordinator
201 East King Street
King, NC 27021
< www.petsit.com >

Accreditation, legal services, and a referral line. Publishes a networking directory. Send an SASE for membership information or visit the Web site.

Books

Pet Sitting for Profit: A Complete Manual for Success, by Patti Moran (New York: Howell Books, 1997).

The Professional Pet Sitter: Your Guide to Starting and Operating a Successful Service, rev. ed., by Lori and Scott Mangold (Ashland, OR: Paw-sitive Press, 1999).

Supplies

American Pet Products Manufacturers Association
255 Glenville Road
Greenwich, CT 06831
< www.appma.org >

Additional Business Ideas

- Housesitting. Many pet sitters combine their services with housesitting for homeowners who are away; or they do routine checks of vacation home for owners during off-season periods.
- Specialize in exotic or large animal care.
- Add additional services such as sales of animal-related products: food, stain and odor removers.
- Have a pet sitters' referral service.
- Dog walking or a dog "day care" for pets belonging to persons who work during the day. See *The Face in the Window: A Guide to Professional Dogwalking,* by Dianne Eibner (Toronto, Ontario: Hushion House Publishing Limited, 2001).
- Yard-waste cleanup.
- Livestock care and even milking if you have experience with dairy cows.

46
PET TRANSPORTATION

This business involves transporting dogs, cats, rabbits, birds, and other animals including small livestock such as sheep and goats to veterinarian visits, grooming appointments, boarding facilities, or other destinations the owner wishes. You provide a useful service for people who are not able to transport their animals, who have busy work schedules, or who just like the convenience of the service.

Janet, who had worked with all kinds of animals for more than 15 years, started her Pet-Mo-Bile service when friends and family repeatedly asked her to take their animals to one place or another. "They knew I worked at night and that I was free during the day to take their pets to appointments, so I decided to have my own pet taxi and do what I love best—working with animals."

Start-Up Costs

$2,000 to $3,000 if you already own a truck or van. Start with a used one at first to see how you like this business.

Pricing Guidelines

$20 to $35 for one-way transportation. Prices vary according to the distance, size of the pet, and the number of pets an owner wants transported.

Marketing and Advertising Methods and Tips

- Post flyers and your business cards on community bulletin boards and in pet grooming shops, veterinarian offices, pet stores, and livestock feed and supply centers.
- Encourage word-of-mouth referrals.
- Place magnetic or painted signs advertising your service on your vehicle.
- Advertise in local newspapers and pet publications.
- Donate your services to an animal shelter and send out a press release about it.

Essential Equipment

Van or truck equipped with animal crates of different sizes, leashes, harnesses, car phone or pager, business telephone line and answering machine or service, billing and record-keeping systems.

Recommended Training, Experience, or Needed Skills

- Get experience working with animals at a veterinarian's office, an animal shelter, or a pet store.
- Attend classes at a local technical or agricultural school.
- Understand the types and breeds of animals and how to best handle them.
- Need strength, energy, and an empathy for animals.

Income Potential

$200 per day or more. Expect more income if you sell or deliver food and supplies. Janet also offers an ambulance service for sick animals but enjoys the pet taxi part better. She also designs and builds outdoor, enclosed cat yards for places where cats cannot roam free. These cost $3,000 to $4,000.

Type of Business

An out-of-the-home business.

Target Market

Busy people with full-time jobs, older people who cannot transport their animals, pet owners who do not have a vehicle or do not want their pet in their car.

Success Tips

- Give efficient, reliable, and good care to the animals, and people will refer others to you.
- Check with your auto insurance agent as to what insurance you should be carrying. Janet's agent put a livestock rider on her van insurance so she would be covered when transporting animals.

For More Information

Association

Independent Pet and Animal Transportation Association International
Holly Lake Ranch
Route 5, Box 747, Highway 2869
Big Sandy, Texas 75755
< www.ipata.com >

Trade association of pet-care professionals who transport pets locally, nationally, and internationally (does not have start-up business information).

Book

The Portable Pet, by Barbara Nicolas (Landham, MD: Harvard Common Press, 1990).

Home Study Course

Educational Direct, Veterinary Assistant
P.O. Box 1900
Scranton, PA 18501
< www.educationdirect.com >

Additional Business Ideas

- Animal hauling. Take horses, cows, sheep, or other animals to 4-H, horse, or farm shows, to the vet, or to new owners when sold. Need a sturdy truck or trailer and a good driving record. Must know how to load and unload certain animals.

  One woman who owns a horse trailer charges $30 for one animal and $40 for two animals for a one-way trip within 20 miles of her home. Beyond 20 miles, she charges an additional $1 per mile for one animal and $1.75 a mile for two animals.
- Deliver pet food. Save people time by delivering their favorite pet foods.

Business-to-Business Services

47
ANSWERING SERVICE

This is an excellent niche for home-based businesses. Even though answering machines, cellular phones, voice mail, and call forwarding abound, many businesses still prefer a personalized answering service, and customers often prefer talking to a person when they have a question, problem, or complaint.

Some successful answering services that were started in the home moved to larger offices when they needed more space. Others still operate from their homes because they prefer to stay small. The physically challenged find this a good business to fit their special needs.

Start-Up Costs

$27,000 to $47,000. You can start, however, by having your clients use call forwarding to your home business telephone number.

Pricing Guidelines

Charge according to a set number of calls per month, say 100 calls, for $80 per month. Add a surcharge for each call beyond the 100 calls. Rates may vary from state to state and community to community. Find out what other answering services in your area charge.

Marketing and Advertising Methods and Tips

- Advertise in the business telephone directory.
- Place classified ads or small display ads in the weekly business section of local newspapers.
- Send direct mailings to small businesses, individual contractors, and professionals.

Essential Equipment

Telephone lines or switchboard, computer with billing and bookkeeping software, fax machine, promotional materials for direct mailing, and business cards.

Recommended Training, Experience, or Needed Skills

- Work for an answering service, operator, or telemarketer.
- Have a pleasant and professional phone manner.
- Keep accurate records of calls received for your clients.

Income Potential

$20,000 to $34,000.

Type of Business

An in-home business.

Target Market

Professionals, independent contractors, salespersons, repair persons.

Success Tips

- Be efficient and accurate in taking and then relaying messages to your clients.
- Check with local zoning laws to see if you need special permits.
- Use the Internet to offer the services of routing voice mail messages or faxes to clients electronically; or offer to lease clients e-mail accounts that you can buy from your ISP (Internet service provider); notify clients through their pagers

when they have received e-mails or automatically route e-mail messages to customers' alphanumeric pagers; or you can set up e-mail accounts for customers who do not have a PC or Internet access; you can also automatically fax any incoming e-mails to your client.

For More Information

Association

Association of TeleServices International (ATSI)
12 Academy Avenue
Atkinson, NH 03811
<www.atsi.org>

ATSI is not for home-based telemessagers, but ATSI's trade magazine and information may be helpful to your business.

Books

How to Start and Manage an Answering Service Business, by Leslie Renn and Jerre G. Lewis (Interlochen, MI: Lewis & Renn Associates, 1999). Order from Lewis & Renn Associates, 10315 Harmony Drive, Interlochen, MI 49643.

Publications

Connections magazine, 48955 West Hickory Lane, Mattawan, MI 49071; <www.connectionsmagazine.com>. Practical, relevant information for the teleservices industry.

Additional Business Ideas

Add additional services: make appointments, give referrals, take orders, provide information for specific organizations or companies.

48
BOOKKEEPING

If you took basic bookkeeping and/or accounting courses in high school or have worked in the bookkeeping department of a company, you may already have the basic skills and knowledge needed to start your own bookkeeping service.

Many smaller businesses or independent contractors often dump bookkeeping responsibilities on their spouses, who may hate this job and will welcome you to take it off their hands. These are just the customers who hire Pam to do their bookkeeping.

Pam started her bookkeeping business from her home part-time when she discovered she was only clearing $20 per week from her company bookkeeping job after paying day care expenses, keeping up her business wardrobe, and buying gas for her commute. Her first client was a friend who owned an antique business. That friend then referred her to another contractor. That was seven years ago. Today her business grosses more than $40,000 per year.

Many of Pam's clients are in seasonal lines of work—concrete, lawn care, and other services—which works out great for her. "When one business is slow, another may be busy, which enables me to have steady work year-round," she says. She likes, too, the way she can manage her business hours around her children's school and other activities. "I like being my own boss," she says. "I can never picture myself working for anyone else again."

Start-Up Costs

$500 for basic home office supplies. $3,000 to $5,000 for a computer, software, and other equipment. Start out with good used equipment or rent and then buy your equipment from your first earnings.

Pricing Guidelines

$65 for a first meeting and evaluation of a business's bookkeeping records. $40 to $65 per hour after that.

Marketing and Advertising Methods and Tips

- Encourage word-of-mouth referrals from your customers.

- Look in the classified or business sections of local newspapers to find small businesses. Call to make an appointment with them.
- Place classified ads in the business section of newspapers.

Essential Equipment

You can start with just a typewriter and a calculator, but most bookkeeping and accounting businesses use a computer and bookkeeping and accounting software. You'll also need a separate business telephone, answering machine or service, fax machine, copier.

Recommended Training, Experience, or Needed Skills

- Work in a bookkeeping department of a company.
- Take a home study course or courses at a local business school or college.
- Volunteer to help friends or relatives with small businesses do their bookkeeping.

Income Potential

$30,000 to $50,000 or more.

Type of Business

One-half in-home; one-half out-of-the-home at your clients' businesses.

Target Market

Small businesses that gross between $100,000 and $500,000 a year. Often these are seasonal businesses such as concrete contractors, landscapers, and pool cleaners. Pam says that small businesses run by one spouse with the other spouse doing the bookkeeping is an especially good market. "Most of the spouses who do the bookkeeping for the business hate it and have told me that my service has eliminated a number of arguments and maybe even saved a few marriages," she says with a laugh.

Success Tips

- ✤ Be honest with your customers. Know what resources can help you and your client.
- ✤ Work with your customers' accountants to make sure you have the right tax forms, and so forth. Accountants may often refer other customers to you because you will make their jobs easier.
- ✤ Back up all important files and have copies stored away from your office in the event of a disaster.

For More Information

Association

American Institute of Professional Bookkeepers (AIPB)
Suite 500
6001 Montrose Road
Rockville, MD 20852
< www.aipb.com >

Networking and support organization; certification; also offers home study courses.

Bookkeeping System

Safeguard Business Systems
< www.gosafeguard.com >
Business checks system and other related products.

Books

Bookkeeping & Tax Preparation: Start & Build a Prosperous Bookkeeping, Tax, & Financial Services Business, by Gordon P. Lewis (Ukiah, CA: Acton Circle Publishing Company, 1996).

Bookkeeping Made Simple, by Louis W. Fields, rev. by Richard R. Gallagher (New York: Doubleday & Company, 1989).

Home Study Courses

Distance Education and Training Council
1601 18th Street, NW
Washington, DC 20009
< www.detc.org >

Write for a brochure of schools offering bookkeeping home study courses or visit the Web site.

Graduate School, USDA (U.S. Department of Agriculture)
Ag Box 9911, Room 1112
South Agriculture Building
1400 Independence Avenue, SW
Washington, DC 20250
<www.grad.usda.gov>

Offers correspondence courses on accounting, auditing library technology, and others. Write for a current listing or visit the Web site.

EAgle Business Center
P.O. Box 1460
Wildomar, CA 92595
<www.eaglevip.com/html/onb.html>

Bookkeeping audio and computerized tutorial; write for prices or visit the Web site.

Software

Peachtree Bookkeeping software. (800) 247-3224.

Timeslips, by Best U.S. Holdings; (972) 818-3900; <www.timeslips.com>. A billing program for service professionals.

Additional Business Ideas

Add services such as billings, mailings, correspondence, payrolls, collection calls, and preparation of tax forms.

49

BUSINESS AND OFFICE SUPPORT SERVICES

More and more, businesses are using independent business and office support services. Business and office support services may include typing, letter writing and mailing, transcription, general bookkeeping, dictation, copying, and other office support services. These could include producing the following: résumés, flyers, press releases, reports, term papers, catalogs and brochures, directories, and reports.

Your business can start by offering a wide range of secretarial and word processing services. Then by seeing what services are most in demand and/or profitable for you, you can determine what areas to specialize in. Your work history, training, and expertise will also help determine areas of specialization. Joining professional associations (see "For More Information," later in this section), reading trade publications, and networking with other secretarial or word processing services will keep you up to date with the industry.

Start-Up Costs and Financing Sources

- $7,000 to $30,000.
- Personal savings, small business loan, lines of credit from your bank, loans from friends, family.

Pricing Guidelines

$40 to $50 per hour. See the Association of Business Support Services International's pricing manual (see "For More Information," later in this section) for the best advice on pricing guidelines.

Marketing and Advertising Methods and Tips

- Advertise in the business telephone directory.
- Network with business owners at local conferences.
- Join and attend meetings of the local chamber of commerce.
- Print business cards and brochures describing the exact services you offer.
- Offer fast service and free pickup and delivery.
- Send direct mailings to small businesses that do not have a secretarial staff.
- Ask printers, copy centers, and satisfied customers to refer other clients to you.

Essential Equipment

PC computer with a modem, laser printer, desktop publishing and word processing software, database and simple spreadsheet program that downloads addresses, charts, and graphs to documents. Also need a business telephone line, answering machine or service, fax machine, and dependable vehicle if you make pickups or deliveries.

Recommended Training, Experience, or Needed Skills

- Need office and business writing skills obtained through business school or college courses. It is also helpful to have worked in an office that was in the same industry as your customers.
- Project a professional image, be fast and accurate with your assignments.

Income Potential

$35,000 to $65,000 or more.

Type of Business

In-home, except to pick up and deliver work.

Target Market

Small firms that cannot afford to have a full-time office support staff.

Success Tips

- Start out taking a variety of assignments until you have enough clients to handle and to see which are the most fun and profitable for you.
- Talk to friends or acquaintances to see if they know of any potential clients who might need your services.

Franchises, Distributorships, and Licenses

See the regular issues of such print publications as *Entrepreneur* <www.entrepreneur.com> and *Home Business* <www.home

businessmag.com > magazines (find at newsstands and bookstores) and their Web sites for listings of related office and business support business opportunities and franchises.

For More Information

Association

Association of Business Support Services International (ABSSI)
5852 Oak Meadow Drive
Yorba Linda, CA 92887
< www.abssi.org >

Publishes a monthly newsletter as well as updated editions of their *Industry Production Standards Guide* and various business and pricing manuals for various types of office support services such as desktop publishing, Web services, and others; membership directory; small business resources; and more.

Books and Publications

Starting a Successful Business Support Service, 2nd ed., by Lynette M. Smith (Yorba Linda, CA: ABSSI, 1998).

Pricing Manual, Association of Business Support Services International (address is given earlier in this section).

Home Study Courses

Distance Education and Training Council
1601 18th Street, NW
Washington, DC 20009
< www.detc.org >

Write for a brochure of schools offering home study courses for office support training or visit the Web site.

Start-Up Guides

Entrepreneur's Start-Up Guide, *How to Start a Business Support Service.* For pricing and ordering information, visit < www.smallbizbooks.com > or call (800) 421-2300.

E-book: *Bizy's Guide to Starting a Profitable Home-Based Word Processing Business,* by Diana Ennen. Visit <www.bizymoms.com> for ordering information.

Additional Business Ideas
Court scopist (recorder).

50
BUSINESS AND TECHNICAL WRITING

Freelance business writing has endless markets. Corporations may need writers for the following: manuals, annual reports, press releases, sales letters, critiques, direct mail packages, and catalog descriptions. Nonprofit organizations frequently need writers to help them with brochures, press releases, and promotional and fund-raising articles and literature.

All businesses and organizations also need proofreaders for the copy they produce in their promotional materials, for example, their Web site and its content.

What you write and for whom depends on your interests, experience, and training. Finding a niche is particularly helpful. One retired real estate agent makes more than $50,000 a year writing brochures for local real estate agencies.

With technical writing, scientific and technical data is presented in an understandable form that can be comprehended by readers who are not scientists or engineers. Technical writers assist scientists, engineers, computer technologists and other experts in communicating their information and instructions to their readers so that the readers, in turn, can put the information to practical use. Having a specialization and/or education in the fields in which you will be writing is usually what qualifies you to be hired. Few attempt to write in a field with which they have had little experience. Your writing may also involve organizing and writing reports and articles about new discoveries and theories in your field.

Start-Up Costs and Financing Sources

- $3,000 to $15,000.
- Small business loan, personal savings.

Pricing Guidelines

Business public relations writing prices can run from $20 to $100 per hour; $250 or more per day; $1,000 to $2,000 for a monthly retainer. The *Writer's Market* (see later in this section) gives pricing suggestions for a multitude of business writing assignments and projects.

Technical writers charge from $35 to $85 an hour, depending on the complexity of the project, with an average of $45 to $50 an hour.

Marketing and Advertising Methods and Tips

Business Writing

- Send introductory letters and a follow-up with telephone calls to the advertising departments of large companies and to small business owners.
- Network with other writers for possible writing assignments.
- Place classified ads in local newspapers to get individual clients.
- Join local business ownership organizations and trade industry groups.
- Have a listing in a women's business ownership directory.
- Send out postcards to targeted clients.
- Write articles in local and national publications.
- Set up a Web site and offer articles and tips for visitors.

Technical Writing

- Contact those in your specialized industry with letters and then phone calls for presentations.
- Ask for referrals from satisfied clients.
- Have a portfolio that includes samples of your writing.
- Place ads in trade journals or publications.

Essential Equipment

Word processor or computer with word processing software, ink jet or laser printer, modem for online research and Internet access, copier, business telephone and answering machine or service, fax machine, promotional materials, home office suitable for meeting with clients (unless you meet with them at their businesses or residences), a few classic suits for business appointments.

Recommended Training, Experience, or Needed Skills

Business Writing

- Work in an advertising or public relations firm.
- Take business writing, journalism, and ad writing courses at a local community college.
- Be able to contact experts when writing about subjects unfamiliar to you.
- Know how to write clearly and concisely.

Technical Writing

- A degree in the area in which you plan to specialize will help qualify you.
- Have the talent to take scientific and trade jargon and turn it into informative but not boring writing.

Income Potential

Business Writing

$15,000, part-time; $35,000 to $85,000+, full-time.

Technical Writing

$30,000 to $55,000.

Type of Business

In-home business, except when consulting with clients.

Success Tips

- Take as many types of assignments as possible when you start out to determine what assignments are most profitable.

- Build up your client list gradually until you are able to run your business full-time.
- Market your services, nonstop. Janet Tilden, a professional business writer and owner of the company Exec-rewrites <www.exec-rewrites.com>, says, "Strive for long-term relationships with your clients by treating each one as a VIP. Provide exemplary service that exceeds their expectations, and they will keep coming back for more."

For More Information

Association

National Writers Union (West)
337 17th Street, #101
Oakland, CA 94612

National Writers Union (East)
113 University Place, 6th Floor
New York, NY 10003

Web site <www.nwu.org> has articles for business, instructional, technical, and electronic writers.

Books

The Business Writer's Handbook, 6th ed., by Charles T. Brusaw, Gerald J. Alred, and Walter E. Oliu (New York: St. Martin's Press, 2000).

The Complete Idiot's Guide to Technical Writing, by Krista Van Laan and Catherin Julian (Indianapolis, IN: Macmillan, 2001).

The Handbook of Technical Writing, 6th ed., by Gerald J. Alred, Walter E. Oliu, and Charles T. Brusaw (New York: St. Martin's Press, 2000).

How to Start a Home-Based Communications Business, by Louann Nagy Werksma (Old Saybrook, CT: Globe Pequot Press, 1995).

The $100,000 Writer: How to Make a Six Figure Income as a Freelance Business Writer, by Nancy Flynn (Holbrook, MA: Adams Media, 2000).

Secrets of a Freelance Writer: How to Make $85,000 a Year, 2nd ed., by Robert W. Bly (New York: Henry Holt & Company, 1997).

The Well-Fed Writer: Financial Self-Sufficiency as a Freelance Writer in Six Months or Less, by Peter Bowerman (Atlanta, GA: Fanove Publishing, 2000); <www.wellfedwriter.com>.

Writer's Market. Writer's Digest Books <www.writersdigest.com>. An annual market guide and book club of all types of business, nonfiction, and fiction genres of writing.

Additional Business Ideas

- Freelance proofreading and editing services. Bruce Noeske, owner of wwWebEditor <www.wwwebeditor.com> and author of the BizyMom's e-book *Bizy's Guide to Website Proofreading As A Business* (visit <www.bizymoms.com> for ordering information), says "Freelance proofreading is a great business to start from home. And one of the easiest ways to get your foot in the door is to become a Web site editor/proofreader."

  Noeske continues, "More and more businesses are developing a Web presence. The problem is, they don't spend enough time ensuring that their Web sites are clear of writing errors. This is your chance! Search the Web for error-filled sites, contact the owner (usually through a "contact" link somewhere on the site), and explain how you can add a touch of professionalism to the site. Then, and this is most important, ASK FOR THEIR BUSINESS.

  "It may take a while to get that first client, but you won't get ANY clients until you begin. Once you get one client, ask him or her to supply a reference describing your good work. Then begin approaching other potential clients in the same line of business, tell them that you are a Web site editor for realtors, lawyers, candle makers, coffee sellers, or whatever that 'niche' that you've just established happens to be, and once again, ask for their business."

  "The Internet is growing at a phenomenal rate; begin your Web site editing and proofreading business now and become a recognized expert in no time!"
- Letter writing: consumer complaint letters, letters of appeal, general correspondence.

51
BUSINESS CONSULTANT/ COACH

As the economy fluctuates and businesses are downsizing and laying off workers, it may be a good time for you to become a business consultant or coach. For many companies, it is less expensive to purchase a consultant's or coach's services than to pay a full-time staff member. Business coaches assess the qualities of individuals who have been laid off or are seeking to find another position within their company or with another firm or who even want to start a business. Business consultants assess a business's present status and management methods and make recommendations to help increase a business's efficiency.

Experts recommend holding on to your present job while starting your consulting/coaching business. Network with former employers and friends. Keep your ears open to any prospective customers in your industry or trade. Potential clients could be former employers, customers, or even competitors. These are ideal clients to start with since they are already familiar with your work.

Work out a complete and thorough business plan and consider your insurance and credit needs. Get any additional training or information before you quit your job.

A consultant can make a good living and have the independence of working for himself or herself. Plenty of research and planning will only help to ensure your success.

A professional coach's services include helping individuals and business owners to focus and follow through on their goals. They monitor their clients to see if they are following through on their daily tasks to ensure their clients are moving forward to what they want to achieve. Coach training programs emphasize that coaches work with their clients in a collaborative relationship, a type of partnership.

Start-Up Costs and Financing Sources

- $5,000 to $20,000. You should have savings equivalent to three to six months of your present salary to cushion you while you search for clients.
- Personal savings, small business loan.

Pricing Guidelines

Network with other consultants in your trade or industry and/or follow any related trade association guidelines. Average billing rate for all consultants is approximately $1,000 per day. This will vary with your specialty.

Marketing and Advertising Methods and Tips

- Place ads in business and trade publications.
- Rent a booth at your industry's trade show and distribute promotional materials.
- Offer talks, seminars, and workshops in your field.
- Encourage word-of-mouth referrals from clients.
- Network with other consultants.
- Make your promotional materials professional and dynamic looking.

Essential Equipment

Computer with word processing, database, and spreadsheet software; modem; business telephone line; answering machine, answering service, or voice mail; fax machine; copier.

Recommended Training, Experience, or Needed Skills

- Have broad enough experience to serve the varied needs of your clients.
- Have confidence in your expertise.
- For a consultant, you should be well known and respected in your field.
- For a business coach, professional coaches are individuals who come from a variety of work experiences in their industry

and profession and have a natural inclination and desire to help others achieve what they really want in their lives, careers, and businesses. A coach should be people oriented and have good communication skills.

Income Potential

$25,000 to $100,000.

Type of Business

Approximately one-half in-home and one-half out-of-the-home, depending on whether work needs to be done at your client's place of business.

Target Market

Businesses that need an expert, but not on a full-time basis. Business professionals or business owners who need to set new life and career goals.

Success Tips

- Be flexible. Expect the worst and plan for it.
- Be professional, ethical, and honest with your clients.
- Be prepared to put in long hours, especially in getting your business started.
- Keep up to date with your specialty.
- Charge what you are worth.
- Continue marketing and advertising no matter how many clients you have at the moment.
- Check with the IRS for tax guidelines on professional consulting.
- Have your lawyer draw up business contracts.
- Terri Levine, M.S., a high-performance coach who founded the coaching company Comprehensive Coaching <www.comprehensivecoaching.com> as well as a Coach Training Program for Professionals <www.comprehensivecoaching

u.com>, says about finding clients when first starting out: "It is easiest to begin with those you know—friends, family, coworkers, neighbors, or people in any clubs or organizations you belong to. I highly recommend that new coaches already have a business card file, address book, or contact manager with names, addresses, and phone numbers of at least 100 people that they feel comfortable speaking about coaching to. I also train new coaches to find their own way of naturally marketing themselves. For some that may mean writing articles, for others public speaking, for others mailing letters, and for some, making phone calls. My advice to new coaches is to 'do coaching' or 'coach everyone' versus describing coaching to people. Let them sample it by giving complimentary sessions where people can try coaching on and see if they enjoy it."

For More Information

Coaching

International Coach Federation, 1444 "I" Street NW, Suite 700, Washington, DC 20005; <www.coachfederation.com>. A professional organization with chapters in most states and more than 20 other countries. Offers a listing of coach training schools.

Books

Co-Active Coaching: New Skills for Coaching People Toward Success in Work and Life, by Laura Whitworth, Henry House, Phil Sandahl and Henry Kimsey-House (Palo Alto, CA: Consulting Psychologists Press, 1998).

Course

Comprehensive Coaching U, "Training Professionals to be Coaches" <www.comprehensivecoachingu.com>. For a free newsletter, send an e-mail to <CoachesCorner-On@lists.webvalence.com>.

Management Consulting

The Association of Management Consulting Firms
380 Lexington Avenue, Suite 1700
New York, NY 10168
<www.amcf.org>

Provides a free referral service.

The Institute of Management Consultants
2025 M Street, NW, Suite 800
Washington, DC 20036
<www.imcusa.org>

Awards certification.

The Consultant's Quick Start Guide: An Action Plan for Your First Year in Business, by Elaine Biech (New York: John Wiley & Sons, 2001).

Consulting for Dummies, by Bob Nelson and Peter Economy (Foster City, CA: IDG Books Worldwide, 1997).

Management Consulting: A Complete Guide to the Industry, 2nd ed., by Sugata Biswas and Daryl Twitchell (New York: John Wiley & Sons, 2001).

Additional Business Ideas

- Start a print newsletter or an e-newsletter for other consultants in your field or in the area of your specialty or to keep in touch with your coaching clients
- Business etiquette coach. Work with clients to develop a professional image or for communicating with business owners in other countries.

52

BUSINESS PLAN CONSULTANT

People who want to start a business or small businesses that want to expand need a business plan to get loans or additional financing. As the consultant, using business software as the blueprint, you write a formal business plan according to your client's goals, including the report that presents the plan to potential lenders. Business plan consultants also assist business owners in setting up their accounting systems and in figuring cost estimates and sales forecasts.

A typical business plan includes a description of the business, data on current assets and income, present and potential markets, and a financial projection of the business's earnings. You can type up the plan or use one of the many computer software programs available.

Your fee is based on the complexity and length of the plan your customer needs.

Start-Up Costs and Financing Sources

- $5,000 to $8,000 to start, for your office setup and supplies, your office suite software, and your business plan software.
- Personal savings, small business loan, lines of credit with your bank.

Pricing Guidelines

$2,000 to $6,000+ per plan. $60 to $100+ per hour.

Marketing and Advertising Methods and Tips

- Contact an SBA Small Business Development Center <www.sba.gove/sbdc> or a Women's Business Center <www.onlinewbc.gov> to see if they can refer potential clients to you. In turn, you might be able to direct business plan seminars and workshops for them.
- Send direct mailings to community colleges and adult evening and technical schools that offer business start-up courses.
- Attend workshops and seminars on small business issues.
- Rent a booth at small business development shows.
- Place classified ads in business sections of local newspapers.
- Make presentations describing your business to lending institutions. They may send you referrals.

- Teach business start-up courses in your community schools and colleges.
- Place an ad in the business section of your phone directory.
- Write articles for business publications.

Essential Equipment

Computer, business planning software, laser printer, telephone, fax machine, answering machine or service, copier.

Recommended Training, Experience, or Needed Skills

- Background in banking; experience working at lending institutions.
- Should have started at least one business yourself and/or be a current successful business owner.
- Enroll in courses on how to write business plans (check with your SBA Small Business Development Office for seminars and workshops).
- Ask local lending institutions what they like to see in business plans.
- Talk with accountants for tips on what to include in business plans.
- Professional degree in business, accounting, or financial management is preferred.

Income Potential

You can charge $2,000 to $6,000 (per plan), depending on your client (individual, corporate, organization, other), the length and complexity of the plan, and your expertise (if you are a certified professional, your rates will be higher than those of someone who is not).

Type of Business

In-home business except for research, interviews, presentations, show exhibits, and so forth.

Target Market

Individual entrepreneurs needing start-up money or small businesses or corportions seeking money for expansion or diversification from banks, venture capitalists, or other investors.

For More Information

See also chapter 3, "Your Business Plan."

Book

Anatomy of a Business Plan: A Step-by-Step Guide to Building a Business and Securing Your Company's Future, 5th ed., by Linda Pinson (Chicago, IL: Kaplan Professional Company, 2001).

Software

Automate Your Business Plan, version 10, by Linda Pinson. 2002. (See "Web Sites," for more information.)

BizPlan Builder 8, by Jian <www.jian.com>.

Business Plan Pro 2002, by Palo Alto <www.paloalto.com>.

Start-Up Guide

Entrepreneur's Start-Up Guide, *Ultimate Business Planner.* For pricing and ordering information, visit <www.smallbizbooks.com> or call (800) 421-2300.

Web Sites

<www.onlinewbc.gov/docs/starting/basics.html>

Women's Online Business Center document—"Business Plan Basics."

<www.business-plan.com>

Web site of Linda Pinson—Business plan expert. Lists her book and companion business planning software, *Automate Your Business Plan.*

Additional Business Ideas

- Help others fill out SBA loan applications. Refer to *The SBA Loan Book: How to Get a Small Business Loan, Even with Poor*

Credit, Weak Collateral, and No Experience, by Charles H. Green (Holbrook, MA: Adams Media Corp., 1999).

53

CONSULTANT FOR HOME-BASED BUSINESSES

With the growth and success of millions of home-based businesses, many people would like to join this movement in working from home but have no idea where to start. If you have a business background and own a successful home-based business, you might consider assisting others in choosing a home business that matches their skills and one that has a profitable potential.

In this consulting business, you evaluate the expertise, experience, business idea, finances, and future business plans of either home-based entrepreneurs or those considering starting a home-based business. You then provide them with financing options, market breakdowns, sources for products and supplies, and advertising strategies.

With the growth of home-based businesses expected to continue, the services of a consultant specializing in this field will be in continual demand.

Start-Up Costs and Financing Sources

- $5,000 to $8,000.
- Personal savings, lines of credit from your bank. Start part-time and put those earnings back into your business.

Pricing Guidelines

You can charge a one-time consultation fee or an hourly fee. Average is $100 to $150 for the one-time consultation and evaluation fee; $55 to $75 per hour for as-needed consulting.

Marketing and Advertising Methods and Tips

- Place ads in local publications and on cable television.
- Teach courses on business start-ups and offer consulting to your students when the course is over.
- Give presentations on starting a home-based business to local women's groups.
- Rent a booth at a small business fair.
- Write articles in local business publications and approach the editors of your local newspapers about writing a regular column about home business start-ups.

Essential Equipment

Computer with modem for gathering online information about home-based businesses; database of home-based business resources; copier; business telephone line and answering machine or service; fax machine; books on marketing and writing business plans and start-up manuals and publications on specific home-based businesses; suitable office or room in which to receive clients.

Recommended Training, Experience, or Needed Skills

- Take entrepreneurial courses at business schools or local community colleges.
- Attend small business fairs.
- Be familiar with home-based businesses and their special requirements or problems.

Income Potential

$26,000 to $50,000 or more.

Type of Business

In-home, except when giving talks, courses, or attending shows.

Target Market

People of all ages who are looking to start a business from their homes.

Success Tips

- Help people become more effective time managers (or recommend a course they can take).
- Teach them the tools to find the information they may need in the future and how to make the most of their available money and resources.
- Launch your business with an effective press release along with ads in local papers and on radio and cable television.
- Teaching start-up courses at local schools and colleges will also help promote your image as a home business expert.
- Provide your clients with financing options, market research, sources for equipment and supplies, and advertising strategies.

For More Information

Association

American Association of Home-Based Businesses (AAHBB)
P.O. Box 10023
Rockville, MD 20849
<www.aahbb.org>

A nonprofit support organization for home-based businesses.

Books

See more in the beginning chapters of this book and additional ones in the "Resources" chapter.

The Home-Business Sourcebook: Everything You Need to Know About Starting and Running a Business from Home, by Maxye and Lou Henry (Los Angeles, CA: Lowell House, 1998).

Homemade Money, 5th ed., by Barbara Brabec (Cincinnati, OH: Betterway Books, 1987); (800) 289-0963.

Working from Home: Everything You Need to Know About Living and Working Under the Same Roof, by Paul and Sarah Edwards (New York: Jeremy P. Tarcher/Putnam, 1994).

Seminars and Workshops

Contact your local offices of the U.S. SBA's Small Business Development Center <www.sba.gov/sbdc> for low-cost business seminars and Women's Business Centers <www.onlinewbc.gov> and offices of SCORE <www.score.org>.

Additional Business Ideas

- Sell home office supplies, books, planners.

54
INFORMATION BROKER

Because having the right information is vital to our lives and business success, information overload has created a fast-growing, much-in-demand service business with markets in both the consumer and business world for a new professional—the information broker. Using available technology and Internet resources such as online databases, a person with a background in research skills and techniques can have a thriving home business finding and reporting the specialized data her clients need.

The right information can often give one business the edge over a competitor. You will search not only the growing number of computerized databases but also look through library sources, reference books, and publications as well as interview experts to find the information your clients require. Many information brokers diversify by doing market research, conducting surveys, and scouting out competitors.

Start-Up Costs

Depending if you need to purchase or update the capabilities of your computer, the start-up costs can range from $3,000 to $11,000. This also includes subscriptions to online databases and industry publications, memberships in trade organizations, plus seminars and courses in which you may want to enroll.

Pricing Guidelines

Some professionals charge for their time in quarter-hour increments and for expenses that include online database usage, postage, charges for long distance calls, and shipping charges.

Most information professionals give a quote or estimate for the client's proposed project. This will be based on your rate per hour (anywhere from $80 to $125 or more), your expenses incurred, and the time you spend in the actual preparation of the report. The more you do this kind of work, the better at estimating you will be.

Marketing and Advertising Methods and Tips

- Directly contact your target clients through letters of introduction, personal appointments, or presentations.
- Place advertisements in business publications and magazines.
- Attend and network at trade conventions, meetings, and conferences.
- Seek recommendations and referrals among business associates and clients.

Essential Equipment

Computer with high-speed connection, plenty of RAM, a CD-ROM drive, and the capability to run various business software and information retrieval programs; subscriptions to your needed online information resources; several e-mail addresses for customer contact; printer; fax machine; two phone lines (ground) to handle modem, fax, and client demands; answering service or voice mail; cell phone.

Recommended Training, Experience, or Needed Skills

- Need expertise in operating computers and accessing online information.
- Take computer courses at local schools or colleges and business seminars at colleges, schools, or SBA Small Business Development Centers.
- Work in a research firm. Marketing and advertising experience in business is also helpful.

- Take one- or two-day courses offered by database vendors.
- Be willing to spend longer than eight-hour days to keep your business growing.
- Have tenacity and persistence in finding the information your client needs.
- One information specialist says, "You need computer skills, Internet search skills, online database searching skills and some subject expertise, whether it is medical, chemical, business, marketing, construction, or some other industry."
- Many information professionals have library science degrees and backgrounds, but what professionals recommend more in this business is being able to communicate with your client—knowing how to determine what data they actually need.
- Should be a fast typist, good at computer keyboarding.
- Good at grammar, spelling, and writing reports.

Income Potential

$35,000 to $85,000 if your business is a sole proprietorship; more if you hire part-time researchers.

Type of Business

In-home, except for any presentations or attendance at meetings, and so forth.

Target Market

Companies that do not have the employees or time to do the research they need. Individuals that need specific information for personal or business reasons. Other potential customers are companies and institutions, advertising and public relations firms, international corporations, and individuals who need market research for business start-ups.

Success Tips

- Decide what kind of clients and research you wish to specialize in and target your marketing techniques in that direction.

- Provide fast, accurate service.
- Diversify your research services by offering more than one information service (for example, market research reports), and become a specialist in just one or two areas and market specifically to that industry.

For More Information

Association

Association of Independent Information Professionals (AIIP)
7044 So. 13th Street
Oak Creek, WI 53154
< www.aiip.org >

Click on the sidebar "What Is an Independent Information Professional?"

Seminars

Burwell Enterprises, Inc. Founded by Helen Burwell, well-known expert in the field of information research. Visit < www.burwellinc.com > for details about related seminars and publications listing information professionals.

Book

The Information Broker's Handbook, 3rd ed., by Sue Rugge and Alfred Glossbrenner (New York: McGraw-Hill, 1997). The quintessential text about becoming an information professional, with resources to help a person start an information business.

Start-Up Guide

Entrepreneur's Start-Up Guide, *How to Be an Information Consultant.* For pricing and ordering information, visit < www.smallbizbooks.com > or call (800) 421-2300.

Additional Business Ideas

- Researching public records.
- Health information specialist. Help clients find health data and sell the information to them in reports.

- Research birth dates. Charge $100 to compile the news events that happened on people's birthdays, anniversaries, or other special dates.
- Create newsletters for customers based on the topics they choose.

55
JANITORIAL SERVICES

Cleaning buildings and offices is a competitive business. It is predicted to be one of the faster-growing services in the next few years. You will have to study the industry and then aggressively market your business. Maybe you can find a particular style of service that other larger janitorial services are not covering.

If you hire others, you will have to combat the high turnover rate. Maybe you can offer baby-sitting services or job-sharing with any single parents you hire. Getting one contract at a time and doing high-quality work may be the best way to success.

Start-Up Costs and Financing Sources

- $7,000 to $15,000.
- Personal savings, small business loan, lines of credit from your bank.

Pricing Guidelines

Most janitorial services charge so many cents per square foot (follow industry standards; see "For More Information," later in this section); call offices and other services to see what the going rate is in your area.

Marketing and Advertising Methods and Tips

- Advertise in the business telephone directory.
- Look for new buildings being erected and call their owners to see if they signed a janitorial contract yet.

- Send direct mail and make calls to owners of shopping centers, malls, industrial parks.
- Find out what type of interiors a building has, then pitch to the owners that you specialize in those types of floors or fabrics (furniture, carpets, drapes, etc.).

Essential Equipment

Basic cleaning supplies, power equipment (can rent at first).

Recommended Training, Experience, or Needed Skills

- Work part- or full-time in one or more janitorial services.
- Need stamina, strength, energy, and attention to detail.

Income Potential

$35,000 to $60,000 is about the maximum if you are a sole proprietor. If you are able to expand and manage the business, much more is possible.

Type of Business

Out-of-the-home if you are a one- or two-person business. Many husbands and wives start this business together.

Target Market

For a one-person business, look for those small or unusual businesses that need professional cleaning.

Success Tips

- Combine other services—carpet, window, upholstery cleaning.
- Tackle the companies that bigger janitorial services often overlook.
- Many small janitorial businesses are finding that the best money is made in specializing in a certain type of cleaning,

especially a type not offered by the larger janitorial services in their area.

Franchises, Distributorships, and Licenses

Franchise

See the regular issues of such print publications as *Entrepreneur* <www.entrepreneur.com> and *Home Business* <www.home-businessmag.com> magazines (find at newsstands and bookstores) and their Web sites for listings of related cleaning and janitorial business opportunities and franchises.

For More Information

See also Cleaning, page 100.

Association

Building Service Contractors Association International
10201 Lee Highway, Suite 225
Fairfax, VA 22031
<www.bscai.org>

Offers publications, seminars.

Books

Inside the Janitorial Business: How to Start from Scratch & Succeed in Professional Cleaning, 2nd ed., by Frederick R. Massey (Valley Center, CA: MBM Books, 1989).

Order other janitorial business books from Clean-Pro, P.O. Box 6350, Portland, OR 97228; <www.janitorial-books.com>.

Consultant Service

Cleaning Consultant Services
P.O. Box 1273
Seattle, WA 98111
<www.cleaningconsultants.com>

Contact for listing of books, videos, and software related to cleaning and self-employment.

Home Study and Seminars

Cleaning and Maintenance Management
National Trade Publications
13 Century Hill Drive
Latham, NY 12110
<www.cmmonline.com>

Videos, handbooks, seminars, industry publication, articles. Write or visit the Web site for information.

Magazine

Cleaning Business, 1512 Western Avenue, P.O. Box 1273, Seattle, WA 98111. Geared toward self-employed cleaning professionals.

Software

Rimrock Technologies, 1919 Montana Avenue, Billings, MT 59101; <www.rimrocktech.com>.

Additional Business Ideas

- Cleaning office ceilings.
- Window washing. Refer to the magazine *American Window Cleaner,* P.O. Box 70888, Point Richmond, CA 94807; <www.awcmag.com>. "Voice of the professional window cleaner."
- Sell lightbulbs, paper, and soap as a sideline.

56
MARKETING CONSULTANT

Every entrepreneur and business needs customers to make money. Marketing consultants help entrepreneurs and business owners analyze past customer responses to products and services and create effective marketing plans to acquire new customers.

Start-Up Costs and Financing Sources

- $6,000 to $10,000.
- Small bank loan, personal savings.

Pricing Guidelines

$45 to $175 + per hour; fees may be set per project.

Marketing and Advertising Methods and Tips

Next to financing, marketing is the most important part of any business, especially a new business. You can market to owners or new business owners with direct mail, meeting them at business expos, and getting word-of-mouth referrals.

Essential Equipment

PC and laptop computer; mobile technology; promotional materials with a creative flair; standard office supplies and equipment.

Recommended Training, Experience, or Needed Skills

- A degree or extensive work experience in marketing is preferred.
- Excellent communication skills.
- Must be able to emphasize the benefits of clients' products and services to potential customers.
- Should be creative and adept at problem solving.
- Network with media and others in the industry you specialize in for leads and referrals.

Income Potential

$60,000 to $100,000 or more.

Type of Business

About one-half in-home, working on a marketing campaign; and one-half out-of-the-home, working with your clients and "getting the word out."

Target Market

Those needing marketing strategies to start a business or expand or revive their businesses after a sales slump.

Success Tips

Raleigh Pinskey, visibility marketing expert, says, "Join local business organizations, attend trade shows and other business events. Then shake as many hands as you can; follow up on any leads; create as many strategic alliances as you can." Remember to be consistent in your communications with potential clients.

Franchises, Distributorships, and Licenses

See the regular issues of such print publications as *Entrepreneur* <www.entrepreneur.com> and *HomeBusiness* <www.homebusinessmag.com> magazines (find at newsstands and bookstores) and their Web sites for listings of related marketing business opportunities and franchises.

For More Information

Association

American Marketing Association
311 South Wacker Drive, Suite #5800
Chicago, IL 60606
<www.marketingpower.com>

Books, magazines, journals.

Books

Getting Business to Come to You: A Complete Do-It-Yourself Guide to Attracting All the Business You Can Handle, 2nd ed., by Paul and Sarah Edwards and Laura Clampitt Douglas (New York: Putnam Publishing Group, 1998).

101 Ways to Promote Yourself, by Raleigh Pinskey (New York: Avon Books, 1997) <www.promoteyourself.com>.

Web Sites of Marketing Experts

Excellent articles and tips!

< www.dobkin.com >

Jeffrey Dobkin—"America's Master Marketer" and author of *How to Market a Product for Under $500!*

< www.gmarketing.com >

Guerrilla Marketing Online—Small business marketing tips by Jay Conrad Levison, author of *Guerrilla Marketing* books (including one on home-based business marketing), newsletter, and columns.

< www.yudkin.com/marketing.htm >

Marcia Yudkin—"Creative Marketing Solutions" and tips.

Additional Business Ideas

If you are a good speaker, give talks and marketing seminars to small business owners.

57

MEDICAL TRANSCRIBING SERVICES

With staff cutbacks in hospitals and medical facilities these days, one home business that is in demand is a medical transcription business. However, this is a medical services profession requiring training, practice, and hard work to be successful and involves much more than just taking a correspondence course or buying the software that you see advertised in local papers and magazines. Many of these ads you see in publications that offer to teach you medical transcription or to sell you software are nothing more than scams designed to take your money. Always check a company's or school's credentials before investing any of your money!

If you are a medical transcriptionist, you will type up physicians' and other health professionals' dictation. You must be able to edit and rewrite from the audiotapes; know medical terms, English grammar, and spelling; be able to operate transcription equipment; and write clearly without changing the medical professionals' meaning or directions.

Many transcriptionists specialize in different fields of medicine. As a professional, you must stay abreast of the changing terminology and medical techniques. It is a challenging career, but one that can provide steady work once your business is established.

Start-Up Costs

$4,000 to $9,000, depending if you have a computer and office already set up.

Pricing Guidelines

Follow the industry standards (see information on associations later in this section). Some charge so many cents per line or charge by the character. Hourly rates run from $30 to $75.

Marketing and Advertising Methods and Tips

- Contact transcriptionist services for overflow work.
- Make direct contact with physicians, health professionals, and hospitals.
- Producing a high-quality product will give you valuable word-of-mouth referrals from satisfied clients. Also promote your medical transcription business through networking contacts in the medical field. Independent transcriptionists often directly contact hospitals for overflow work and/or smaller medical group offices, which may not be able to afford to have in-house transcriptionists.

Essential Equipment

Computer, modem, printer, transcriber or transcribing unit with conversion capabilities to different sizes of audiotapes, word processing and specialized software, business line with answering capabilities, fax machine. Reference books, journals, pharmaceutical references, and medical dictionaries and texts.

Recommended Training, Experience, or Needed Skills

- Take medical transcription courses at local business schools.
- Work for a hospital, doctor, or transcription service to get experience and make contacts.
- Be attentive to detail; be accurate.
- According to the "Tip Sheet for Becoming a Self-Employed Medical Transcriptionist" from the American Association of Medical Transcriptionists (AAMT; see "For More Information," later in this section), a person needs to have a thorough background in medicine, English, medicolegal issues, transcription technology, and ethics and business practices, as well as work experience or externship in a medical setting under the supervision and direction of a qualified medical transcriptionist *before* thinking of becoming an independent medical transcriptionist.
- You also must be competent in your transcriptionist skills and proficient in English grammar and in the terminology of the medical specialties in which you work. You also need keyboard speed and the discipline to be able to work long hours while balancing client demands (many want fast turnaround times) with family activities and crises (vacations, illnesses, etc.).

Income Potential

$30,000 to $60,000 or more (depends on the number of billable hours you work—plus you must factor in your taxes, including Social Security, health and other insurances, supplies, overhead, etc.).

Type of Business

In-home.

Success Tips

One experienced (and very busy) medical transcriptionist said she (and her four employees) do transcription from her home office for approximately 40 doctors in her area. She recommends a person should enroll in a medical transcription course (she prefers colleges or business schools) and then work in positions where one can get an extensive knowledge and experience of the profession *before* starting a medical transcription home business.

She also advises, "You should be able to understand diverse dialects and accents, because our clients include doctors from China, India, Korea, Pakistan, Poland, Portugal, and other countries."

For More Information

Association

American Association for Medical Transcription (AAMT)
100 Sycamore Avenue
Modesto, CA 95354
<www.aamt.org>

This association will send medical transcription career information to anyone who sends an LSASE to them. Or interested persons can visit the AAMT Web site for the same information. The Web site presents tips, articles, and an overview of the profession and important industry resources. It also presents a number of professional publications, videos, medical transcription tools and other products for sale.

Books

How to Become a Medical Transcriptionist, by George Morton, CMT (Spring Valley, CA: Medical Language Development, 1998).

The Independent Medical Transcriptionist, 4th ed., by Donna Avila-Weil, RHIT, and Mary Glaccum (Windsor, CA: Rayve Productions, 2002).

Additional Business Ideas

Medical records specialist (organizes health records in doctors' offices and hospitals; can freelance).

58
PROCESS SERVER

A process server delivers legal documents to individuals and business entities involved in court cases. A process server is hired by lawyers, collection agencies, banks and financial institutions, and some state and federal agencies. State laws govern who may serve state court papers, so be aware of the regulations covering your delivery area.

In 1981 the U.S. Marshal's office was relieved of much of its process serving duties. Since then most federal civil processes have been served by private process servers (any person over the age of 18 and not a party to the lawsuit). Sheriffs and constables serve in state courts. Funding cutbacks in many counties, however, have left sheriffs with fewer personnel and more work. This has opened the door for private process servers (where permitted by law) to step in and compete with the sheriff for those services.

Start-Up Costs and Financing Sources

- $6,000 minimum (not including the price of a reliable vehicle).
- Private savings, small business loan, credit cards.

Pricing Guidelines

$35 and up per service (rate will vary from state to state).

Marketing and Advertising Methods and Tips

- Call lawyers, collection agencies, and others who use process servers.
- Call other process servers who may have overflow work and provide you with referrals.

Essential Equipment

Computer with filing and bookkeeping software (Quicken is one of the best low-cost bookkeeping and check writing programs available; *MyInvoices* is an excellent program for preparing invoices), business line with an answering service or voice mail saying you will get back to your caller within 15 minutes, cellular, pager, reliable vehicle.

Recommended Training, Experience, or Needed Skills

- Call a process serving business and ask if they need your services. Try it for a time to see if it is something you can see yourself doing.
- Be persistent at tracking people down.
- Be professional and reliable.

Income Potential

$15,000 to $30,000; $85 to $150 per delivery of document (of course, income and rates will vary with the region and the demand for your services).

Type of Business

One-fourth in-home, conducting business matters; three-fourths out-of-the-home, picking up and delivering papers.

Target Market

Lawyers, who are notorious for waiting until the last minute to file or serve papers and need a lot of immediate personal attention for which process servers can charge extra fees.

Success Tips

- This business is more profitable part-time in a rural rather than urban setting. Call a larger agency located in an urban area and tell them you are available to serve papers in your vicinity. Otherwise, provide services full-time and be available for your clients at all times.

For More Information

Association

National Association of Professional Process Servers (NAPPS)
P.O. Box 4547
Portland, OR 97208
< www.napps.com >

This is a not-for-profit, professional organization of more than 1,300 members worldwide. Association promotes code of ethics, publishes an industry publication, and sponsors an annual conference and other activities for its members. To join NAPS, a person must have worked at least one year as a process server. Web site provides news, products, and database of process servers. (Does not have start-up information).

Additional Business Ideas

- Courier services. Many process serving companies in larger cities provide courier services for delivery of business documents in downtown areas and between local communities.
- Private investigators. Many private investigators do process serving as part of their work. They frequently are hired to serve subpoenas upon witnesses who are called to testify at trials.
- Become a public notary with a home office.

59

PROMOTIONAL PRODUCTS CONSULTANT

In this business, which is also known as advertising specialties, you help business clients choose promotional products (such as pens, calendars, refrigerator magnets, bookmarks, paperweights, calculators, freestanding clocks, personalized pocket magnifiers, among many other items) they can use for displaying their business logo and contact information to be used in business promotions as free giveaways or gifts. You consult with business clients and help them choose the best promotional product (from a list of vendors that make these items) that will fit their businesses' images and their budgets and that will be the most effective for their money.

Iris Kapustein, a trade show exhibition specialist (Trade Show Xpress), expanded her consulting services by offering a sideline business, Premier Promotions <www.premierpromos.com>, of advertising specialty gifts that her clients could hand out at trade shows and/or to their customers.

Start-Up Costs and Financing Sources

- $5,000 to $7,000 for a basic home office setup and your own business's promotional materials.
- Personal savings; small business loan for inventory.

Pricing Guidelines

You would receive a commission from the vendors for the products of theirs that you sell to your clients.

Marketing and Advertising Methods and Tips

- Join your local business ownership organizations for potential clients and for networking opportunities. Carry samples with you.
- Give out samples with your own business name on them.
- Set up a Web site with photos of your products and marketing articles.
- Articles about how to thank your customers in business publications.
- Ads in business publications and directories.

Essential Equipment

Basic home office equipment, PC, or laptop to take with you when you travel to clients and vendors; cell phone, pager, PDA; carrying case for your samples.

Recommended Training, Experience, or Needed Skills

- Join the industry organization Promotional Products Association International and enroll in its training and certification courses.
- Possess good sales and communication skills.

Income Potential

$25,000 to $45,000 or more.

Type of Business

About one-third in-home for managing your business and two-thirds visiting your customers and vendors (producers of the products).

Target Market

Just about any type of business can use a related product to help promote business.

Success Tips

- Find dependable vendors with quality products for your customers.
- The promotional products you recommend for your client should always enhance the client's business relationship with her customers.
- Choose useful products for your clients to use in their promotions so they will be used often.

Franchises, Distributorships, and Licenses

See the regular issues of such print publications as *Entrepreneur* <www.entrepreneur.com> and *Home Business* <www.homebusinessmag.com> magazines (find at newsstands and bookstores) and their Web sites for listings of related promotional products or advertising specialties business opportunities and franchises.

For More Information

Association

Promotional Products Association International (PPAI)
3125 Skyway Circle North
Irving, TX 75038
<www.ppa.org>

This organization serves more than 5,000 manufacturers and distributors of imprinted promotional products and services; offers certification.

Books

Industry-specific books, audio- and videotapes, training materials are available from Promotional Products Association International. See the PPAI Web site <www.ppa.org>.

Grow Your Business!: 125 Success Tips for Small or Home-Based Promotional Products Distributors, by Rosalie Marcus <www.best-biztips.com> and Robert Winthrop, CPA. Order from Lasting Impressions, 1039 Wellington Road, Jenkintown, PA 19046; <promoteyourbiz.com>. $10 by mail; $8 e-book.

Additional Business Ideas

Create personalized products for businesses to give away to their customers.

60

TEMPORARY STAFFING SERVICES

The American Staffing Association says that 2.2 million people per day are employed by staffing companies and that this type of business service is a $66 billion U.S. industry. With the economy swinging in periodic ups and downs, as well as the increasing cost of employee benefits, businesses turn to temporary help agencies to supply them with temporary help to adapt to these conditions. Many temporary agencies used to offer only clerical and secretarial workers, but today's agencies also supply professionals in health care, business, law, and other areas. The Internet is used to find potential employees all across the country and even the world!

Start-Up Costs and Financing Sources

- $5,000 to $80,000. Costs will be less if you are starting with small businesses and more if you plan on a larger number of temps. You need this amount for your payroll since you pay your employees and you bill the businesses—which may not pay you for 30 days or more.
- Bank loan until the businesses that hire your temps pay you, line of credit to cover your payroll.

Pricing Guidelines

You will charge either a percentage of the going salary for a position that you fill or a commission for placing an employee. Keep up with the going pay rates for the positions you fill.

Marketing and Advertising Methods and Tips

For Clients

- Advertise in the business telephone directory and in the business section of local newspapers and publications.
- Make calls and presentations to potential business clients.
- Conduct surveys. Contact the businesses in the area(s) you plan to concentrate on and ask them what times in their fiscal year they need help to fill in for or back up their employees.
- Network with the local chambers of commerce.
- Use mailing lists to businesses, scan publication help-wanted ads; establish a business network for referrals.

For Employees

- Advertise in the business telephone directory.
- Place want ads in employment sections of newspapers and on cable television.

- Give talks to retirees' groups.
- Contact local schools, technical schools, and colleges for student help and recent graduates.
- Print professional-looking brochures and advertising literature.

Essential Equipment

Home office suitable for interviewing employees (unless you rent a conference room periodically, once a week or so, to conduct interviews); computer with billing, payroll, and temporary help software, modem, desktop publishing capabilities to create forms you need; business telephone line with answering service or voice mail; fax machine.

Recommended Training, Experience, or Needed Skills

- Work in a temporary employment office (the management part of it) to see how business is conducted.
- Have basic business management skills—from previous work experience and/or from taking courses at colleges or business schools.
- If you specialize in certain types of employee placements (nannies, medical professionals, etc.), have training in that same field.

Income Potential

$40,000 to $100,000, and potentially much more.

Type of Business

About two-thirds in-home, scheduling employees, billing, record keeping; about one-third out-of-the-home, making presentations to clients, interviewing employees if you rent a conference room.

Target Market

Companies, practices, and other businesses that need short-term labor.

Success Tips

- Understand the changes in this industry in that many potential employees like the flexibility that working for a staffing agency gives them and many like being an independent professional instead of looking for a permanent position.
- Research to see if there is a market for your services in your area and enough workers to supply it.
- Requires strict and constant organization at all times to keep both marketing your business to find clients and recruiting (and keeping) reliable and qualified temporary employees.
- Hold periodic training for updating employees' skills to be qualified to work for your clients.
- Check with your business professionals—lawyers, insurance agents, accountant, and tax expert—for procedures on reporting taxes, paying employees, contracts, and so forth.
- Start small and concentrate at first on getting the best employees and best clients possible.
- May be a business to start with a relative or friend, but have a legal partnership agreement drawn up if you do.

Franchises, Distributorships, and Licenses

Franchises

See the regular issues of such print publications as *Entrepreneur* <www.entrepreneur.com> and *Home Business* <www.homebusinessmag.com> magazines (find at newsstands and bookstores) and their Web sites for listings of related employment staffing business opportunities and franchises.

For More Information

Association

American Staffing Association
277 South Washington Street, Suite 200
Alexandria, VA 22314
<www.staffingtoday.com>

Start-Up Guides

Entrepreneur's Start-Up Guide, *How to Start a Staffing Service.* For pricing and ordering information, visit <www.smallbiz-books.com> or call (800) 421-2300.

Additional Business Ideas

Placement services for nannies, day care workers, nurses, home health care workers; executive recruiting service.

61

VIDEO PRODUCTION SERVICES

With little more than a home video camera and an idea, you can either produce your own educational and training tapes for schools and businesses or make and sell one yourself on a topic in which you have expertise or interest.

Just about any how-to topic makes for a good video. Topics for business videos could include safety tips, basic step-by-step training (could be a series), descriptions of new products, or business management techniques. Educational videos could be made in conjunction with textbooks or school classes or for sports instruction or training. Videos for consumers could cover endless how-to topics, such as gardening, sports, crafts, and art instructions.

Once you have basic videotaping knowledge and skills, the possibilities are endless.

Start-Up Costs and Financing Sources

- $12,000 to $60,000.
- Personal savings, small business loan, line of credit.

Pricing Guidelines

Charge per video or project. Follow the industry-suggested rates or survey the rates of video production services.

Marketing and Advertising Methods and Tips

- Market your services or tapes to the businesses, associations, schools, and video distribution companies that sell videos on your topics.
- Send direct mail to potential customers (send an introductory tape to show samples of your work).
- Sell to catalog companies that serve customers interested in your specialized topics.

Essential Equipment

Video cameras, at least one (preferably two or three) VCR, editing equipment, digital switcher, computer with software for editing purposes, digital camera, modem, business phone, fax machine, answering machine or service. You can start out renting your video camera and other necessary equipment, as well as using the services of video reproduction houses.

Recommended Training, Experience, or Needed Skills

- Take videotaping, editing, and production courses at local technical schools or local community colleges or a get four-year degree.
- Work in a video reproduction house or for a video production service.

Income Potential

$30,000 to $100,000 or more.

Type of Business

In-home business except when making a video in a rented studio or on location.

Success Tips

- Know target markets from your in-depth research.

- Try a small test-marketing of your videos to see how they sell and are received.
- Try different topics and different markets to find your niche in the industry.

Franchises, Distributorships, and Licenses

See the regular issues of such print publications as *Entrepreneur* <www.entrepreneur.com> and *Home Business* <www.homebusinessmag.com> magazines (find at newsstands and bookstores) and their Web sites for listings of video-related business opportunities and franchises.

For More Information

Books

The Computer Videomaker Handbook, 2nd ed., from the editors of *Videomaker* magazine, section introductions by Stephen Muratore (Newton, MA: Butterworth-Heinemann, 2001).

The Video Camera Operator's Handbook, by Peter Hodges (Newton, MA: Butterworth-Heinemann, 1995).

Magazine

Videomaker magazine, P.O. Box 4591, Chico, CA 95927; <www.videomaker.com>. Site is a rich resource of many video topics—books, workshops, and much more.

Additional Business Ideas

- Video yearbooks, video portfolios, sports videos.
- Video scriptwriting.
- Video editing service.

62
VIRTUAL ASSISTANT

Many women find that becoming a home-based entrepreneur has a number of advantages—such as having more independence and the flexibility to arrange their work hours. One drawback, however, is that much of their time will be involved in administrative duties—billing, print and online (e-mail) correspondence, handling telephone calls, and other related office duties—all tasks that use valuable hours that could be spent on income-producing operations. These managerial responsibilities will continue to grow, too, as your business advances.

Enter the virtual assistant (VA), one of the newest and fastest-growing office support professionals. Shane Bowlin <www.askshane.com>, a certified VA, says, "A VA is a professional assistant working in partnership with an individual to provide support—without being physically present. They [VAs] are more than just remote secretaries. They learn their clients' businesses and work closely in helping their clients take their businesses to the next level, becoming more productive and effective."

Start-Up Costs and Financing Sources

- $5,000 to $8,000 for a complete home office setup.
- Personal savings, small business or SBA microloan.

Pricing Guidelines

$30 to $40 per hour or by the project.

Marketing and Advertising Methods and Tips

- How does a VA find clients? Bowlin says, "The first step in finding clients is to identify a few things. . . . What type of services do you want to provide? What types of businesses would use these services? Then as with any marketing campaign, you need to contact potential customers. There are many ways to do this—through direct marketing, networking, articles, and through local and civic organizations."
- Many VAs find clients through referrals, word of mouth, or online job postings.

Essential Equipment

PC and office suite software; high-speed Internet connection. Cellular phone, pager; personal digital assistant.

Recommended Training, Experience, or Needed Skills

- Bowlin says, "To become a VA you first need to have good administrative skills. Although some people become VAs without any training, I found that the program at AssistU .com was invaluable to building my practice. Because of their guidance (and my hard work), I was able to build a successful business within a year. Note: The program doesn't teach you administrative skills, you need to possess those—what it does is guide you in how to work with others virtually and how to use your services virtually."

Income Potential

$20,000 to $40,000.

Type of Business

In-home, working over the Internet and phone.

Target Market

Small business owners, especially e-business owners because of all the administrative duties that an online business involves.

Success Tips

- Kelly Poelker, master VA and owner of Another 8 Hours <www.another8hours.com>, says, "Always remember that anyone you come in contact with is a potential client for your business, including fellow virtual assistants. All contacts should be met with courtesy and professionalism projecting a consistent, positive image about you and your company. By contact I mean every possible way of communicating with another person. Whether it be in an e-mail, your business card, your marketing material, or an introductory letter. All of these things are a reflection of you and often times the only opportunity you have to make an impression on someone—make it a good one."

- Stacy Brice of AssistU says, "VA professionals want to work closely in long-term, one-on-one relationships with their clients, and they know that it's only in those relationships where they can find job satisfaction and really impact the life and work of their clients."

  Brice adds, "Currently, very small businesses understand that kind of partnership, and the power created in one. The corporate world isn't ready for it . . . yet. My belief continues to be that, for now, the question is, 'What is a VA?' By 2005, that question will be, 'Who is your VA?' A radical difference, and one we're building toward!"

For More Information

Association Web site

<www.ivaa.org>

International Virtual Assistants Association—Member benefits; accreditation and professional development.

E-Book

BizyMom's *Bizy's Guide to Starting a Successful Virtual Assistant Business,* by Kelly Poelker. Visit <www.bizymoms.com> for ordering information.

Training

AssistU <www.assistu.com>. Stacy Brice, one of the forerunner VAs and the founder of AssistU, says of her program, "It is the only organization providing comprehensive training for virtual assistants in their field. We also have the only free members association, and the only free referral service that endorses the people in it." AssistU students earn a CPVA

(Certified Professional Virtual Assistant) designation after completing close to 400 hours of training and study, and after proving themselves as proficient in close to 100 critical skills in an eight-week-long client-simulated experience.

VA Referral and Employment Services Web Sites

< www.va4hire.com >

VA4Hire—"Virtual Assistant Referral Web site."

< www.staffcentrix.com >

Staffcentrix—"The Virtual Assistant Center."

Entertainment Businesses

63
CHILDREN'S PARTIES

Birthdays are special days, especially for children. If you enjoy children and have a unique skill or talent or are just a kid at heart, then this business may be for you. Here are just a few of the types of parties you can offer in this business:

- Character parties. Make up your own costume and character (don't copy any protected well-known, commercial ones). Your character can sponsor such activities as singing, dancing, balloons, pictures, prizes, and a special gift for the birthday boy or girl.
- Magic parties. Start with simple tricks and work up to more complicated ones. Teach the children a few simple tricks to do (they love to show their families and friends). Give them each a magic trick gimmick to take home.
- Fiesta parties. Have Mexican songs, dances, games, piñatas, and so forth. Bring a sombrero (Mexican hat) for each child. Teach them some simple Spanish phrases.
- Western parties. Have square dances, cowboy hats, and pony rides.
- Craft parties. Take several simple crafts appropriate for the season or holiday and have the children choose one or more to make. One woman has sand art parties—children love it because each work is different.

- Music parties. Have an hour of dancing, singing, or playing simple rhythm instruments. You can even have the children make simple instruments to take home.
- Puppet shows. Buy or make your own puppets. Write skits or simple plays. Also have the children make their own simple puppets to take home.
- Obstacle courses or field day games. Come with your own obstacle course equipment and let the children challenge themselves or one another. Have fun field day events (for ideas, see *The Cooperative Indoor and Outdoor Game Book,* listed later in this section).

See also the Clowning entry, page 309.

Start-Up Costs and Financing Sources

- $500 to $3,000 for advertising, props, supplies, promotional materials and equipment.
- Personal savings; line of credit from your local bank.

Pricing Guidelines

$75 to $150 or more per hour; add extra for craft supplies, materials, and mileage.

Marketing and Advertising Methods and Tips

- Print business cards, flyers, coloring pictures with your name and business number on them.
- Have a business stamp made. Stamp paper bags and hand out to each child at the party for them to carry their prizes, candy, and crafts home.
- Place ads in local publications, especially parenting newspapers and on cable television.
- Hang flyers on grocery store and other community bulletin boards and at party supply stores.

Essential Equipment

Props, party supplies, your own costume(s), mats; play equipment such as a play parachute, padded tubes, and other items for your games and activities.

Recommended Training, Experience, or Needed Skills

- Work or volunteer in schools or day care centers. Notice the likes and dislikes of different age groups.
- Enroll in college child psychology courses.
- Be flexible—substitute another game if the one you chose does not go over well.

Income Potential

$600 to $1,000 per week.

Type of Business

Out-of-the-home.

Target Market

Families with children in suburban or affluent neighborhoods, schools, churches, day care centers, intermediate units for physically or mentally challenged children, day camps, company family picnics or banquets, scouting banquets.

Success Tips

- Have a signed contract between you and your client as to payment, date, and time of the party. Confirm this information several days in advance.
- Never cancel. Have a standby substitute in case of an emergency. No mother wants to have 15 active children to entertain by herself for three hours!
- Check with your insurance agent and lawyer on your liability needs.

- Have age-appropriate activities.
- Have enough supplies on hand for each child. Always bring extras.
- Volunteer to do family or friends' parties to see how your acts go over.
- Keep up to date on what is popular with children of all ages.

For More Information

Books - Party Planning

It's Party Time: How to Start & Operate Your Own Home-Based Party Planning Business, by M. L. Hine (New York: Carlton Press, 1996).

The Complete Idiot's Guide to Throwing a Great Party, by Phyllis Cambria and Patty Sachs (Indianapolis, IN: Alpha Books, 2000). The authors provide further excellent tips and resources for party planners on their Web site <www.partyplansplus.com>.

Magazine

Family Fun magazine <www.familyfun.com>. Magazine with many monthly activities for children, including party ideas.

Additional Party Ideas and Activities Books

For other excellent party books, do not forget to look at your local public library and at your favorite online bookstore.

Einstein's Science Parties: Easy Parties for Curious Kids, by Shar Levine and Allison Grafton, Terry Chui (illustrator) (New York: John Wiley & Sons, 1994).

50 Fabulous Parties for Kids, by Linda Hetzer and Meg Hartigan (New York: Crown Publishers, 1994).

52 Fun Party Activities for Kids/Includes Edible Jewelry, Wishing Web, and Balloon Races, by Lynn Gordon (San Francisco: Chronicle Books, 1996).

Hit of the Party: The Complete Planner for Children's Theme Birthday Parties, by Amy Vangsgard (Collingdale, PA: Diane Publishing Company, 2000).

The Indoor & Outdoor Cooperative Game Book: Easy Classroom and Field Games for Fitness and Fun, by Priscilla Y. Huff (New York: Scholastic Professional Books, 1992).

Party Supplies

M & N International, 13860 West Laurel Drive, Lake Forest, IL 60045. Write for the latest catalog.

1-800PARTYSHOP and Theme Parties in a Box <www.1800partyshop.com>. A wide variety of party kits (also a home-based business opportunity).

Sweeter Celebrations <www.sweetercelebrations.com>. An online party supply Web site offering a large selection of individually priced party items to make your own party creations. Features many themes and patterns, along with an array of party supplies: balloons, candles, decorations, piñatas, and other celebration items. Everything delivered to your door.

E-Book

BizyMom's *Bizy's Guide to Starting a Children's Party Business,* by Priscilla Y. Huff. Visit <www.bizymoms.com> for ordering information.

Additional Business Ideas

Offer children's cooking classes.

64
CLOWNING

For a number of years, Donna Huff and Cindy Longacre enjoyed working together as codirectors of a summer day camp for mentally challenged children. They often made up skits to help their campers understand certain educational concepts. A clown they hired to entertain the children invited them to visit a local clown club. The club members gave Donna and Cindy basic clowning tips and suggestions on where they could begin clowning.

Donna and Cindy then enrolled in a high school evening course taught by a former mime. They came up with their duo name, Whoopsie and Daisy, and began to do birthday parties, picnics, and other special events. After attending a clown convention, they came up with the idea to teach educational units as clowns. Being former teachers, this came easily to them—they worked out skits on fire safety, how to clean your room, and other themes.

In addition to parties, they were hired at preschools and elementary schools to perform educational skits. The teachers and children loved it. Donna and Cindy keep files on each party, event, and school at which they perform and what skits they do. They also leave evaluation sheets for both teachers and students. Their clowning career is hectic for their families, but both say it's given them an income while their children are small. Not only that, but it's fun, too!

Start-Up Costs and Financing Sources

- $1,000 to $3000.
- Personal savings, loans from family and friends, bank loan.

Pricing Guidelines

$75 to $250 per hour, depending on the number of children or people at the event. Network with other clowns, entertainers, clubs for current entertainment rates.

Marketing and Advertising Methods and Tips

- Print business cards. Donna and Cindy had an artist draw their clown faces on colorful business cards, which they hand out to teachers and parents after their performances. They also give away pens with their names and phone numbers on them.
- Volunteer to be the clown at a parade or a community event.
- Be creative. Donna and Cindy give away pictures for children to color, with their names and numbers listed on the bottom.

- Approach schools or institutions by personal visits (in your clown suit) or send out brochures. Follow up with phone calls.
- Post your business cards and flyers on every community bulletin board you can.

Essential Equipment

Clown makeup supplies (best found in a costume, theater, or dance supply store); gimmicks like oversized sunglasses, kazoos, simple magic tricks (may be found at your costume or magic store); old suitcase to carry your props (decorate it for your acts); clothes (can buy suits or sew ones from patterns or find at thrift shops and create your own look); hair (use a clown wig, spray your hair, use a hat—whatever you decide your look to be); answering machine; contract to give to your customers; promotional materials.

Recommended Training, Experience, or Needed Skills

- Take pantomime courses, acting courses.
- Work with another clown or clowns in a club.
- Volunteer at different events until you decide if you like this business. It's good practice and will help you decide your look and style.

Income Potential

$500 to $1,500 per week.

Type of Business

Out-of-the-home.

Target Market

Birthday parties (for children and adults), company picnics, opening or sales days, special community events, fairs, carnivals, Sunday schools, scouting troops, retirement dinners, roasts, preschools, residential institutions for children with special needs, hospitals, retirement homes.

Success Tips

- Network with other professional clowns and clubs.
- Be professional and keep clown ethics, such as not smoking or doing anything inappropriate while in your clown suit.
- Volunteer at different places in your community—everyone needs to laugh now and then!
- Make sure you have a signed contract or call in advance to confirm the date, place, time, and payment.

For More Information

Association

World Clown Association
Administration Office
P.O. Box 77236
Corona, CA 92877
< www.worldclownassociation.com >

Publishes a trade magazine, *Clowning Around,* and offers other information on clowning.

Books

Be a Clown: The Complete Guide to Instant Clowning, by Turk Pipin, (New York: Workman, 1989).

Clown Act Omnibus: Everything You Need to Know About Clowning Plus Over 200 Clown Stunts, 2nd ed., by Wes McVicar, Michelle Gallardo (illustrator) (Colorado Springs, CO: Meriwether Publishing, 1988).

Creative Clowning, by Bruce Fife (Colorado Springs, CO: Picadilly Books, 1992).

Additional Business Ideas

Learn how to do clown makeup and have a booth to do the makeup and face painting at fairs, festivals, resort towns, and at other events.

65
GAME INVENTOR

If you love playing games and are always modifying games or thinking up new ones, you may want to investigate selling your ideas to toy companies. To start your own game company could cost thousands, even millions, of dollars. A more practical way to start is to sell the manufacturing and marketing rights to your game to a large toy company that already has distributorships in the United States and around the world. It takes quite a bit of persistence to get your game noticed by a company—but if it is purchased, you receive a percentage of the gross revenues.

Here are a few guidelines:

1. Develop your idea. Make it original, simple, and direct. Games where players work together toward a common goal are most popular.
2. Decide if your game is for a specific age group or for general entertainment.
3. Test-market your game with many people and get their reactions.
4. Make a prototype closely resembling the finished product. It should look professionally designed and be easy for the consumer to tell what kind of game it is from the box.
5. Decide which toy companies would be the best buyers for your game. Research them to find out what games they carry, and then select several to contact for a presentation of your game. If possible, attend toy company trade shows and talk to company representatives.
6. To protect your game idea from being copied, you may have to obtain a patent. Seek advice at your local SBA Business Development Center.

Mary Couzin, of DiscoverGames.com, an online game promotion Web community, offers this tip, "Don't give up! No one will 'discover' you, unless you work hard at it. Most of the big hit games took three years to become 'overnight' successes."

For More Information

Book

Toy & Game Inventor's Guide, 2nd ed., by Gregory J. Battersby and Charles W. Grimes. (Stamford, CT: Kent Communications, 1996).

Also, for more information, see *Toy Industry Fact Book,* from the Toy Industry Association (see address later in this section).

Government Assistance

Small Business Development Centers <www.sba.gov/sbdc> can provide information on the patent application process.

Patent and Trademark Office, U.S. Department of Commerce, Washington, DC 20231; <www.uspto.gov>. Will send you information about patents and trademarks.

Magazine

Playthings, 345 Hudson Street, 4th Floor, New York, NY 10014; <www.playthings.com>. Monthly magazine covering toys and hobbies, aimed mainly at mass-market toy retailers.

Trade Shows

International Toy Fair (trade only, not for consumers). Contact Toy Industry Association, 1115 Broadway, Suite 400, New York, NY 10010; (212) 645-3246; <www.toy-tia.org>. Held each February, attended by buyers from 93 countries.

Web site

<www.discovergames.com>

Discover Games—An online game promotion community offering resources, articles, and other information for game and toy inventors. Visit Web site for information about membership fees and services.

Additional Business Ideas

If you are adept in woodworking, create unique versions of old toys from past centuries—whirligigs, tops, jigsaw puzzles, and other games and toys to sell at art and or craft shows. Be sure, though, that you do not make and sell ones that have a trademark or copyright.

66

NOVELTY MESSAGE SERVICE

If you are outgoing or have a special talent or product that people would enjoy receiving as a gift or gag, then this unusual and creative business may be for you. You present a gift, card, or bouquet of balloons or flowers with a signed message from the client to the designated person. You may perform a short routine along with it. Here are some ideas for novelty messenger services:

- Exotic dancers, belly dancers, tap dancers.
- Characters: gorillas, seasonal characters (Santa-grams, witch- or ghost-grams, Easter Bunny–grams), favorite children's storybook characters, clowns, or whatever costumed character you create (don't copy any protected well-known, commercial ones).
- Balloon deliveries, chocolate-grams, teddy bear–grams.

Start-Up Costs and Financing Sources

- $2,000 to $4,000.
- Personal savings, lines of credit from your bank, loans from family or friends.

Pricing Guidelines

$65 to $100+ per delivery. Charge more if you provide a short entertainment act.

Marketing and Advertising Methods and Tips

- Place ads in the business telephone directory, bridal supplements and personal sections in newspapers.
- Leave business cards where you deliver your messages.

- Post flyers on community bulletin boards.
- Donate a coupon for one free message for a community auction.
- Buy ads on cable television and on local radio stations or national radio stations (if your product is mailed).

Essential Equipment

Business line with answering machine or service, cell phone, costumes (rented or your own), 800 number for ordering, dependable vehicle, distinctive costumes and props, billing and filing system (computerized or manual).

Recommended Training, Experience, or Needed Skills

- Can work in a novelty delivery service.
- Have some dance or acting, comedy, or entertaining experiences.

Income Potential

$35,000 to $55,000.

Type of Business

Out-of-the-home, except for scheduling, marketing, billing.

Target Market

Engaged couples, recent graduates, new parents or grandparents, new retirees, recipients of awards, those celebrating birthdays, confirmations, bar mitzvahs.

Success Tips

- Be professional and tasteful.
- Confirm date, time, and place a few days before you deliver the service.
- Describe your service accurately so your clients know what they will be getting.
- Have an entertaining answering voice mail or machine message.
- Do your own market research to determine who are your best customers and how you can reach them and to see if

there is a big enough population in your area that will hire your service to make it worthwhile and profitable for you.

For More Information

E-Book

Bizy's Guide to Making Money with Balloons by Joyce Gowens. Visit < www.bizymoms.com > for ordering information.

Additional Business Ideas

Start a messenger courier service. Basic needs are a pickup truck, several incoming telephone lines, pager, and cell phone.

67

SCHOOL PROGRAMS AND ASSEMBLIES

If you are an expert in history, animals and nature, science, environmental sciences, or different cultures, or you are a children's writer or work in some other occupation of interest to children, you have a market to bring your knowledge to public and private schools, institutions, and nursery and day care centers. These institutions are always looking for high-quality, educational programs for their students to add to their standard programs.

Donna Weiss Hill, a musician-composer who is blind, performs a variety of music on her acoustic guitar at schools, youth groups, family concerts, and churches. She takes along her guide dog, Curly Connor, and answers questions about her blindness and Curly Connor.

You can choose to limit your presentations to your immediate area or you can bring your program across county and state lines. Most presenters offer rates for one-hour, two-hour, or all-day presentations. Set your prices according to your expertise (are you certified or a professional in your subject?), distance traveled, and what other presenters charge.

Here are some of the programs offered by various presenters:

- ✤ Science: Space programs, fun and exciting science experiments.
- ✤ Animals: Endangered animals, odd or unusual animals (bats, snakes, reptiles).
- ✤ History: Reenactments, pioneer life (food, customs, dress, tools, crafts), folktales.
- ✤ Environment: Recycling, earth in danger.
- ✤ Music: Unusual instruments and their history.
- ✤ Authors: Presentations related to their books.

Start-Up Costs and Financing Sources

- ✤ $500 to $5,000, depending on your needed home office supplies and technology, cost of your promotional materials and postage to mail them, transportation costs.
- ✤ Personal savings, a small business loan, or a line of credit from your local bank.

Pricing Guidelines

$175 to $400 for an hour presentation; $400 to $700 for a two-hour program; $1,000 to $1,200+ for a full-day presentation. Often your time at a full-day program will be divided to accommodate different age groups. For example, one hour will include grades K–3; the second hour, grades 4–6. Some presenters visit individual classrooms to answer questions and offer additional information.

Marketing and Advertising Methods and Tips

- ✤ Get a copy of the directories of a state's private and public schools and institutions and send direct mail advertising to the person(s) responsible for scheduling special programs.
- ✤ Contact school parents' groups, who often provide the funding for special programs.

Essential Equipment

Audiovisual equipment (always bring your own equipment to ensure you have working equipment!), extension cords, cages and crates if you have animals, dependable transportation, props, promotional materials.

Recommended Training, Experience, or Needed Skills

- Start giving your presentations to small groups for free or for a low fee until you feel your program is ready for a larger audience.
- Know children's interests at different age levels.
- Be familiar with the school's curriculum and see if you can relate your program to a part or parts of it.

Income Potential

$1,500 to $4,000 per week.

Type of Business

Out-of-the-home.

Target Market

Private, public, and nursery schools; institutions and/or group homes; churches; youth, scouting groups; museums, nature centers; local cable television programs; summer camps.

Success Tips

- Involve your audience in your presentation to keep up their interest.
- Keep your program lively and fun. Children love humor. Stay within the time allotted.
- Have a signed contract with terms stated (space needed, electrical requirements, time allotted, grade levels, etc.). Several days in advance, call to confirm time, date, and location.
- If showing wild or endangered animals, make sure you are following regulations and/or have the licenses required by state or federal departments.
- Check with your insurance agent and/or lawyer as to insurance coverage and liability concerns.

- Obviously, educational professionals prefer programs to be educational and enriching for their students. However, do not forget that children want programs that are entertaining, or they will become bored very quickly! If you can provide all three, then you will have well-received programs that will be in demand.

Additional Business Ideas

Make your own videos and sell them to educational catalogs or advertise in parent and/or teacher trade publications.

68
TOUR SERVICES

If you live in or near historic or interesting places, you may want to start your own local tour service. If you live in a town or a major city, you could give walking tours. Offer interesting facts or feature places not covered in standard tours or guidebooks. One woman who wrote about ghost stories in her historic town gives walking tours to the ghosts' haunts, ending the tour with dinner at one of the local restaurants (also a "haunt" location). She has copies of her book for sale for additional profits.

You could charter a bus or rent a van and specialize in tours like visiting caves in your county or state, nature preserves, or public gardens.

Start-Up Costs and Financing Sources

- $8,000 to $28,000, depending on whether you need transportation.
- Personal savings, a small business loan, or a line of credit from your local bank.

Pricing Guidelines

$20 to $45 per person for a one- or two-hour tour. Charge more if the tour is by van or bus.

Marketing and Advertising Methods and Tips

- Contact historic places, travel agencies, restaurants, museums, and bus companies that regularly bring tourists to your town or city to make them aware of your services and that you could provide such services as door-to-door pick-up or even travel to and from public transportation (airports, train and bus stations), for example.
- Place ads in travel and family magazines.
- Place ads in local publications. Post flyers on community bulletin boards.
- Buy ads on local radio or cable television stations.
- Send out press releases to the travel section editors of local newspapers.
- Print brochures describing your tour and rates. Place them in the lobbies and offices of local hotels, motels, and bed-and-breakfast establishments.
- Advertise on the local cable television channels.
- Have a Web page on your local chamber of commerce's Web site.

Essential Equipment

Business line with answering capabilities, cell phone; PC with business suite software; promotional materials; van or rental bus if needed.

Recommended Training, Experience, or Needed Skills

- Enroll in travel training courses.
- Work as a tour guide or in a travel agency.
- Be an expert in the area of your tours.

Income Potential

$50,000 to $85,000 or more, depending on the length of your tours and the tourist season. Follow industry suggestions and guidelines.

Type of Business

One-third in-home for booking and arranging tours; two-thirds out-of-the-home for conducting the tours.

Target Market

Tourists or business travelers, local senior citizens' groups, youth and small school groups or classes, special clubs or hobbyists, companies that attend conventions or seminars in your area.

Success Tips

- Follow licensing, bonding, and tax laws.
- Check with your insurance agent and lawyer for insurance and liability needs.
- Offer a variety of tours.
- Sell souvenirs, booklets, books, and videos for additional profits.
- Make the history interesting with little-known tidbits of information not found in the usual tour books.
- Jennifer Dugan, owner of Dugan's Travels <www.dugans travels.com>, says, "The most important thing I feel people who are starting a home business should know is that success takes time. So many people start up a business and then when they don't see results immediately they give up. Or they are so 'gung ho' in the beginning but fade off the marketing and promoting after a little while. A good business needs to be taken care of like a flower garden. Each season you have to maintain it in order for the flowers to continue to come up each year. If you don't tend to it and expect it to take care of itself, you end up with a bunch of weeds. If you continue to take care of it by each month caring for it depending on what it needs, you will have a beautiful garden of flowers."

  Dugan continues, "My successful (travel) agents are the ones that have promoted every month whether they were busy or not. Each month they sent customers thank-you cards and made sure all customers were cared for. It is important to not forget about those who have given you a sale or business just because they have paid you already. It takes dedication, but those who commit to their home business are the successful ones."

Franchises, Distributorships, and Licenses

See the regular issues of such print publications as *Entrepreneur* <www.entrepreneur.com> and *Home Business* <www.home businessmag.com> magazines (find at newsstands and bookstores) and their Web sites for additional listings of travel-related business opportunities and franchises.

Travel Network
560 Sylvan Avenue
Englewood Cliffs, NJ 07632
<www.travelnetwork.com>

A recognized global chain of travel agencies. For more information, write or visit the Web site.

For More Information

Books

The Business of Tour Operations, by Pat Yale (Philadelphia, PA: TransAtlantic Publications, 1994).

Tour Guiding Business, by Richard Cropp, Barbara Braidwood, and Susan M. Boyce (Bellingham, WA: Self-Counsel Press, 2000).

Additional Business Ideas

- Lead overnight tours—camping, wagon train, rafting, hiking, mountain climbing.
- Make videos of your areas of interest and sell them to travel agencies that book tours in your area.
- Home-based travel agency. Have an office suitable for meeting with clients. Provide a relaxed environment and give individual attention. Refer to the BizyMom's e-book *Bizy's Guide to How to Start Your Own Home-Based Travel Agency*, by Jennifer Dugan <www.duganstravels.com> or <www.travelathome.com>. Visit <www.bizymoms.com> for ordering information.

Green Businesses

Green Resources

Associations

American Horticultural Society
7931 East Boulevard Drive
Alexandria, VA 22308
(800) 777-7931
< www.ahs.org >

Journal, gardening information for gardeners.

Books

Christmas Trees: Growing and Selling Trees, Wreaths, and Greens, by Lewis Hill (Pownal, VT: Storey Books, 1991).

The Flower Farmer: An Organic Grower's Guide to Raising and Selling Cut Flowers (White River Junction, VT: Chelsea Green Publishing Company, 1997).

Flowers for Sale: Growing and Marketing Cut Flowers—Backyard to Small Acreage: A Bootstrap Guide, by Lee Sturdivant (Friday Harbor, WA: San Juan Naturals, 1994).

The Four-Season Landscape: Easy-Care Plants and Plans for Year-Round Color, by Susan A. Roth (Emmaus, PA: Rodale Press, 1996).

The Greenhouse and Nursery Handbook—A Complete Guide to Growing and Selling Ornamental Plants, by F. X. Jorwik (Mills, WY: Andmar Press, 1992).

Herbs for Sale: Growing and Marketing Herbs, Herbal Products, and Herbal Know-How, by Lee Sturdivant (Friday Harbor, WA: San Juan Naturals,1994).

Lawn Care and Gardening: A Down-to-Earth Guide to the Business, by Kevin Rossi (Ukiah, CA: Acton Circle,1996).

Successful Small Scale Gardening, 2nd ed., by Karl Schwenke (Pownal, VT: Storey Books, 1991).

Wreath Magic, by Leslie Dierks (Asheville, NC: Lark Books, 1996).

Gardening Book Publishers

Send an SASE for a listing or catalog of publishers' current books.

Better Homes and Gardens Books, 1100 Walnut Street, Des Moines, IA 50309.

Rodale Books, 33 E. Minor Street, Emmaus, PA 18099; <www.rodale.com>.

Storey/Garden Way Publishing, 210 Mass Moca Way, North Adams, MA 01247; <www.storey.com>.

Government Assistance—
Cooperative Extension Service

The U.S. Department of Agriculture has an extension office in every county in the United States. Originally formed to assist farmers, these offices operate in conjunction with state universities and are good sources for information on plants and insects. In recent years, they have also assisted in forming crafts cooperatives and providing information on small business start-ups. Call your local directory assistance for the number of the extension office nearest you. Or visit the Web site <www.reeusda.gov>.

Publications, Gardening

Visit your local bookstore, newsstand, or public library to see all the gardening and landscaping publications.

Miscellaneous

To establish a backyard habitat, order the packet from the National Wildlife Federation, 1400 Sixteenth Street, NW, Washington, DC 20036; <www.nwf.org>.

Gardening by Mail: A Source Book, 5th ed., by Barbara J. Barton (Boston, MA: Houghton Mifflin, 1997). A directory of mail order sources for gardeners.

69
ENVIRONMENTALLY CONCERNED BUSINESSES

Air and water pollution, accumulation of toxic chemicals and wastes, and overflowing landfills are just some of the environmental problems we face. If you can come up with a unique business or an original idea to fix an ecological problem, you will not only help the earth, but you can also make some handsome profits in the process.

There are a number of existing businesses, franchises, and other opportunities that you can invest in or operate. Or look in your community to see what environmental problems exist and come up with your own ecologically based business to handle them.

Here are just a few of the kinds of environmentally concerned businesses that presently exist:

- Ecotourism. There are two kinds of ecotourism—one is termed "soft," in which people take hiking, mountain biking, photo, rafting, or other nontraditional excursions and do not disturb the ecosystems; and the other is termed "hard," in which people work toward common goals such as restoring habitats or working at archaeological sites. You may live in a special area in which you can offer such tours.
- Selling natural products. These include non-animal-tested cosmetics and environmentally safe home cleaning and pet care products.
- Recycling materials. Collect materials for industries and "green" businesses.
- Recycling consultant broker. Help communities set up and implement or improve their recycling programs.
- Recycling inventor. Come up with a unique way to use recycled materials in a product you devise.
- Grower of organic produce and herbs. Sell to health food stores, grocery stores, and restaurants.
- Natural garden service. Offer chemical-free lawn and garden care service and products.

Start-Up Costs and Financing Sources

- $3,000 to $50,000, depending on whether you start a service business or need an inventory.
- Personal savings, a small business loan from your local bank, or a loan or grant from your state or the federal government if your business qualifies for any existing government programs that encourage the growth of businesses designed to improve the environment.

Pricing Guidelines

Compare your business to a similar commercial business's prices to give you a starting point. Consider, too, your time and cost of materials involved. Talk to an SBA expert at your local SBA Small Business Development Center <www.sba.gov/sbdc>. (See "Government Resources" in part III.)

Recommended Training, Experience, or Needed Skills

- Work in a business similar to one you want to start.
- Read environmental publications.
- Have a degree, training, or experience in the industry in which you wish to conduct your business.

Income Potential

$10,000 to $100,000+, depending on the market and demand for your product or services.

Type of Business

Can be either in-home or out-of-the-home.

Target Market

Middle- to upper-income people, businesses that want to save money through recycling and want to use recycled products.

Franchises, Distributorships, and Licenses

There are a number of franchises that are concerned with the environment.

For More Information

Association

National Recycling Coalition
1727 King Street, Suite 105
Alexandria, VA 22314
<www.nrc-recycle.org>

Recycling information and helpful resource links.

Books and Publications

Choose to Reuse: An Encyclopedia of Services, Businesses, Tools & Charitable Programs That Facilitate Reuse, by Nikki and David Goldbeck (Woodstock, NY: Ceres Press, 1995).

Ecopreneuring: The Complete Guide to Small Business Opportunities from the Environmental Revolution, by Steven J. Bennett (New York: John Wiley & Sons, 1991).

Additional Business Ideas

Send an LSASE for more information.

- Papermaking. Recycle junk mail and other paper scraps to make handmade paper to sell at art and craft shows. *Papermaking Techniques Book: Over 50 Techniques for Making and Embellishing Handmade Paper* by John Plowman (Cincinnati, OH: North Light Books, 2001).
- Create fashion jewelry from paper. *The Paper Jewelry Book* by Jessica Wrobel (Gloucester, MA: Rockport Publishers, 1998).

70
FLOWERSCAPING SERVICE

In this business, you buy flowers from a wholesaler or raise them yourself, then plant them in your clients' flower beds. Give advice on what kind of flowers should go where. After you plant the flowers, you can either let your client maintain them, or, for a weekly fee, you can do the weeding, watering, and pruning.

You can specialize in flowers or small bushes (leave the planting of trees and large shrubs to the bigger landscapers in your area).

Start-Up Costs

$3,000 to $8,000. Personal savings; borrowing from family, friends; small business loan.

Pricing Guidelines

Charge an additional 50 percent to 100 percent of the wholesale price of the flowers plus your hourly wage ($25 to $40 per hour, more if you have a degree in landscape design or horticulture).

Marketing and Advertising Methods and Tips

- Post flyers and your business cards on community bulletin boards.
- Make direct calls to landscapers who plant only trees and shrubs and not flowers.
- Leave business cards at garden centers.
- Encourage word-of-mouth referrals.
- Donate your services to "flowerscaping" the gardens of an area historic house or a new school and distribute a press release about it for the media.

Essential Equipment

Truck, van, or station wagon. Gardening equipment: pruners, edger, clippers, shovels/spade/hoe, rakes, wheelbarrow, trowels, weed puller, washable gloves, drop cloths (for dirt), scissors, measuring tape, watering can. Office equipment: telephone and answering machine, computer for record keeping, billing and gardening software, promotional materials.

Recommended Training, Experience, or Needed Skills

- Work in a nursery, garden center, or greenhouse or for a landscaper.
- Take gardening and horticulture courses at local vo-tech schools or colleges.
- Volunteer to do your friends' and neighbors' gardens and experiment in your own with various flowers.
- Need to have a green thumb and enjoy working long hours in the growing seasons.

Income Potential

$35,000 to $50,000 in a growing season.

Type of Business

Out-of-the-home.

Target Market

Working couples, elderly adults who need assistance in maintaining their gardens, local businesses and institutions that have flower beds, homeowners in new developments.

Success Tips

- Charge an evaluation fee, but credit it toward the customers' bill if they decide to hire you.
- Study landscape design books.
- Know the best flowers for certain soil, light, and weather conditions.
- Constantly learn and try new horticultural techniques.

- Attend garden shows, read up on the latest garden advances, give talks and/or courses to gardening clubs or at adult evening schools in the off-season.
- Make your business unique; for example, advertise that you use "old-fashioned" flowers that were common in the early part of our country's history.

For More Information

The New Flower Gardener, by Pippa Greenwood (New York: DK Publishing, 2001).

Additional Business Ideas

- Lawn care service (mow, clip, rake—no chemical applications).
- Raise and sell your own flowers, plants, and shrubs to your customers.
- Set up container gardens for homeowners' and businesses' entrances, for example.

71
GARDEN CONSULTING

The popularity of gardening as a hobby—one of the biggest in the United States—has created a demand for gardening information of all kinds. Each spring, homeowners invest money in flowers, trees, shrubs, and lawns to beautify their house and gardens and are willing to pay gardening experts for tips to keep their plants alive and healthy. You help people plan and design their gardens, suggesting the best flowers, shrubs, trees, and even decorative structures for the area. Clients may also call on you to recommend solutions to insect infestations, plant diseases, and other gardening problems.

You can either supply the plantings yourself or refer your client to a suitable garden center. A client may hire you for a one-time consultation or have you come on a regular or as-needed basis.

Start-Up Costs and Financing Sources

- $5,000 to $9,000.
- Personal savings, line of credit from your bank, small business loan.

Pricing Guidelines

$30 to $45 per hour; $75 to $200 per hour if you have a degree or certification in landscape design, architecture, or horticulture.

Marketing and Advertising Methods and Tips

- Place signs on your customers' lawns while you are working there.
- Rent booths at home and garden shows.
- Write a gardening column for your local paper.
- Place a magnetic sign or paint a sign on your vehicle.
- Make direct calls to builders of new housing developments.
- Place an ad in the business telephone directory, as well as in the home and garden supplement of your local newspaper.

Essential Equipment

Garden reference books, access to online gardening databases, graph paper and drafting tools or computer with garden designing software.

Recommended Training, Experience, or Needed Skills

- Have a degree or training in ornamental horticulture or attend classes at a local agricultural school or community college.
- Work for an established landscaper or established nursery.
- Be creative.

Income Potential

$35,000 to $80,000 or more.

Type of Business

Out-of-the-home, except for designing on paper.

Success Tips

- Take the necessary courses or have training or work experience to be properly qualified.
- Keep up on the latest environmental and organic studies related to gardening, as many homeowners are concerned about chemicals and their effects on living organisms.
- Specialize in designs for small gardens or lots because many homes are built on smaller lots these days.
- Make each one of your customers' properties the envy of their neighbors!
- Many gardening consultants are horticulturalists and/or have expertise and experience with certain types of specialty plants and garden designs. One consultant had more business than she could handle from the publicity she received from teaching gardening courses at local adult education programs and at retirement centers. She also conducted children's workshops at local plant nurseries.

For More Information

Books

Easy Garden Design: 12 Simple Steps to Creating Successful Gardens and Landscapes, by Janet Macunovich (North Adams, MA: Storey/Garden Way Publishing, 1992).

Garden Blueprints: 25 Easy-to-Follow Designs for Beautiful Landscapes, by Becke Davis, Harriet Cramer, and Daria Price Bowman (New York: Sterling Publishing Company, 2000).

Software

Home Gardener Package and *Professional Package,* by Lafayette Landscape Designs, 6323 Lafayette Road, Medina, OH 44256; (303) 725-7442; < www.neobright.net/lldesign >. Landscape software.

Additional Business Ideas

- Plan natural backyard habitats.

- Plan and design decorative, backyard water ponds. Refer to *Quick and Easy Container Water Gardens,* by Philip Swindells (North Adams, MA: Storey Communications, 1998).

72
GROWING HERBS

Herbs in the past few years have become popular for use in home remedies, in potpourris, in gourmet cooking, and by gardeners who want to grow them for their beauty and practical uses. You can make money growing herbs by selling them wholesale or retail or by making and selling your own herbal products.

You need less space than for growing other cash crops. A small greenhouse (either attached to your house or freestanding) will allow you to grow them all year, or at least get them started for the growing season in your area.

Start-Up Costs and Financing Sources

- $8,000 to $40,000 for equipment, seeds, greenhouse, drying shed, vehicle, advertising.
- Personal savings, small business loan.

Pricing Guidelines

$2 to $10 per plant. Check with other growers in your area for prices.

Marketing and Advertising Methods and Tips

- Wholesale. Contact garden centers, nurseries, hardware and grocery stores, and restaurants.
- Teach continuing education courses at local schools and colleges.
- Take a booth at home and garden trade shows.
- Offer to give talks to local gardening clubs.
- Approach your local cable television producer with a proposal for a weekly show about growing herbs and their uses for cooking.

- Retail. Place classified ads in local publications, give talks to garden clubs, hand out flyers and business cards, and rent a table at a flea market or farmer's market.
- Mail order. Advertise in gardening and herbal publications. Add shipping and handling costs and taxes for some states. Check with state regulations regarding transportation of plants.

Essential Equipment

Greenhouse(s), outside area for beds, gardening equipment, lumber for tables, plants, dirt, vehicle for transporting plants, markers, pots, seeds. Office supplies: phone with fax, answering machine or service, billing system.

Recommended Training, Experience, or Needed Skills

- Work in a nursery or a commercial greenhouse, or apprentice with a person who grows herbs.
- Take courses, workshops, and seminars on herbs at vo-tech schools or agricultural colleges.
- Know all the different herbs, their properties and characteristics.
- Know propagation techniques and have basic gardening skills.

Income Potential

$30,000 to $60,000 or more.

Type of Business

In-home business, except when out-of-the-home selling.

Target Market

Weekend gardeners, gardening centers, nurseries, restaurants that use herbs, grocery stores and farm stands that carry local produce. Growing your own specialty herbs—different and unusual varieties—will help you compete with larger, commercial and foreign markets.

For More Information

Associations

Send an LSASE for more information.

Herb Growing and Marketing Network
P.O. Box 254
Silver Springs, PA 17575
< www.herbworld.com >

International Herb Association
4456 Corporation Lane, Suite 120
Virginia Beach, VA 23462

American Botanical Council
P.O. Box 144345
Austin, TX 78714
< www.herbalgram.org >

Publishes *HerbalGram*.

Books

Growing Your Herb Business, by Bertha Reppert (North Adams, MA: Storey/Garden Way Publishing, 1994).

Herb Resource Directory. Northwind Farm Publications, Route 2 Box 246, Sevlin, MN 56676.

Herb Topiaries, by Sally Gallo (Loveland, CO: Interweave Press, 1992).

The Pleasure of Herbs, by Phyllis Shaudys (North Adams, MA: Storey/Garden Way Publishing, 1994).

Book Publisher

Wood Violet Books
3814 Sunhill Drive
Madison, WI 53704

Offers hundreds of herb and garden books; will do special searches. $2 for catalog.

Magazines

The Business of Herbs, published by Paula Oliver. Send an SASE to Northwind Farm Publications, 439 Ponderosa Way, Jemez

Springs, NM 87025; <www.herb-biz.com>. Excellent resource for herb businesses.

The Herb Companion, Interweave Press, 201 East Fourth Street, Loveland, CO 80537.

Additional Business Ideas

- Create and sell herbal vinegars, gifts, or potpourris. Teach how-to classes at adult evening schools or at your home.
- Plan and install herbal gardens.
- Grow cactus and other plants for states with desert or arid climates.

73
PLANT MAINTENANCE SERVICE

In this business, you maintain businesses' or institutions' plants and keep them looking healthy. You may also be called on to be a plant "doctor"—that is, to revive sickly plants.

Recent studies have shown that green plants help filter out air pollutants, including toxic chemicals produced by cigarette smoke. Plants also give banks, restaurants, or offices a welcoming and comforting appeal. Plants can be a major investment. For this reason alone, plant care professionals are needed by establishments to keep their plants alive and looking healthy.

Start-Up Costs and Financing Sources

- $1,500 to $6,000.
- Personal savings, small business loan, loan from family or friends, lines of credit from your bank.

Pricing Guidelines

Plant maintenance: $2 to $3.50 per plant, but charges are determined by the number and size of the plants and can be bid separately with each client. Time at each location can range from 10 to 30 minutes or more. Plant "doctoring": $2.75 per plant.

Marketing and Advertising Methods and Tips

- Send direct mail and place calls to business offices, restaurants, banks, and other institutions.
- Place classified ads in local newspapers and magazines.
- Post flyers on community bulletin boards.
- Buy ads on local cable television or radio stations.
- Encourage word-of-mouth referrals.

Essential Equipment

Small ladders, watering devices, soil, pruners, scissors, fertilizer, filing and billing systems (manual or computerized), business phone and answering machine or service, maintenance contracts.

Recommended Training, Experience, or Needed Skills

- Work in a commercial greenhouse specializing in houseplants.
- Enroll in horticultural courses at local vo-tech schools or agricultural colleges.
- Study your own plant reference books or the many available in public libraries.
- Volunteer to take care of friends' houseplants.

Income Potential

$10,000 to $65,000.

Type of Business

Out-of-the-home.

Target Market

Institutions, banks, museums, hospitals, restaurants, offices, building lobbies, persons with higher incomes that have little time to care for plants.

Success Tips

- Offer free replacement guarantees if plants die, but insist that only you care for the plants.
- Keep up to date on the latest plant care techniques.

Books

Interior Plantscapes: Installation, Maintenance, and Management, 3rd ed., by George H. Manaker (Upper Saddle River, NJ: Prentice-Hall, 1996).

Interior Plantscapes: A Guide to Plantscapes in Work and Leisure Spaces, by Lynne Lockwood (Brookfield, VT: Ashgate Publishing, 2000).

Additional Business Ideas

- Rent or lease plants that you have grown yourself or purchased from wholesalers. Charge $2 to $3 a plant for rental. Charge $80 to $1,000 a month to lease plants to office buildings and institutions.
- Work with caterers, event planners, and convention centers to set up seasonal displays or displays for special occasions.

74
WREATHS

Once only around during the holiday season, wreaths have become an indoor and outdoor decorative fixture. The popularity of the "country" look has helped to give this craft popularity, but wreaths can be created to fit the decor of even the most contemporary style.

This is a business that can be started easily part-time and then expanded to full-time as you gather more customers and markets. You can purchase wreath supplies from wholesale growers or craft shops or gather natural materials if you live in a rural area. You might also grow the materials you need if you choose.

Start-Up Costs and Financing Sources

- $8 to $25 for materials for a single wreath. $600 to $2,000 for additional supplies, advertising, promotional materials.
- Personal savings, lines of credit from your bank, loans from family or friends.

Pricing Guidelines

$30 to $350 per wreath, depending on the materials and if it is custom designed.

Marketing and Advertising Methods and Tips

- Begin selling at craft shows, then to home and holiday boutiques.
- Donate wreaths to a community auction.
- Contact interior decorators for referrals.
- Rent booths at home shows.
- Contact real estate agents and ask to decorate sample homes.
- Make direct calls to stores, businesses, and institutions that are being built or redecorated.

Essential Equipment

Glue, glue gun, pruning shears, wreath frames, dried flowers, vines, weeds, other natural materials, decorative accessories, drying shed (if drying your own materials), workroom, display rack, large cardboard boxes for carrying and storing wreaths, flexible wire, hangers, telephone with answering machine.

Recommended Training, Experience, or Needed Skills

- Take wreath-making courses at craft shops, craft centers, or adult evening schools.
- Work in a dried flower or wreath shop.
- Know various dried flowers and weeds.
- Have a creative flair for design.

Income Potential

$700 to $2,000 or more at a weekend craft show.

Type of Business

About one-half in-home, making the wreaths; one-half out-of-the-home, selling, delivering, and marketing.

Target Market

Business offices, interior decorators, stores for seasonal decorations, individuals for decorating their living spaces.

Success Tips

- Develop your own styles and designs.
- Be active marketing your wares and seek out as many places to show your work as possible.
- Keep a list of the people who buy from you. Mail them brochures and notify them of shows where you will be selling your wreaths.
- Join a craft guild for networking information and referrals.

For More Information

Books

Everlasting Flowers: Making and Arranging Dried, Preserved, and Artificial Flowers, by Patricia Crosher (Mineola, NY: Dover Publications, 1997).

How to Do Wreaths, Even If You Think You Can't, by Leisure Arts staff (Palm Coast, FL: Leisure Arts, 1997).

Wreath Making Basics, by Dawn Cusick (New York: Sterling Publishing, 1993).

Supplies

Vermont Wreath Company
Route 7A
Danby, VT 05739
<www.vermontwreath.com/supplies.shtml>

Has a section for supplies for pro wreath makers.

Additional Business Ideas

Make and sell grapevine wreaths, undecorated, to craft shops. Refer to *Grapevine Wreaths,* by Gayle O'Donnell (North Adams, MA: Storey Communications, 1996).

Craft Businesses

Craft Resources

Craftspersons advise trying a variety of ways to market your items. Here are a few:

Craft Mall or Barn

These first opened in Texas and have since spread out over the country. In a craft mall you rent spaces with shelves for a set period of time—one, three, or six months—during which you can decorate and set up your display as you wish. Craftspeople often share the space and rent with another crafter-friend. The mall's owner sells your items and sends you your profits, minus an advertising fee. The mall's owner pays any sales taxes.

The advantage of this method is that you do not have to be present for the sale of your crafts. A disadvantage is that you do not get a chance to talk to your customers.

To open a craft mall yourself in a busy shopping center, for example, can cost as much as $150,000+ for rent, advertising, equipment, and displays. You might start on a smaller scale by remodeling and using a barn or other structure on your property. To be successful, though, you must be open at least six days a week and be near an area frequented by shoppers.

Craft mall software is available from companies like Infinity Data Products, P.O. Box 548, Jackson, MO 63755; <www.infinitydata.com/cccs.htm>.

Craft Home Parties

If you make a variety of crafts and know others who do, too, you may want to sell items through a craft home party business. You have to enjoy talking to and meeting new people and working afternoons and evenings.

If you want to start a craft home party business, first see if there are any others in your area, and find out what types of crafts are the most profitable to sell. Then check with an accountant for tax advice, hire craft demonstrators if needed, and have your lawyer draw up a contract for the demonstrators that supply you with crafts. You make money by selling your own crafts. Or you take a percentage, say 25 percent, of the demonstrators' selling price for their crafts.

You may want to just sell your crafts through someone else's home party business. You will usually have two weeks to fill orders given to you. Make sure you have a contract if you are the supplier.

Crafts Retail

Selling your crafts retail entails face-to-face selling to customers. Most craftspersons start out by selling their crafts at the following places: shopping mall kiosks and carts (temporary or seasonal); craft shows, fairs, festivals; holiday boutiques and home parties; custom orders from promotional materials, ads, referrals; your own home shop. (See "Books," later in this section.)

Crafts Wholesale

This involves selling your crafts in large quantities to retail outlets. You set a wholesale price, and the buyer adds on her price to come up with the retail selling price. You have to be able to produce enough of your craft in a certain time to fill orders received. Some wholesale markets include the following: trade shows—take a booth or hire sales reps (can be expensive, but if you receive enough orders, you may only have to attend one or two a year); sales representatives; galleries or shops (often come to trade shows); mail order catalog houses. (See "Books.")

Association

American Craft Council
72 Spring Street
New York, NY 10012
<www.craftcouncil.org>

Professional organization supporting artists and fine craft artisans; various member benefits, including receiving the prestigious magazine *American Craft*. Yearly membership dues.

Books

Crafting As a Business, by Wendy Rosen, 1998. Rosen Group, 3000 Chestnut Avenue, Suite 300, Baltimore, MD 21211.

The Crafts Business Answer Book and Resource Guide, by Barbara Brabec (New York: M. Evans, 1998).

The Crafts Supply Sourcebook, by Margaret Boyd (Cincinnati, OH: Betterway Books, 1994); (800) 289-0963.

Creative Cash, How to Profit from Your Special Artistry, Creativity, Hand Skills, and Related Know-How, 6th ed., by Barbara Brabec (Roseville, CA: Prima Communications, 1998).

How to Start a Home-Based Craft Business, by Kenn Oberrecht (Old Saybrook, CT: Globe Pequot Press, 2000).

Book Club

Better Homes and Gardens Crafts Club, 1716 Locust Street, P.O. Box 4724, Des Moines, IA 50336.

Crafter's Choice, a Bookspan Club, P.O. Box 6432, Indianapolis, IN 46206; <www.crafterschoice.com>. The latest books on a wide range of creative crafts.

Book Publishers and Sellers

Write for their current book catalogs. Some may charge a fee.

Chester Book Company
28 Ferry Road
Chester, CT 06412
<www.chesterbookco.com>

A bookseller of many fine arts and crafts books from other publishers. View their catalog of current offerings online or write for a current listing.

Dover Publications
31 East Second Street
Mineola, NY 11501
< http://store.doverpublications.com >

Many books, stencils, patterns, copyright-free designs.

North Light Books
F & W Publications, Inc.
1507 Dana Avenue
Cincinnati, OH 45236

Publisher of many art-related books.

Sterling Publishing Company
387 Park Avenue S
New York, NY 10016
< www.sterlingpublishing.com >

Publisher of many how-books of fine arts, crafts, woodworking and hobbies.

Magazines and Newsletters

American Craft, P.O. Box 3000, Denville, NJ 07834. $40/year, bimonthly.

Country Sampler's Country Business, (subscriptions) P.O. Box 420839, Palm Coast, FL 32142. For country business retailers but has regular creative business features and the latest craft trends.

Crafts 'n Things, Clapper Communications Companies, 2400 Devon, Suite 375, Des Plaines, IL 60018; < www.craftideas.com >. Many craft ideas and projects.

The Crafts Report, P.O. Box 1992, Wilmington, DE 19899; < www.craftsreport.com >. Highly recommended for the professional craftsperson and artist.

ProCrafter, "The Trade Magazine for the Professional Crafter." Krause Publications, 700 E. State Street, Iola, WI 54990. Information and articles for those interested in selling their handmade products.

Show Guides

Arts 'n Crafts Showguide. ACN Publications, P.O. 25, Jefferson City, MO 65110; <www.events2000.com>.

The Ronay Guides. A Step Ahead, Ltd., 2090 Shadow Lake Drive, Buckhead, GA 30625. Lists a few thousand arts and crafts shows, fairs, festivals, competitions, and art exhibits for a number of Southern states. Each guide is sold separately. Write for current pricing.

SAC Newsmonthly, P.O. Box 159, Bogalusa, LA 70429; <www.sacnewsmonthly.com>. Listing of thousands of art or craft festivals.

Start-Up Guides

Entrepreneur's Start-Up Guide, *How to Start a Craft Business.* For pricing and ordering information, visit <www.smallbizbooks.com> or call (800) 421-2300.

Software

Artisan POS (point of sale) Plus, by CerTek Software Designs, 933 Grant Avenue, Plainfield, NJ 07060; <www.certek-software.com>. Point-of-sale-based system for retailers (though home-based craft business owners can use it). Track customers and inventory, create mailing lists and labels, and other helpful features.

Supplies

Dick Blick Art Materials
P.O. Box 1267
Galesburg, IL 61402
<www.dickblick.com>

Order from *Dick Blick's Art Materials Catalog.*

75
AIRBRUSH ART

In airbrush art, an atomized brush is used to create the pictures, which can be applied to windows, walls, vehicles, T-shirts, store windows, helmets, and most other surfaces. Bianca, custom airbrush artist, says her business <www.angelfire.com/tx3/phoenixxx/mairbrush> just "fell right into my lap, so if things are meant to be, they will happen!" She also advises, "Do what you love in life and good things will come to you. Believe in yourself and the rest will follow."

Start-Up Costs and Financing Sources

- $3,000 to $9,000 for basic equipment, promotional materials, advertising.
- Personal savings, small business loan, line of credit from your local bank.

Pricing Guidelines

$100 to $200+ per hour and/or per project.

Marketing and Advertising Methods and Tips

- Airbrush a design and business number on your vehicle(s).
- Leave business cards at custom van shops and auto centers.
- Place ads in local auto publications.
- Post flyers on community bulletin boards.
- Set up a Web site to show samples of your work.

Essential Equipment

Atomizer operated by compressed air that propels paint or ink as a fine spray (a low-line brush is not recommended); business telephone with answering capabilities; PC with office software billing, filing, and record-keeping systems.

Recommended Training, Experience, or Needed Skills

- Take courses at art schools.
- Apprentice with an airbrush artist.
- Need basic artistic talent and training.

Income Potential

$35,000 to $85,000.

Type of Business

One-half in-home for working on customers' smaller items; one-half out-of-the-home traveling to shows, doing custom work directly onto larger items (store windows, walls, other).

Target Market

Businesses that have storefront windows and individuals' vehicles, mailboxes, walls, motorcycle helmets.

Success Tips

- Keep a photo record of each job along with data on the supplies used and time it took. This will help you calculate your costs and subsequent profits so that you can give accurate estimates to future customers.
- Give estimates. It's up to you whether to charge for the estimate. Ask questions like: What type of paint(s) will be needed? Is the project for indoors or outdoors? How large an area is to be painted? How much detail work is involved? What type of surface is to be painted?
- Keep track of business records to make sure you are charging enough to cover your expenses, time, and costs for running the business.
- Network with other freelance artists.

For More Information

Books

Airbrush: The Complete Studio Handbook, by Radu Vero (New York: Watson-Guptill Publications, 1997).

Getting Started in Airbrush, by David Miller and Diana Martin (Cincinnati, OH: F & W Publications, 1993).

How to Make Money with Your Airbrush, by Joseph Sanchez (Cincinnati, OH: F & W Publications, 1992).

The Ultimate Airbrush Handbook, by Pamela and Donn Shanteau (New York: Watson-Guptill Publications, 2001).

Supplies

Badger Air-Brush Company
9128 West Belmont Avenue
Franklin Park, IL 60131

Dick Blick Art Materials
P.O. Box 1267
Galesburg, IL 61402
<www.dickblick.com>

Order from *Dick Blick's Art Materials Catalog.*

Paache Airbrush Company
7440 West Lawrence Avenue
Harwood Heights, IL 60656

Magazine

Airbrush Action, Airbrush Action, Inc., 3209 Atlantic Avenue, Allenwood, NJ 08720; <www.airbrushaction.com>. Web site has videos, books for sale, information about airbrush workshops, and subscription information.

Video

Bob Ross's art-video series, *Airbrush.* Bob Ross Company, P.O. Box 946, Sterling, VA 20167; <www.bobross.com>.

76
CANDLES

Candlemaking is a popular home-based business because the demand for candles continues with homeowners. There continues to be a profitable market for new lines of uniquely designed candles and related products. Some candle artisans have home shops for the public. Others sell their candles at craft shows, at malls, or through sales representatives or retail outlets.

Start-Up Costs and Financing Sources

- $1,500 to $10,000 for supplies, to set up a workroom, and for home office supplies and equipment.
- Personal savings, small business loan, line of credit at your bank.

Pricing Guidelines

Prices depend on the materials and scents used and the size of the candle. They range from $10 or $15 to $25 for simple candles, $38 to $60 for more elaborate ones. Network with other candle artisans for guidelines. (See the association listing in "For More Information," later in this section.)

Marketing and Advertising Methods and Tips

- Print business cards, flyers, and brochures.
- Take booths at home and/or gift shows.
- Place classified ads in local publications.
- Buy ads in trade publications such as *Giftware News* and *Gift and Decorative Accessories* to attract buyers and sales reps.
- Make presentations to small gift and country business stores.
- Create a Web site for a photo display and ordering.

Essential Equipment

Wax (paraffin or beeswax), stearin (adds hardness), wax dyes, perfumes, wick holder and wicks, thermometer, equipment to melt and hold waxes, molds and mold seal, enameled containers for dipped candles, knives, stirrers. Home office supplies: phone with answering service; computer for record keeping and billing.

Recommended Training, Experience, or Needed Skills

- Work in a candlemaking shop.
- Take classes or workshops in candlemaking.

- Experiment to develop your individual unique technique and style.

Income Potential

$45,000 to $95,000 per year (with sales representatives). As much as $300 per weekend at a busy mall or craft show.

Type of Business

About one-half in-home, making the candles; one-half out-of-the-home, selling the candles.

Target Market

Gift shops, bridal accessories shops, craft show attendees, mall shoppers, professional decorators.

Success Tip

Anna Campbell of Anna's Candles < www.annascandles.com > says, "Truly enjoying what your business is about has a great impact on how well your business will do. When customers know that you care about your product and them, they are going to come back."

For More Information

Association

International Guild of Candle Artisans (IGCA)
1640 Garfield
Fremont, NE 68025
< www.igca.net >

Holds an annual convention. Web site provides list of suppliers; chat room; and more.

Books

The Candlemaker's Companion, by Betty Oppenheimer (North Adams, MA: Storey Communications, 1997).

Candlemaking, by David Constable. Order from Chester Book Company (see "Book Publishers and Sellers" in "Craft Resources," page 344).

Candlemaking for Fun and Profit, by Michelle Espino (Roseville, CA: Prima Communications, 2000).

Candles That Earn: Starting and Operating a Candle Business, by Don Olsen. Order from Barker Enterprises (see address under "Supplies"). $14.95.

Ye Old Candle Instruction Book. Order from Barker Enterprises. $1.75.

Supplies

The Wax House-Scentmasters
15009 Held Circle
Cold Spring, MN 56320
<www.waxhouse.com>

Has a booklet for sale, *Starting a Candle Business,* rev. ed. Send $3 for a catalog or order online.

Additional Business Ideas

- Make paperweights or other objects out of wax.
- Press home-raised flowers and attach them to plain candles with a thin layer of paraffin.

77

CHAIR CANING, RUSHWORK, AND WEAVING

In this business, you revive the traditional craft of caning, doing rushwork on, or weaving the seats and backs of old and new chairs. Antiques and reproductions are always in demand by collectors and early American furniture makers, as well by individuals who want to restore and preserve family heirlooms. Antique shows on television have helped to renew the interest again in vintage furniture and collectibles.

Start-Up Costs and Financing Sources

- $500 to $5,000 for equipment and supplies, promotional materials, advertising, and setup of a work area or home shop.
- Personal savings; loans from family or friends; reinvest earnings back into your business to purchase more supplies and inventory.

Pricing Guidelines

Usually charged by the hole, $1.35 to $2.50 each, depending on the technique and style used. Cane Webbing $3 to $3.25 per inch. Compare your prices with others in your area. The following equation may also be used:

(Your hourly wage × the number of hours)
+ cost of supplies + overhead

Marketing and Advertising Methods and Tips

- Leave your business cards and flyers at antique shops, folk fairs, folk museums, and historical societies.
- Place ads in antique trade publications and country lifestyle magazines.
- Exhibit or demonstrate at folk and craft fairs. Have your brochures available.
- Teach chair caning classes at adult evening schools, craft shops or centers, or community colleges.
- Encourage word-of-mouth referrals.

Essential Equipment

High-quality cane—buy from a specialty craft or caning store or order from mail order suppliers. Various tools according to technique used: bucket, pliers, pick or awl, wooden pegs, scissors, glue, chisel, hammer.

Recommended Training, Experience, or Needed Skills

- Take courses or private lessons in chair caning.

- ✤ Practice on old furniture or frames you find at flea markets and thrift shops.

Income Potential

$100+ for a chair that has 100 holes.

Type of Business

In-home business, except for exhibiting at fairs or crafts shows or when teaching courses.

Target Market

Antique shops, antique collectors (professional and amateur), museums, historical societies that have collections of furniture.

Success Tips

Cathryn Peters, owner of The Wicker Woman <www.wickerwoman.com>, offers these tips:

> If you find yourself procrastinating or your mind begins to wander and you don't complete your projects on time, set an exact amount of time aside to complete the project and track it using an oven timer!
>
> For example, if you set aside one hour to complete a particular step of your project, set the timer for one hour. Focus on completing the step in one hour and when the bell rings, stop and move on to something else.
>
> Also, during that hour's time, don't answer the phone, doorbell, watch TV, or get on the computer, just focus on the task at hand and assigned for that period of time. You'll be amazed at how much you can accomplish using this method.
>
> Nothing beats free advertising like writing press releases for the local newspapers! If you are beginning a new line of your product, just opening your business, started your own domain Web site, or are giving free demonstrations, be sure to whip up a smart, catchy press release and submit it to all your local newspapers. Finding an interesting angle is impor-

tant, so put on your thinking cap and come up with some good copy.

For More Information

Books

Also check your local and/or historical libraries for out-of-print books on chair caning and weaving.

The Caner's Handbook, by Bruce W. Miller and Jim Widess (Asheville, NC: Lark Books, 1992). (See The Caning Shop listing under "Supplies," later in this section, for ordering information.)

Chair Seating: Techniques in Cane, Rush, Willow, and Cords, by Kay Johnson, Olivia E. Barratt, and Bary Butcher (London: Dryad, 1988).

Chair Seat Weaving, by George Sterns, 1990. Interweave Press, 201 East Fourth Street, Loveland, CO 80537.

Supplies

The Caning Shop
926 Gilman Street
Berkeley, CA 94710
< www.caning.com >

Source for gourds and basketry and caning supplies. The owner of The Caning Shop, Jim Widess, is also coauthor of the bestselling how-to book, *The Caner's Handbook* (Asheville, NC: Lark Books, 1992), that gives detailed instructions for restoring all types of woven furniture and is available from The Caning Shop for $18.95 plus shipping and handling.

GH Productions
Box 261
521 East Walnut Street, Department EM-Box 621
Scottsville, KY 42164
< www.basketmakerscatalog.com >

Basket-making and chair-seating supplies.

Additional Business Ideas

- Teach, private instruction or classes. $40 to $50 per hour.
- Make and sell unique baskets (especially research the heritage of your area to see what baskets were made and used a century or two ago—e.g., Native American, African American, European).
- Collect old wicker furniture, old baskets, old chairs to repair and refinish them for resale at $40+ an hour.
- Make twig furniture or miniature twig furniture for country-style decor. Read *Willow Chair: How to Build Your Own,* by Joseph S. Stone and Carollyn Wolff. Genesis Publications, North Andover, MA.

78
DOLLHOUSES

You can build dollhouses from kits, create replicas of customers' homes or businesses, or design and build your own unique dollhouses. As a sideline to this business, you can sell commercial or handmade miniature furniture and/or accessories. Though many of your dollhouses will be ordered as gifts for children, many will be made for adults who will display them for their own pleasure.

Start-Up Costs and Financing Sources

- $7,000 to $15,000, depending on whether you have a home retail shop on your property or not.
- Personal savings; loans from family or friends.

Pricing Guidelines

Go by industry standards. Join the Miniatures Industry Association of America (see association listing under "For More Information," later in this section) and attend dollhouse and miniatures trade shows to check out prices. Handmade, innovative, and original houses and accessories are more expensive than those that are mass-produced. A dollhouse can sell for $400 to $6,000 or more, depending on its size and detail.

Marketing and Advertising Methods and Tips

- Donate a replica of a historic building in your town for a charity auction or work with a local school's shop or vo-tech students to make a dollhouse to give to a day care center.
- Place your business cards in toy shops.
- Attend craft and mall shows and industry wholesale shows; show samples, take orders.
- Teach dollhouse-building classes in your home shop, at local crafts shops, or at adult evening schools.
- Place ads in national trade publications (see "For More Information") and magazines. Buy display ads (when you can afford it) in doll and children's magazines and catalogs.
- Rent booths at trade shows (see MIAA in "For More Information").
- Keep a mailing list of customers, and send out a small newsletter or sales flyer on new miniatures or dollhouses you have made.
- Display your dollhouses in your local library's showcase in October, which is National Dollhouse and Miniatures Month.
- Set up a Web site to display photos of your samples and ordering information.

Essential Equipment

Assorted woodworking and hand tools and supplies: hammers, hand saws, scroll saw. Sewing machine and notions for making miniatures and decorating; paints, odds and ends of materials. Basic drafting tools and graph paper for drawing up designs, plans. PC with drafting software to design your own.

Recommended Training, Experience, or Needed Skills

- Have experience in sewing, carpentry, woodworking, interior decorating.

- Enroll in dollhouse-building courses or take woodworking, sewing, and other related courses at adult evening schools or vo-tech schools.
- Practice building and decorating dollhouses from kits. Then try your own designs.

Income Potential

$25,000 to $80,000 or more.

Type of Business

Two-thirds in-home, building, creating; one-third out-of-the-home, marketing, exhibiting at shows, teaching classes.

Success Tips

- Keep in touch with loyal customers with regular mailings and news—print or an e-newsletter.
- Recycle throwaway materials into unusual miniatures.
- Keep current with the latest trends in the field by reading industry publications and attending related trade shows (see "For More Information").

For More Information

Association

Miniatures Industry Association of America (MIAA)
P.O. Box 3388
Zanesville, OH 43702
< www.miaa.com >

Publishes a newsletter with industry and marketing information and show dates.

Books

Also check your library's shelves for out-of-print books on building dollhouses and furniture.

A Beginner's Guide to the Dolls' House Hobby, by Jean Nisbett (New York: Sterling Publishing Company, 1997).
The Complete Guide to Remodeling and Expanding Your Dollhouse, by Nola Theiss (New York: Sterling Publishing Company, 1993).
The Doll's House Do-It-Yourself Book, by Venus A. Dodge (New York: Sterling Publishing, 1993).
Dolls' House Details: Over 350 Craft Projects in 1/12 Scale by Kath Dalmeny (New York: Sterling Publishing, 2000).

Magazine
Dollhouse Miniatures, Kalmbach Publishing Company, 21027 Crossroads Circle, Waukesha, WI 53187; <www.dhminiatures.com>.

79
FRAMING

Cindy Smith opened her professional framing and matting service in conjunction with a small art gallery on the lower floor of her house. She also sells original artwork, prints, and posters, framed or just matted.

Smith says, "I began to think of opening up my own framing shop when my husband and I were given an estimate of several hundred dollars to frame two prints." She took a course on framing and assisted her photographer husband in framing his work for shows. She also gained experience by working part-time in two framing shops.

Start-Up Costs and Financing Sources

- $30,000 to $50,000, but costs can be less if you buy good, used equipment.
- Small business loan, personal savings, refinancing your home.

Pricing Guidelines

Follow the guidelines of the Professional Picture Framers Association (see "For More Information"). Cindy Smith, however, says that "you have to charge the going rate for your community. You can charge more for your service in affluent neighborhoods where art is supported and art enthusiasts live."

Marketing and Advertising Methods and Tips

- Place classified ads in local publications and in the business telephone directory.
- Offer an art contest for local high school students with local artists as judges. Frame the winning entry.
- Network with various artists' groups.
- Send flyers to and/or contact local art instructors.
- Join your local chamber of commerce.

Essential Equipment

Mat cutter, knives, wood for frames. You will need a work area that you can screen off to receive clients.

Recommended Training, Experience, or Needed Skills

- Take framing courses at art schools or institutes.
- Work in framing shops for experience.
- Practice framing friends' and relatives' work.

Income Potential

$25,000 to $45,000 is possible in a small community, $90,000 to $100,000 or more is possible in a larger, art-conscious community.

Type of Business

In-home.

Target Market

Art enthusiasts, art collectors, artists, photographers, calligraphers, graduates, people wanting to preserve old photographs, those who want their wedding or baptism certificates framed, needlework hobbyists.

Success Tips

- ✤ Work in a framing shop before you open one.
- ✤ Specialize in different types of matting—French, gold leaf, and so forth—depending on the demand for it and your training. Cindy also learned conservation and archival processes to preserve old paper, paintings, and prints.
- ✤ Follow professional standards in your work and pricing.

For More Information

Association

Professional Picture Framers Association
4305 Sarellen Road
Richmond, VA 23231
<www.ppfa.com>

Generally, the organization is for retail shop owners, but the business information is helpful.

Books

Home Book of Framing: Professional Secrets of Mounting, Matting, Framing, and Displaying Artworks, Photographs, Posters, Fabrics, Collectibles, by Kenn Oberrecht (Mechanicsburg, PA: Stackpole Books, 1998).

Matting, Mounting, and Framing Art, by Max Hyder (New York: Watson-Guptill, 1998).

Picture Framing, by Vivian C. Kistler. Order from *Dick Blick's Art Materials Catalog.* This is a comprehensive reference for the professional framer.

Picture Framing: A Practical Guide from Basic to Baroque, by Desmond MacNamara. Sterling Publishing (see "Book Publishers" in "Craft Resources," page 345).

See also *Dick Blick's Art Materials Catalog* for other framing books.

Supplies

Art Supply Warehouse Express (ASW)
5325 Departure Drive
North Raleigh, NC 27616
< aswexpress.com >

Art and framing supplies.

Dick Blick Art Materials
P.O. Box 1267
Galesburg, IL 61402
< www.dickblick.com >

Order from *Dick Blick's Art Materials Catalog.*

Additional Business Ideas

- Sell local artists', artisans', and craftspersons' work.
- Make your own unique frames—sell them to artists, art galleries, framing shops. Refer to *Making and Decorating Fantastic Frames,* by Thom Boswell (New York: Sterling Publishing, 1994) and *Making & Decorating Picture Frames,* by Janet Bridge (Cincinnati, OH: F & W Publications, 1996).

80
FURNITURE ART

In this business, old or used furniture and household items are decorated with original art. Pieces you find for a few dollars at garage sales, flea markets, or auctions can be refinished and/or decorated to sell for 10 or more times that amount. If you are not skilled in freehand painting, there are stencils and other techniques to use that will make your work look like a master's. Think of this business as turning junk into someone else's treasure and helping recycle items that would just be tossed away.

Start-Up Costs and Financing Sources

- $1,000 to $3,000.
- Personal savings, loans from friends or family.

Pricing Guidelines

Your time (total hours to complete) × your rate per hour
+ the cost of the piece of furniture + cost of supplies
= total × 2 or 3 (for profit) = Final price

Prices also depend on what your customers are willing to pay in your selling area. For example, a $5 table might sell for $65 finished. If you have made a "name" for yourself, you can, of course, ask for more.

Marketing and Advertising Methods and Tips

- Post business cards and flyers on community bulletin boards.
- Make presentations to owners of small furniture or used furniture shops, baby and children's furniture stores, and country stores to sell your items.
- Rent a booth at a craft mall or home show.
- Give a demonstration at a paint or hardware store.
- Donate a piece of furniture art to a community charity auction.
- Contact interior decorators.
- Set up a Web site with a photo display of your items. Sell some items on online auction sites to attract people to your site.

Essential Equipment

Refinishing supplies, paints, good brushes, tracing paper, paper towels, rags, well-ventilated workspace, promotional materials.

Recommended Training, Experience, or Needed Skills

- Know how to recognize good, used furniture and other salvageable pieces.
- Know basic refinishing and painting techniques.

- Take courses at vo-tech schools or work in a refinishing shop.
- Practice on old pieces you find.
- Must have an artistic eye.

Income Potential

Your profits will vary with each piece, from $50 to $900 or more. Annual earnings can average $30,000 to $80,000 + , depending on how much custom work you do for customers.

Type of Business

Two-thirds in-home, refinishing and painting the furniture; one-third out-of-the-home, looking for pieces and marketing.

Target Market

People who love original art and hand-painted pieces, people who like nontraditional and accent pieces, people who want a new look for a piece of furniture, small antique furniture shops, some interior decorators who may want you to do custom pieces for their clients.

Success Tips

- Take the time to look for customers and markets for your pieces.
- Network with friends and family—they can refer people to you who may want custom work.
- Let the piece you are painting "guide" you as to what design to use.
- Develop your own original, recognizable style.

For More Information

Association

The Society of Decorative Painters
393 N. Mclean Boulevard
Wichita, KS 67203

Promotes the art of decorative painting through member chapters located throughout the U.S. Membership includes subscription to the society's publication, *The Decorative Painter* <www.decorativepainters.org>.

Books

Decorative Painting: How to Start Making Money with Your Decorative Painting, by Dorothy Egan (Cincinnati, OH: F & W Publications, 1998).

Folk Art and Tole Painting: New Designs for Decorative Paintwork, by Kate Coombe (New York: Sterling Publishing, 1993) (see "Book Publishers" in "Craft Resources," page 345).

Priscilla Hauser's Book of Decorative Painting by Priscilla Wait Hauser (Cincinnati, OH: F & W Publications, 1997).

Publications

Decorative Artist's Workbook, 4700 E. Galbraith Rd., Cincinnati, OH 45236; <www.decorativeartist.com>.

Decorative Painter (see the Society of Decorative Painters).

Supplies

Dick Blick Art Materials
P.O. Box 1267
Galesburg, IL 61402
<www.dickblick.com>

Order from *Dick Blick's Art Materials Catalog.*

Hofcraft!
P.O. Box 72
Grand Haven, MI 49417
<www.hofcraft.com>

Offers a full line of supplies and paints for decorative arts. Send $5 for a catalog. Also sells decorative painting books at the Web site <www.decorativepaintingbooks.com>.

Additional Business Ideas

- Repairing and refinishing furniture. Refer to *How to Recognize and Refinish Antiques for Pleasure and Profit,* by Jacquelyn Peake (Old Saybrook, CT: Globe Pequot Press, 1997).
- Building and painting birdhouses. Refer to *Painting and Decorating Birdhouses: 22 Step-by-Step Projects to Beautify Your Home and Garden,* by Dorothy Egan (Cincinnati, OH, F & W Publications, 1997).

81
GREETING CARDS

In the past few years there has been an explosion of variety in the greeting card market. Greeting cards now cover themes ranging from the sentimental and poetic to the humorous, sometimes to the point of being almost off-color; and the Internet is enabling many smaller greeting card businesses to sell their line of products.

Kathy Davis is an artist who started her own line of greeting cards and products, called Kathy Davis Designs <www.kathydavis.com>. She sells them in her own gift shop and also to various shops around the country. Davis sends out flyers to customers on her mailing list, including a calendar of events advertising contests, specials, and other activities she holds at her store. This designer, illustrator, and writer says, "Work hard and love your work."

Start-Up Costs

$8,000 to $15,000.

Pricing Guidelines

Printed packs of cards with your designs—20 cards for $10 to $20. Add other items with your designs, such as mugs—$7.95; recipe cards—$6.50; canvas tote bag—$19.95; sweatshirts (preshrunk)—

$29.95. Individual printed cards (stamped, embossed, hand-colored)—$3 to $4 each.

Marketing and Advertising Methods and Tips

- Design your own line and market directly to shops and companies.
- Attend trade shows to show your portfolio (see "For More Information").
- Sell your cards at craft and art shows, to gift stores or small, unique shops (big shops already have cards).
- Design your own promotional materials to send out to greeting card companies.
- Mail out a periodic flyer with your new line of cards and products. Have customers buy through mail order (get names at craft and art shows).
- Set up a Web site to showcase your designs.

Essential Equipment

Art and graphic arts supplies, computer with graphic arts design capabilities and laser printer, standard home office setup with a design and work area.

Recommended Training, Experience, or Needed Skills

- Take courses or get training in graphic arts and/or design.
- Research what types of greeting cards are on the market and what greeting card companies look for in submissions. See if you can come up with your own distinctive cards.

Income Potential

Depends on your materials, your reputation as a designer, the contract you sign (a percentage). Network with others in the industry for the going rate paid.

Type of Business

In-home.

Success Tips

- Davis says, "Believe in yourself. Do the work you want to do, and do not give up. Take satisfaction in every job you do however small."
- Stay current with industry news.
- Sally Silagy, owner of the home-based greeting card business Gardening Greetings <www.gardeninggreetings.com>, featuring the "Garden Lady," says, "Starting and operating your own home-based greeting card business is one of the most exciting and satisfying challenges you will ever undertake. There are no limitations on income potential when you're investing time and energy in your own enterprise."

For More Information

Associations

The Greeting Card Association
1156 15th Street, NW, Suite 900
Washington, DC 20005
<www.greetingcard.org>

Holds a trade show and publishes a variety of books, audiotapes, and CD-ROMs to help greeting card entrepreneurs, including the *Directory of Greeting Card Representatives.*

The Graphic Artists Guild
90 John Street, Suite 403
New York, NY 10038
(212) 791-3400

For full information, see the Graphic Artist/Designer entry in "Computer Businesses," page 399.

Books

See also the Graphic Artist/Designer entry in "Computer Businesses," page 399.

The Artist's and Graphic Designer's Market: How to Sell Your Illustrations, Fine Art, Graphic Design & Cartoons (Cincinnati, OH: F & W Publications, 2001). An annual listing of markets for your art and designs.

Card Crafting: Over 45 Ideas for Making Greeting Cards and Stationery, 2nd printing, by Gillian Souter (New York: Sterling Publishing Company, 1993).

How to Make Money Publishing from Home: Everything You Need to Know to Successfully Publish Books, Newsletters, Greeting Cards, Zines, and Software, by Lisa Shaw (Roseville, CA: Prima Communications, 1997).

Home Business Opportunity

Gardening Greetings features cards with the "Garden Lady" character. For prices and information about the *Home-Based Greeting Card Kit,* send an LSASE to Gardening Greetings, 189a Paradise Circle, Woodland Park, CO 80863 or visit the Web site <www.gardeninggreetings.com>.

Trade Show

National Stationery Show
George Little Management, LLC
10 Bank Street
White Plains, NY 10606
<www.nationalstationeryshow.com>

Held each May at the Jacob K. Javits Center in New York City. Attendance is for those in the industry only, but you may register at the door as an artist if you have a business card and artwork to show. Great opportunity to see companies' greeting cards firsthand and possibly meet with their creative directors. Write or visit the Web site for admission and exhibition information.

Additional Business Ideas

Freelance writing for greeting cards. Author and professional greeting card writer Sandra Miller-Louden <www.greetingcardwriting.com> provides these tips:

> Greeting card verse payments today run anywhere from $25 to $150 per verse. Most beginning writers channel all their energy—and their verse submissions—to the companies

paying the highest amounts. So I pose this question to my students: Which is better—selling one verse to a company for $150 or selling three verses to three different companies at $50 each? My answer never varies—while the dazzling $150 for a few, choice words (generally under 20) can overwhelm a writer, the second scenario is always preferable.

The savvy writer constantly cultivates as many clients as she can—in the world of greeting card writing, the ideal situation is to have 3 or 4 companies with whom the writer works closely and another 6 to 8 companies where she submits work on a semi-regular basis. Just as in other businesses, greeting card companies come and go, freelance writing needs change often and there is always a tendency for large companies to buy the smaller, independent ones. For someone to be truly successful as a greeting card writer, she must always remain flexible—and one component of flexibility means writing for as many diverse companies as possible.

For further information, refer to these books by Louden: *Write Well & Sell: Greeting Cards, A Few, Choice Words: Short, "Do-Able" Writing That Sells,* BizyMom's e-book *Greeting Card Writing.* Visit < www.bizymoms.com > for ordering information.

82
JEWELRY

Today jewelry can be made of anything from gold and silver to clay and cloth, with styles ranging from formal to funky. Research where and to whom you will sell your pieces based on your style of design and materials. Your potential markets will also depend on your expertise and what people are willing to pay. By attending craft and trade shows, reading trade publications, and networking with other jewelry makers, you will be able to determine where your pieces can sell best.

The jewelry crafts referred to here pertain to pieces made from a variety of materials: metal, glass, ceramics, wood, paper, leather, fabric, plastic, stones, and recycled items.

Start-Up Costs and Financing Sources

- $4,000 to $10,000 for supplies and advertising.
- Personal savings, loans from friends and family.

Pricing Guidelines

Depends on cost of materials, cost of running your business, the time it takes to make your pieces, and the demand for your jewelry. Check out other jewelry prices at craft and trade shows.

Marketing and Advertising Methods and Tips

- Rent a booth at jewelry and/or gift trade shows.
- Place a classified or color display ad in craft marketing publications.
- Offer to make custom orders.
- Take samples of your work to jewelry and gift shops.
- Wear your jewelry and have friends and relatives wear it, too.
- Send direct mailings to customers from a mailing list gathered from show attendees or past customers.
- Set up a Web site for displaying your pieces of jewelry.

Essential Equipment

The tools needed depend on the type of jewelry you are making; for example, metalworking requires files, cutters, clamps, pliers, solders. Materials—new or recycled—clasps, fasteners, strings.

Recommended Training, Experience, or Needed Skills

- Study jewelry making at art centers.
- Apprentice with a jewelry maker or work as an assistant in a small jewelry-making business.
- Need an artistic flair for design and a mastery of the technique you use.

Income Potential

$100 to $2,000 per week, depending on your reputation, your customers, and your markets.

Type of Business

In-home, except when at shows or marketing your pieces.

Target Market

Shops selling fine handcrafts, jewelry show attendees, craft show attendees, jewelry catalogs, galleries.

Success Tips

- Try to develop a following and keep a list of customers who buy your jewelry.
- Establish your own individual style.
- Keep up to date with the fashion and style trends.
- Julie Miller, who produces unique, handcrafted, custom-made jewelry <www.julesjewelry.com>, says, "I always try to correspond through e-mail to help me connect with my customers; it helps me get to know them. Many customers enjoy shopping with a small business because of little personal touches, turning them into repeat customers."

For More Information

Books

The Complete Book of Jewelry Making by Charles Codina (New York: Sterling Publishing Company, 2000).

The Encyclopedia of Jewelry-Making, by Jinks McGrath (Philadelphia, PA: Running Press, 1995).

Jewelry: Fundamentals of Metalsmithing by Tim McCreight (Madison, WI: Hand Books Press, 1997).

Jewelry-Making for Fun and Profit, by Maria Given Nerius, Barbara Brabec (editor) (Roseville, CA: Prima Communications, 2000).

Home Study Course

Gemological Institute of America
World Headquarters
The Robert Mouawad Campus
5345 Armada Drive
Carlsbad, CA 92008
<www.gia.org>

Offers gemology, jeweler retail management, design and other jewelry-related courses at their campus and through home study.

Magazines

The Crafts Report <www.craftsreport.com>. Print publication (sold at major bookstores) that has regular features on all the business of arts and crafts.

Jewelry Crafts, Miller Magazines, 4880 Market Stree, Ventura, CA 93003; <www.jewelrycraftsmag.com>. Features techniques and styles of popular jewelry making. Contains ads for jewelry-making suppliers.

Lapidary Journal, P.O. Box 124, Devon, PA 19333. Gem and jewelry-making magazine.

Supplies

Alpha Supply
1225 Hollis Street
P.O. Box 2133
Bremerton, WA 98310
<www.alpha-supply.com>

Thousands of supplies, items for jewelry making, faceting, and lapidary needs. Offers a large selection of books on jewelry making. Online catalog; print costs $5, with a $10 certificate toward your order.

Trade Shows

Check listings of various gem and jewelry trade shows dates in trade publications such as *Jewelry Crafts.* Send an LSASE for information on retail and wholesale sections.

Video

Jewelry making, design, and other related videos are sold by Alpha Supply. See their online or print catalog.

Additional Business Ideas

- Design jewelry for large people or extremely thin people.
- Sew cloth jewelry.

- Make polymer jewelry. Refer to: *Creative Clay Jewelry,* by Leslie Dierks (Ashville, NC: Lark Books, 1994).
- Use recycled materials to make a unique line of artistic or fun jewelry.
- Make antique-looking jewelry: *Creating Your Own Antique Jewelry: Taking Inspiration from Great Museums Around the World,* by Chris Dupouy (Boston, MA: Harry N. Abrams, 2001).

83
PHOTOGRAPHY

Photography is a highly-competitive field to enter; however, there are many business opportunities you can explore. Here are just a few that are open to photographers:

- Pet photographs. People love their pets—you can specialize in taking pet photos at their homes or contact pet and feed stores to hold an annual pet photo day. Owners of purebred and registered animals also need photos of their pets for promotion or on show days when their animals receive awards. Many photographers make a full-time living following horse, dog, and livestock shows. Digital cameras and photography software have made it easy for photographers to take a wide variety of photos and display and send them via e-mail. Despite digital cameras, there continues to be a need for photographers' professional-quality work.
- Portraiture. One woman photographer specializes in wedding and children's portraits. She had a home studio built onto her house for indoor portraits and also had a decorative gazebo and a bridge built over a small stream for outdoor photos. Her sister, who lives nearby, is a makeup artist and hairdresser and she adds her services if a customer wishes.
- Newborn pictures. Take infants' photos at the hospital.
- Children's sports photos. Market to schools and sports associations.
- Photos of people's houses, cars, and gardens. Sell this service to individuals, real estate companies, auto clubs.

- Photos of community events. Contact your local chamber of commerce, historical associations.
- Photos of crafts and artworks. Many artists and craftspeople need professional slides or photos of their work to qualify for entry into shows and contests. Contact local and state craft guilds.
- Children's photos for identification purposes.
- Restored and tinted photographs.
- Sell stock photos to publishers, writers, and so forth.

Start-Up Costs and Financing Sources

- $5,000 to $15,000+ if you are going to have a home studio with a darkroom and special equipment.
- Personal savings; small business loan; line of credit from your local bank.

Pricing Guidelines

Some of the books listed in "For More Information," such as Writer's Digest's *The Photographer's Market,* provide a section of suggested rates for different photography assignments and projects. These references are good guidelines, especially for new photographers just starting out on their own.

Marketing and Advertising Methods and Tips

You may come up with other ideas, such as photographing people's gardens, family reunions, baptisms, or confirmations, to name a few. Whatever kind of photography you do, you must (1) get adequate training, either by enrolling in formal courses or working as an apprentice, and (2) decide your special area of practice. Then you can decide what potential customers you want to target in your marketing plan.

- Create a brochure featuring your specialty and send to a mailing list you compile or rent.
- Advertisements in your local telephone company's business directory pages.

- Establish a Web site to post samples of your work and contact information.
- Magnetic signs on your vehicle.
- Encourage word-of-mouth referrals from satisfied customers.
- Take a booth at local business expo.
- Join your local business ownership organization for referrals.

Essential Equipment

Cameras: 35mm and digital; equipment as needed for your specialty; computer with high-speed Internet connection; scanner; photocopier; cellular phone and pager; home office supplies; darkroom if you develop your photos.

Recommended Training, Experience, or Needed Skills

Photography courses and training; apprentice with a photographer or work in an area in which you hope to specialize. You should have persistence in learning and perfecting your photography skills.

Income Potential

$20,000 to $50,000 or more.

Type of Business

One-third at home working on operating your business and marketing; two-thirds out taking your photos.

Target Market

As mentioned at the beginning of this chapter, there are many business options available to an independent photographer, and you will want to look for a business niche within these and other opportunities.

Success Tips

- Experiment and find the area of photography that you do best before focusing your marketing efforts.

✤ Ann DeCristofaro, professional photographer, offers this tip: "I have found that the best advertising I get for my business is through my Web site. I do a lot of volunteer community work and have a page 'Community' that is linked to the home page. Instead of giving people that link directly, I always send them through the main page <www.anndee.com>. It is a twofold benefit—they have less to remember and a much shorter URL and I get the exposure for the real things that I do—weddings, portraits, and restorations—which they see first before they click on the community link."

DeCristofaro gets additional business in working with a friend of hers whose business is making wedding or christening clothing for children <www.anndee.com/jka>. "The two of us are combining our skills and networking—where I will take the photos of her kids in their gowns/tuxes and hopefully gain the wedding business that they are dressing for!"

Franchises, Distributorships, and Licenses

See the regular issues of such print publications as *Entrepreneur* <www.entrepreneur.com> and *Home Business* <www.home-businessmag.com> magazines (find at newsstands and bookstores) and their Web sites for listings of photography-related business opportunities and franchises.

For More Information

Association

International Freelance Photographers Organization (IFPO)
P.O. Box 777
Lewisville, NC 27023
<www.aipress.com>

Membership benefits include subscription to *Today's Photographer International* (See "Trade Magazine"). Write or visit the Web site for information.

Books and Publications

See also "Books" in part III.

Business and Legal Forms for Photographers, rev. ed., by Tad Crawford (New York: Allworth Press, 1997).

Guide to Literary Agents and Art/Photo Reps. Writer's Digest Books <www.writersdigest.com>, annual publication.

How to Start a Home-Based Photography Business, 3rd ed., by Kenn Oberrecht (Old Saybrook, CT: Globe Pequot Press, 1999).

Photographer's Market, Writer's Digest Books <www.writersdigest.com>; annual publication.

Home Study Courses

Distance Education and Training Council
1601 18th Street, NW
Washington, DC 20009
<www.detc.org>

Write for a brochure of schools offering photography home study courses or visit the Web site.

Trade Magazine

Today's Photographer International, American Image Press, Inc., P.O. Box 777, Lewisville, NC 27023; <www.aipress.com>. Tips, article for earning money with your camera.

84
RUBBER STAMPING

Many people love rubber stamps and find all kinds of ways to use them in their creative projects. From this demand, talented artists have found making and selling rubber stamps can be a lucrative home business. With improved technology in making the stamps, more and more people are getting into this business.

Start-Up Costs and Financing Sources

- $10,000 to $25,000 to purchase the equipment and supplies.

- Personal savings; small business loan; line of credit from your local bank.

Pricing Guidelines
Follow industry guidelines listed in industry publications.

Marketing and Advertising Methods and Tips
- Catalog of your stamps (start with your desktop publishing software).
- Set up a Web site to show off your samples and designs.
- Rent booths at trade shows—greeting card association, crafts wholesale shows.
- Place ads in consumer crafts and rubber stamp publications.
- Teach stamp classes in local schools or craft centers.

Essential Equipment
Basic home office setup; promotional materials; PC and laser printer and photopolymer system; rubber; vulcanizer; laser engraver; saw to cut wood for the stamps; refrigerator to store the rubber; rubber cement; cushion; wood and other supplies as needed.

Recommended Training, Experience, or Needed Skills
- Artistic gift.
- Attention to detail.

Income Potential
$20,000 to $30,000 or more.

Type of Business
Three-fourths in-house; one-fourth out-of-the-home, marketing your business at shows.

Target Market
Craft hobbiest, stamp clubs.

Success Tips

Melissa Duquette, of StampFolk <www.stampfolk.com>, says, "Never be afraid to ask! Probably my best and simplest piece of advice, but definitely effective. I had finished several rubber-stamped samples of my work using a certain product. I contacted the product's manufacturer and asked if she would be interested in seeing some of my work which used her product. She was delighted and asked to include my projects in an upcoming book. She also included my samples in a magazine column she writes. What this breaks down to is this: It never hurts to ask, they just may say 'Yes,' and all it took was the courage to raise the question!"

For More Information

Books

E-Book: *Bizy's Guide to Rubber Stamping as a Home Business* by Melissa Duquette. Visit <www.bizymoms.com> for ordering information.

The Great Rubber Stamp Book: Designing, Making, Using, by Dee Gruenig (New York: Sterling Publishing Company, 1997).

Simple Printmaking: A Beginner's Guide to Making Relief Prints with Rubber Stamps, Linoleum Blocks, Wood Blocks, Found Objects & More, by Gwen Dieh (New York: Sterling Publishing Company, 2002).

Equipment

Rubber Stamps Unlimited, Inc.
334 South Harvey Street
Plymouth, MI 48170
<www.thestampmaker.com>

Will make custom art/logo stamps from your own work (but not from copyrighted drawings).

Look for other equipment sources and supplies advertised in the rubber stamp craft books and publications.

Publication

Rubber Stamp Madness, P.O. Box 610, Corvallis, OR 97339; <www.rsmadness.com>. For enthusiasts, not professionals, but you can advertise here and get an idea of the stamps being sold.

Additional Business Ideas

- ✤ Sell a line of greeting cards designed with your handmade stamps.
- ✤ Offer to frame your work.

85

SILK AND FABRIC FLOWER AND PLANT ARRANGING

Although fresh flowers are beautiful, many individuals and home and business owners prefer silk or fabric floral arrangements to the real thing. Artificial arrangements are more practical for those who don't have the money or time to care for live plants or flowers. In this business, you make up arrangements to order as well as have a stock of premade floral and plant arrangements. You can buy the silk plants and flowers from wholesalers or make them yourself (if you have the time and skill).

Start-Up Costs and Financing Sources

- ✤ $3,000 to $5,000.
- ✤ Personal savings, small business loan, loans from family and friends.

Pricing Guidelines

Compare prices with others in a similar business. Price according to the cost of supplies, your hourly wage, total time it takes to make an arrangement, plus a percentage of overhead.

Marketing and Advertising Methods and Tips

- ✤ Print business cards and flyers to hand out at shows and post on bulletin boards.

- Rent booths at home, bridal, or craft shows.
- Invite people to sign a mailing list at craft and other shows and send periodic mailings of your specials or places and dates where you will be exhibiting.
- Sell to home accessory or gift shops, also garden centers.
- Contact interior decorators.
- Let your local chamber of commerce members know you are available to decorate offices.
- Contact bridal shops, churches, banks, and hospitals. They often want plants in lounges or public areas.
- Set up a Web site with photos to highlight your arrangements.

Essential Equipment

Business phone line, cell phone; billing and bookkeeping systems; photo portfolio of arrangements you've done; promotional materials. Fabric flowers (cotton, silk, etc.), scissors, standard craft and floral supplies, flower parts, ribbon, and sewing notions. Start with the basic tools until you discover which ones you like to use the most.

Recommended Training, Experience, or Needed Skills

- Take flower-arranging courses at craft shops or through adult education or at horticultural centers.
- Work in a flower shop or at a silk flower distributor.
- Have a good sense of color and balance; know flower arranging.
- Research at your local library for out-of-print books on the various styles of flower arranging or look at used book sales for good instructional books.

Income Potential

$20,000 to $50,000 (full-time).

Type of Business

In-home business, except when doing shows or promotions.

Target Market

Brides, homeowners, businesses, restaurants, institutions, customers at craft shows and craft home parties, boutiques, parents of girls being confirmed (flower-covered headbands are popular), interior decorators.

Success Tips

- Keep a notebook listing the supplies needed for each arrangement, as well as the suppliers, your wholesale and retail price, and a photo. This will help you give accurate estimates to future customers.
- Keep up with trends—attend floral trade shows, study catalogs and trade publications.
- Network with other floral and silk plant designers and producers.
- Have a selection of prices to meet every budget.
- Seasonal pieces for holidays—Mother's Day, Easter, birthdays, and other special occasions.

For More Information

Books

The New Silk Flower Book: Making Stylish Arrangements, Wreaths & Decorations, by Laura Dover Doran (Ashville, NC: Lark Books, 1997).

Fabulous Silk Florals: For the Home by Cele Kahle (Cincinnati, OH: F & W Publications, 2001).

Home Study Course

Lifetime Career Schools
2251 Barry Avenue
Los Angeles, CA 90064

Offers courses in floral arrangement.

Supplies

You will need a sales tax number to make wholesale orders.

Boyle's Silk Flowers
Joe Boyle
Lunenburg, MA 01462
<www.boylesilkfloralsupply.com>

Wholesaler of silk flowers, baskets, and other items.

Silk Tree House
10763 Tucker Street
Beltsville, MD 20705
<www.silktreehouseinc.bigstep.com/catalog.html>

Wholesale distributor of silk, dried flowers, plants, and other seasonal decorations.

Additional Business Ideas

Make dried flower arrangements. See *The Flower Arranger's Encyclopedia of Preserving and Drying,* by Maureen Foster (New York: Sterling Publishing Company, 1992).

Computer Businesses

Computer Resources

Books

How to Earn More Than $30,000 a Year with Your Home Computer: Over 160 Income-Producing Projects, rev. ed., by Phil Philcox (New York: Carol Publishing Group, 1999).

Making Money with Your Computer at Home, 2nd rev. ed., by Paul and Sarah Edwards (New York: Putnam Publishing Group, 1997).

E-Book

BizyMom's *Bizy's Guide to Operating a Computer-Based Business at Little or No Cost,* by LaDonna Vick. Visit <www.bizymoms.com> for ordering information.

Book Club

The Computer Book Club, McGraw-Hill, Blue Ridge Summit, PA 17214.

Home Study Courses

Distance Education and Training Council
1601 18th Street, NW
Washington, DC 20009
<www.detc.org>

Write for a brochure of schools offering computer-related home study courses or visit the Web site.

Magazines

Smart Computing, Sandhills Publishing, P.O. Box 82545, Lincoln, NE 68501; <www.smartcomputing.com>.

Supplies

CDW Computer Centers
200 North Milwaukee Avenue
Vernon Hills, IL 60061
<www.cdw.com>

86
COMPUTER CONSULTING

As a computer consultant, you will be assisting consumers, business owners, or both in all aspects of using the best computer systems and software that meet their needs. Your services will be in demand because it is impossible for people and small business owners who cannot afford a full-time computer specialist to keep up with the latest technology updates. You will assist them with the purchasing, set up, training, and troubleshooting of their computer systems.

You follow up by providing instruction in acclimating the computer system into the client's business. In other words, you help the individual or business owner learn how to use a computer system to make more money or gain access to more information.

Consultants can specialize in PCs or the larger business computer systems used by corporations and large institutions. PC specialists are most in demand because small- and medium-size firms cannot afford full-time computer specialists. Clients can call you for a one-time consultation or have you back as needed.

With the number of home-based businesses growing each year, most of these business owners will need someone to advise them on their computer needs. That someone could be you.

Start-Up Costs

- $800 for simple advising to $1,000 for a home office setup and equipment.
- Personal savings; small business loan; line of credit from your local bank.

Pricing Guidelines

$60 to $100+ per hour, depending on your level of expertise, training, experience, and customers. Go by the industry guidelines and network with others.

Marketing and Advertising Methods and Tips

- Aim your marketing efforts at those clients you determine who will be the best clients for you. Make appointments and presentations to demonstrate to potential clients how to increase their profits with a computer.
- Place classified ads in local business publications.
- Give talks at business meetings and conferences.
- Contact local chambers of commerce members for referrals.
- Print business cards, flyers, and brochures.

Essential Equipment

Business telephone line with answering capabilities, cell phone; fax machine; computer and peripherals; legal contract forms if you will be signed on a retainer.

Recommended Training, Experience, or Needed Skills

- Computer training and education and/or a technology degree.
- Work as a systems analyst, trainer, or teacher.
- Obviously, be skilled at technology "trouble-shooting," and be able to quickly recognize the reason for a computer or software failure.
- Need a thorough knowledge of computers used for the business and their related software.
- Must have patience and be able to teach the system to your client.

Income Potential

Can range from $40,000 to $250,000+ a year.

Type of Business

One-third in-home, running and marketing your consulting service; two-thirds out-of-the-home, working at the client's office.

Target Market

Small- and medium-size businesses (many home-based), individuals who need advice on purchasing a computer or are learning computer basics or how to use a software program.

Success Tips

- Market your service constantly.
- Educate potential clients as to how your computer consulting can help them increase their profits.
- Know your specialization, or if you are a generalist, have sources you can turn to if you do not know an answer.
- Consult with a lawyer for proper wording in your contracts and the IRS for tax-reporting procedures.
- Rochelle Balch <www.rochellebalch.com>, who has generated $17 million from her home-based computer consulting business (started in 1993 when she was downsized from her job), says, "Remember to offer advice that is best for your client, not for your checkbook. And, know when to back away. If it's something where you don't feel you can offer good, honest, accurate advice, be honest with yourself and your client and back away from the assignment; you'll find this approach will keep you busy and get you more referrals."

For More Information

Associations

Independent Computer Consultants' Association (ICCA)
11131 South Towne Square, Suite F
St. Louis, MO 63123
<www.icca.org>

Offers support to independent computer consultants and publishes a bimonthly newsletter.

Books

The Computer Consultant's Workbook, by Janet Ruhl (Leverett, MA: Technion Books, 1999). See also Ruhl's "Computer Consultant's Resource" page <www.realrates.com>.

How to Be a Successful Computer Consultant, 4th ed., by Alan R. Simon (New York: McGraw-Hill, 1998).

Additional Business Ideas

Computer trainer. Train other home-based business owners to use their computers and software programs for their business. Refer to these books:

The Complete Computer Trainer, by Paul Clothier (New York: McGraw-Hill, 1996).

Computer Repair: Start Your Own Computer Repair Business, by Linda Rohrbough and Michael Hordeski (New York: McGraw-Hill Computing, 1995).

87
DESKTOP PUBLISHING

Michelle's tiny office, from where she runs her successful desktop publishing business, Michelle's Design, is literally just off her kitchen and has a window overlooking her backyard where she can monitor her two children's activities. Michelle's clients include local businesses and school districts that contract her for a variety of projects, including calendars, yearbooks, and other related educational materials. She gained her expertise by working in the printing industry and enrolling in desktop publishing technique courses in the early 1980s.

According to the U.S. Bureau of Labor Statistics, desktop publishing (DTP) is one of the fastest-growing professions and will continue to be so well into the 21st century.

Start-Up Costs

$5,000 to $10,000+.

Pricing Guidelines

Go by industry standards and what your market will bear. Suggested reading: *Pricing Guide for Desktop Services,* by Robert C. Brenner (San Diego, CA: Brenner Information Group, 1995).

Essential Equipment

Computer and related software, including page layout (Adobe InDesign or QuarkXPress) and publishing software (Windows or Mac versions of Microsoft Word); printers (quality laser and small color printer); flatbed scanner, removable storage drives, business promotional materials; digital cameras, which have capabilities that are becoming very important in the desktop publishing industry.

Recommended Training, Experience, or Needed Skills

You do not need a degree to run a DTP business, but computer skills, of course, are needed for the area of desktop publishing in which you specialize; also, creativity and basic editorial knowledge (grammar, spelling, manuscript formats). Beginners with no prior experience should take related courses and also work for an experienced desktop publisher for a year or two to better understand the industry, pricing, and so forth, before starting out on their own.

Income Potential

$14,000 to $75,000 per year.

Target Market

Look for customers in the industries in which you are familiar and specialize in that niche market. Desktop publishing businesses produce advertising materials, newsletters, personalized letters, booklets, manuals, reports, and many other documents for businesses, organizations, and/or individuals. Professional desktop publishers have also expanded their services into offering Web page design, art for advertising specialties (such as T-shirts, indoor/outdoor signs), silkscreening or embroidery, and packaging materials (boxes, bags, etc.).

Success Tips

One professional desktop publisher says, "Don't forget that the purpose of design is to communicate a message—not just to be stylish. Lots of ads, brochures, and Web sites read as though the designer never met the sales manager. A design is not a design without an idea that grabs attention, some well-thought-out selling, and a crystal-clear call to action."

For More Information

Books

The Desktop Publisher's Idea Book: One-of-a-Kind Projects, Expert Tips, and Hard-to-Find Sources, 2nd ed., by Chuck Green (New York: Random House Reference, 1997).

How to Start a Home-Based Desktop Publishing Business, by Louise M. Kursmark (Old Saybrook, CT: Globe Pequot Press, 1996).

Start and Run a Profitable Desktop Publishing Business, by Barbara A. Fanson (Bellingham, WA: Self-Counsel Press, 1997).

Web Sites

< www.flashweb.com >

FLASH magazine—Online publication with information on the business of desktop publishing.

< www.ideabook.com >

< www.jumpola.com >

Chuck Green's Web sites—Includes tips and free information.

< www.desktoppublishing.com >

desktopPublishing.com—Many pages of helpful tips.

Journal

Desktop Publishers Journal, 462 Boston Street, Topsfield, MA 01983; < www.dtpjournal.com > .

Additional Business Ideas

Scan old family photos for individuals and compile them into a "family history" book for family reunions and anniversaries; or place on CDs for them for their permanent family records.

88
E-BUSINESS

The U.S. Administration's Office of Advocacy, in its report, *Small Business Expansions in Electronic Commerce* (June, 2000), stated that it expected eighty-five percent of all U.S. small businesses to conduct business via the World Wide Web by the year 2002, Even if you are a sole proprietor of a tiny little business, having an online business or a Web site for an already-existing business is a smart marketing and entrepreneurial move because with a Web presence, the potential exists to reach customers from all over the world. Of course, the challenge is to (1) get potential customers to "find" you on the Internet and (2) stand out in a unique way from all the millions of other businesses with Web sites.

But as with any business, you can start simply and build your Web business as you learn how to use the Internet to the utmost to help your business be profitable.

Start-Up Costs and Financing Sources

As low as $500 to have a simple Web site with a few pages highlighting your business.

Pricing Guidelines

Pricing your products and services for your business is the same as for any type of business, offline. The difference is how your customers will pay and get your product or service—payments and shipping and handling costs for product businesses; e-mail and fax for design, writing, or consulting services.

Marketing and Advertising Methods and Tips

Shannan Hearne-Fortner, Internet marketing specialist and president and "wizard" of Success Promotions <www.successpromotions.com>, has this to say about marketing your e-business site:

> The most important thing to do in today's Internet marketplace is to get your own domain/URL. Don't rely on a self-replicated site like you find with affiliate programs or a page resting on the parent company's domain. It is too hard to attain high search engine rankings. And without them, you cannot get traffic to build a thriving business. You wouldn't put your brick and mortar store at the end of a never-traveled dead end street. Don't do this with your home business either. Free pages at sites like angelfire.com are okay, but ideally a wholly owned domain is much better. It gives you a much more professional image. Once you get traffic to your Web site, it is imperative that you have visitors bookmarking your site and joining your e-mailing list. You can encourage them to do this with contests, or the promise of e-mailed specials and discounts. Your site has to be easy to navigate. Your order form has to be easy to find and use. Make sure that your Web site is clean and crisp. Floating images and sounds are cute, but not particularly professional looking. Content is key, too. If you want to get ranked well in the search engines, you have to put lots of appropriate keywords in both your text and your meta tags.

Essential Equipment

The fastest, best-equipped, most upgradable computer you can afford and a high-speed connection to the Internet. If you are unsure of the type of computer system hardware and software you will need, meet with a computer consultant familiar with e-business needs as technology is ever-changing and it can be overwhelming to the start-up Internet entrepreneur! You will also want to have a scanner; digital camera; photocopier and office suite software, as well as your usual home office supplies.

Recommended Training, Experience, or Needed Skills

- Enroll in e-business and business management seminars or courses held at local colleges and small business and Women's Business Development Centers.
- Know how to do Internet research and conduct business over the Internet.

Type of Business

In-house.

Target Market

Before you spend much money on inventory and money for a complex Web site, take time to research your potential market for your goods and services.

Success Tips

- Darcy Volden Miller, owner and founder of two Web sites, Little Did I Know.com, which sells items made by home-based moms, and Baby Gift Store.com, which sells baby items, says in starting an e-business to "Read! Read! Read! Read everything you can get your hands on to stay on top of the learning curve. Technology, marketing, advertising, and business are constantly in a state of change and exponential growth. It's important to always learn what's going on in the business world to keep your business growing in a positive successful direction. One of the best and easiest ways to fill yourself full of knowledge without having to devote days to reading books is to read things in digestible mini-bites such as weekly e-zines or email newsletters. There are literally thousands of them on every available subject and can be gold mines of information. And . . . don't forget to subscribe to a few good e-zines on motivation and encouragement."

- LaDonna Vick, publisher of the e-book, *A Beginner's Guide to Starting a High Income Business on the Internet,* and founder of the Web site, Mommy's @ Work < http://momsatwork.virtual ave.net > says, "If you are selling an information product on the Internet, you must remember people want value for their dollar. With all the free information on the Web, you must show why your product is worth paying for. Make sure your information will help your customers reach their goals."

Franchises, Distributorships, and Licenses

See the regular issues of such print publications as *Entrepreneur* < www.entrepreneur.com > and *HomeBusiness* < www.home businessmag.com > magazines (find at newsstands and bookstores) and their Web sites for listings of related Internet business opportunities and franchises.

For More Information

Books

HerVenture.com, by Priscilla Y. Huff (Roseville, CA: Prima Communications, 2000).

How to Start a Business Web Site, by Mike Powers (New York: Avon Books, 1999).

121 Internet Businesses You Can Start from Home: Plus a Beginner's Guide to Starting a Business Online, by Ron E. Gielgun (Santa Rosa, CA: Actium Publishing, 1997).

Start-Up Manual

Entrepreneur's Start-Up Guide, *E-Business.* For pricing and ordering information, visit < www.smallbizbooks.com > or call (800) 421-2300.

E-Business Marketing Tips

Subscribe to Hearne-Fortner's free e-newsletter by sending an e-mail to < shearne-marketing-subscribe@yahoogroups.com >.

Internet Tax Issues

A Web site created by The National Retail Federation (NRF), < www.salestaxfairness.com >, provides information about the

Internet taxation issue to inform consumers, legislators, and retailers on equitable sales tax collection.

Additional Business Ideas

- Start an online product "mall" featuring other home-based entrepreneurs' products and/or services.
- Online auctioneer. Sell your specialty items or a specific kind of collectible. Refer to *Starting Your Online Auction Business,* by Dennis L. Prince (Portland, OR: Premier Press, 2000).
- Internet business consultant. Despite the failure of many of the big dot-com businesses over the last couple of years, the number of Internet business start-ups continues to grow. Entrepreneurs seeking to start an online business or owners of existing businesses who wish to have an online presence need advice on finding a Web host, Web design, marketing, communicating with customers, and how to conduct business online.

    Hearne-Fortner says that one of these easiest ways to launch a career as a consultant is to brand yourself and your business by writing and publishing. "Write often, and publish articles on your own Web site, in your e-newsletter, and submit articles to other e-zine publishers," she says. Participation in online groups where your specialty knowledge is of use and signature texts attached to informative e-mails also advertise your expertise.

    Here are some resources:

    The Association of Certified Internet Business Consultants
    c/o Dr. Mosetta M. Penickphillips-Cermak, President
    3308 West 111th Street
    West Park, OH 44111

    Econsultant: Guiding Clients to Net Success, by Rick Freedman (New York: John Wiley & Sons, 2001).

    How to Be a Successful Internet Consultant, by Jessica Keyes (New York: American Management Association, 2002).

89
E-ZINE PUBLISHER

E-zine publishing is becoming one of the fastest growing publishing venues. Many online businesses send out e-zines at no charge to keep in touch with their customers, provide industry tips, and promote special offers. Other entrepreneurs, however, are using the e-zines themselves as a profitable venture, as they can sell their specialized information to a buying market.

Start-Up Costs and Financing Sources

- $5,000 to $8,000 for computer and home office setup.
- Personal finances, small business loan.

Pricing Guidelines

E-zine professionals offer their e-zines free and earn money from their advertisers and subscriber ads; or they charge for monthly or yearly subscriptions.

Marketing and Advertising Methods and Tips

- Promote your e-zine on- and offline.
- Write articles in print publications that target your subscribers.
- Always use your signature on your e-mail to list the title of your e-zine.
- Send out periodic press releases when you do subscriber surveys.

Essential Equipment

Desktop or laptop computer, desktop publishing software, scanner, laser printer, modem, fax machine, business telephone line, answering machine or service, photocopier (or access to one).

Recommended Training, Experience, or Needed Skills

- You are selling information, so you should obviously be an expert in your field or interview experts regularly as well as invite them to contribute articles.
- Publishing and writing experience is helpful.

Income Potential

Depends on the number of subscribers and your subscription prices. One woman who sells information to writers about marketing their books makes thousands each month from the $20-a-month subscribers' fees.

Type of Business

In-home.

Target Market

Special interest groups or businesses, your determined target market. Successful e-zines are ones that cater to a niche market that is willing to pay for your information.

Success Tips

- Kim Essenmacher, an Independent Cognigen Agent (telecom services) her started her BizPreneurNews (bi-monthly) e-zine using Yahoo's offerings. Her goal was to help others to help others grow their businesses and to establish herself as an "accountable" (legitimate) businessperson in her community.

  Essenmacher did research about e-zines and used several sites that helped her devise her e-zine template. "I have found that if you have at least 1,000 subscribers, you will be recognized as having a legitimate e-zine and you can swap ads with other e-zine publishers and barter ads. Of course, I never waited until I reached this level to swap. I began swapping ads with other new e-zine subscribers right away. My newsletter is a tool that opens the 'networking' door." (To subscribe to Kim Essenmacher's newsletter, send an e-mail to: bizpreneurnews-subscribe@yahoogroups.com).

- Need a mailing list that is effective in bringing in subscriptions.
- Be an expert in the field in which you are writing.
- Provide valuable, even exclusive information (not easily obtained elsewhere) to help your readers improve themselves, their businesses, or their profits.

For More Information

Web Sites

< www.ezine-dir.com >

Ezine Directory.

< http://ezine-swap.com >

E-zine-Swap.com—E-zine Publisher's Sponsorship Exchange.

< http://ezine-tips.com >

Ezine Tips—Offers a free newsletter as well as tips.

< http://ezine-universe.com >

Ezine-Universe.com—"Email Newsletter Directory."

< http://e-zinez.com/handbook >

E-Zinez.com—How to write and publish your own e-zine.

< www.freezineweb.com >

The Free Directory of Ezines.

90
GRAPHIC ARTIST/DESIGNER

Using your computer and basic graphic design training and education, you can have your own graphic design studio. You can produce professionally designed logos, mechanicals, layouts, illustrations, presentations, brochures, direct mail, business cards, and other advertising and marketing materials.

You will need a background in design and computer graphics, and it will be helpful if you have worked as a graphic designer for a firm before you start out on your own.

Using graphic software such as Adobe Illustrator and Photoshop; Macromedia Freehand; Microsoft Word; Fractal Design Painter; and QuarkXPress, you can start your own business creating customized graphic output for clients who own small businesses.

The software programs enable you to create professional-looking signs, greeting cards, banners, posters, certificates, and more in minutes. As your ability grows using these programs, you can use the thousands of combinations of graphics, fonts, and special effects to create advanced custom designs, and design one-of-a-kind personalized merchandise—from T-shirts and tote bags to teddy bears.

Possibilities using these programs include designing and creating letterhead, envelopes, and business cards; and making print advertisements, flyers, banners, and signs that clients can use to promote their businesses. They can also be used to create a wide range of promotional items.

You can also design and sell matching stationery and envelopes, greeting cards, postcards, and paper crafts, and you can put your artwork on a variety of items.

Start-Up Costs and Financing Sources

- ✤ $12,500 to $25,000.
- ✤ Small business loan, personal savings, lines of credit from your local bank.

Pricing Guidelines

Go by industry standards (see "For More Information") and compare your prices with other graphic design firms.

Marketing and Advertising Methods and Tips

- Advertise in the business telephone directory.
- Print promotional materials. These are a sampling of what your business can do, so make them look professional and dynamic. Send to your target customers: small businesses, organizations, schools, small ad agencies.
- Place ads in business publications.
- Set up a Web site to showcase your designs and samples.

Essential Equipment

PC or Macintosh to operate your designing software, scanner, digital camera, ink jet or laser printer (preferably color). Other office supplies and equipment: fax machine, modem, telephone, answering machine or service, filing and bookkeeping software, promotional materials, graphic arts reference books.

Recommended Training, Experience, or Needed Skills

- Have a degree in graphic design or a good background or training in basic design principles.
- Work in a design or publishing firm.
- Need to be creative and be able to communicate well with your clients.

Income Potential

$40,000 to $80,000.

Type of Business

In-home business, except for times when meeting with clients (unless your home office is set up for meetings).

Target Market

Small businesses, Netpreneurs for designing their Web sites, advertising companies, organizations, architects, engineers, brides, companies wanting direct mail promotions.

Success Tips

- Create unique layouts and communicate well with your clients. This will help bring you repeat business and referrals.
- Send out a monthly promotional flyer with marketing and/or business tips or a weekly e-zine to those on your mailing list. This will help keep your business in your clients' minds.
- Keep current on advertising and industry trends.
- Use your design software to create promotional items for your business or to create sample designs and sample output to show clients.
- Come up with a list of ideas on how your clients can use the items you produce to promote their businesses.
- Nancy Cleary, graphic designer and owner of Wyatt-MacKenzie Publishing <www.box-is.com>, says, "Be willing (and happy) to go above and beyond the call of duty, be a little more creative than you thought you could, on *every* job *even if* you've reduced your fees. This is the best marketing you can do for your design business."

  Cleary continues, "As a graphic designer, you can help *any* entrepreneur in *any* line of business create *anything* and *everything* they need to succeed. This is powerful. Remember this and serve customers whose mission is in line with your own and help them turn their dreams *and* yours into realities."

For More Information

Association

The Graphic Artists Guild
90 John Street, Suite 403
New York, NY 10038
(212) 791-3400
<www.gag.org>

A national resource and advocacy organization with local chapters. Legal and accounting services and legislative information, newsletters, and a *Pricing and Ethical Guidelines* handbook.

Books

Artist's and Graphic Designer's Market, 2001. F & W Publications, 1507 Dana Avenue, Cincinnati, OH 45207.

The Creative Business Guide to Running a Graphic Design Business, by Cameron S. Foote (New York: W & W Norton & Company, 2001).

Self-Promotion Online, by Ilse Benun (Cincinnati, OH: F & W Publications, 2000). For graphic designers; < www.artofselfpromotion.com > .

Starting Your Small Graphic Design Studio, by Michael Fleishman (Cincinnati, OH: North Light Books, 1993).

Book Club

Graphic Design Book Club
P.O. Box 12526
Cincinnati, OH 45212

Exclusively for graphic design professionals.

Supplies

Dick Blick Art Materials
P.O. Box 1267
Galesburg, IL 61402
< www.dickblick.com >

Order from *Dick Blick's Art Materials Catalog.*

91

WEB DESIGNER

Despite the shake-up and takedown of so many dot-coms several years ago, Web site growth still continues at a phenomenal rate. The number of small businesses with Web sites was estimated at 4.3 million in 2001 (International Data Corporation < www.idc.com >). Even with the easy-to-use Web publishing software that is available, many entrepreneurs prefer to pay someone to design their business's site than to do it themselves.

Businesses hire Web site designers to put together an online graphics package that expresses their mission, gives their company background and accomplishments, and presents their products and/or services to the world and potential customers. The Web designer accomplishes this all in an attractive, yet easy-to-follow order so customers are motivated to buy or find out more information about the business's offerings.

Start-Up Costs and Financing Sources

- $6,500 to $20,000.
- Personal savings, small business loan.

Pricing Guidelines

Anywhere from $45 to $200 per hour or fee per project. One Web designer said that one of his clients paid him $100,000 to do a site.

Marketing and Advertising Methods and Tips

- Join a local business ownership group and offer to give a presentation on Web sites to the membership.
- Advertise in local newspapers and business publications.
- Design your own site as a sample of your work and include links to customers' sites to showcase your work.
- Exhibit at business expos and offer to conduct a workshop on the Internet.

Essential Equipment

Computer with adequate hard drive space for graphic design, removable storage drives, the latest processor with a graphics accelerator; 21-inch monitor; laser printer; graphics software, Web management tool, file transfer software; digital camera; scanner; HTML, XML, and JavaScripting reference books; laptop computer that you can take to clients' offices for presentations. Please note: as computer technology is constantly changing, it is best to contact a computer consultant familiar with the technology needs of

Web design capabilities to help you decide on a system best for your needs. Also talk and network with other designers and experts in the Web designing industry to find out what systems they recommend best for your specific work.

Recommended Training, Experience, or Needed Skills

- Be creative and have some knowledge of basic graphic design as well as basic Web language skills.
- Be able to communicate well with your clients to translate what they want onto the Web site.
- Enroll in Web design classes at local colleges or evening schools to learn the basics and then advanced skills.
- To get started, create your own Web site and offer to do some for friends for free.

Income Potential

$35,000 to $75,000 or more.

Type of Business

Three-fourths in-home, working on the designs; one-fourth out, meeting with clients.

Target Market

Small businesses looking to expand their market, freelance professionals, artists.

Success Tips

Jen Czawlytko, owner of webJENerations.com and Webmaster for BizyMoms.com, offers this success tip: "True Web design success results from a meeting of the minds. You need to really listen to your clients' needs, guide them in areas they are unfamiliar with, and be willing to compromise when necessary. After all, you may be the design expert but your client is the expert on the service and/or product they want to sell."

For More Information

Association

< www.hwg.org >

HTML Writers Guild.

Books

How to Start a Home-Based Web Design Business, by Jim Smith (Old Saybrook, CT: Globe Pequot Press, 2001).

Learning Web Design: A Beginner's Guide to HTML, Graphics and Beyond, by Jennifer Niederst, Richard Koman (editor) (Santa Clara, CA: O'Reilly & Associates, 2001).

E-Book

BizyMom's *Bizy Guide to Creating Success in Web Design,* by Jen Czawlytko. Visit < www.bizymoms.com > for ordering information.

Additional Business Ideas

Offer online and off-line basic Web designing courses for computer enthusiasts and small and home-based business owners.

Food-Related Businesses

92
CATERING

Catering can mean creating romantic dinners for two or making food for a wedding reception of 500 or more. Many start their catering services from their own kitchens or they rent kitchens by the day. The investment is low, and with good management, the profits can be high. Check with your state health department regarding regulations for preparing food.

Start-Up Costs and Financing Sources

- $6,000 to $80,000, depending on whether you have to put in a licensed kitchen.
- Personal savings, loans from friends or small investors, small business loan.

Pricing Guidelines

A set fee per person is usually charged, sometimes two to three times the cost of the food and paper products. Factor in your preparation time, costs of running the business, and any rental fees or commissions you have to pay to party or event planners. Go by industry and expert recommendations (see "For More Information," later in this section).

Marketing and Advertising Methods and Tips

- Encourage word-of-mouth referrals from satisfied clients.
- Stage a catered party to celebrate your business opening. Invite other small business owners with whom you will be working, like wedding and event consultants and planners, owners of banquet halls, DJs and small bands, balloon decorators and florists, and so forth. Give them a sampling of your best dishes and setup. Have business cards, flyers, and brochures listing your specialties available to hand out.
- Advertise in the business telephone directory.
- Rent a booth at bridal shows.
- Send direct mail or make presentations to members of the local chamber of commerce.
- Place classified ads in local publications.
- Donate holiday meals to a local homeless shelter.

Essential Equipment

A professional kitchen (one you can rent), necessary culinary equipment.

Recommended Training, Experience, or Needed Skills

- Enroll in courses at local vo-tech schools or culinary institutes.
- Work for one or more catering businesses.
- Need culinary skills and attention to detail.
- Be well organized yet able to deal with last-minute changes.
- Be creative in your food presentation.

Income Potential

$50,000 to $100,000 or more, depending on the size of the event(s) you cater.

Type of Business

One-half in-home, attending to preparty preparation; one-half out-of-the-home, overseeing each party and marketing.

Target Market

Businesses having seasonal parties, meetings, and company picnics; individuals wanting the following events catered: weddings, retirement parties, graduation parties, small dinner parties, religious and anniversary and other special celebrations.

Success Tips

- Give your best effort with each client—good news travels fast!
- Do something special to make your catering memorable; for example, use ice sculptures or other special food presentations.
- Do not be afraid to suggest ideas to your clients. Your clients may really appreciate it and this could be reflected in your profits.
- Hire help (if needed) with good people skills.
- Offer one-stop catering—add rental of china, tents, and party supplies or work with a party rental service to coordinate everything.
- Offer certain kinds of food catering—ethnic, religious, vegetarian, and other special cuisines.

For More Information

Books

Catering: Start and Run a Money-Making Business, by Judy Richards (Blue Ridge Summit, PA: McGraw-Hill, 1994).

The Complete Caterer: A Practical Guide to the Craft and Business of Catering, by Elizabeth Lawrence (New York: Doubleday & Company, 1992).

How to Open and Operate a Home-Based Catering Business, 3rd ed., by Denise Vivaldo (Old Saybrook, CT: Globe Pequot Press, 1999).

How to Run a Catering Business from Home, by Christopher Egerton-Thomas (New York: John Wiley & Sons, 1996).

Home Study Courses

Distance Education and Training Council
1601 18th Street, NW
Washington, DC 20009
<www.detc.org>

Write for a brochure of schools offering home study courses in catering or gourmet cooking or visit the Web site for information.

Software

Schrek Software, 1420 Interlachen Circle, Woodbury, MN 55125; < www.schrecksoftware.com > .

Additional Business Ideas

- Romantic dinners for two in a couple's home or apartment. Clients pick from a menu beforehand, you bring the food, the china, and a rose, and serve the food in a tuxedo. Charge from $75 to $120 per meal.
- Box lunches for company workers.
- Personal chef. You (and an assistant, if needed) go to a customer's home and cook a gourmet meal for a small dinner party or gathering.
- Catered lunches to child care centers.

93

FOOD/RESTAURANT DELIVERY SERVICE

In this business, you will contract with restaurants to deliver food for the menu price plus your fee for delivery. Usually, your customers will be couples and individuals who prefer to stay at home but want a restaurant menu. Hotels, motels, and businesses sponsoring seminars and workshops may find this service particularly convenient.

Start-Up Costs and Financing Sources

- $12,000 to $30,000 (with your own vehicle).
- Personal savings, small business loan, or line of credit with your local bank. If you decide to purchase one of the food delivery franchises, some offer partial financing.

Pricing Guidelines

Customers pay a $6 to $10 + delivery fee, more for special orders.

Marketing and Advertising Methods and Tips

- Place ads on radio and cable television stations, in local newspapers, telephone directories, and local parents' publications.
- Print and distribute menus in a direct mail campaign to organizations, hotels, college campuses, businesses, and area residents.
- Referrals from the restaurants whose food you serve.
- Donate some services to food shelters and announce it in a press release.

Essential Equipment

Vehicle (some have specialized, built-in compartments to keep prepared food hot and cold); home office setup with computer and database software of customers and restaurants; hand-trucks; containers; pager and cell phone. If cooking your own food, you must have a food license to cook from your own kitchen, an attached kitchen on your property, or access to a licensed kitchen in another facility (church, club hall, and others).

Recommended Training, Experience, or Needed Skills

Restaurant management experience and having worked for a food delivery service is helpful. Food preparation and related courses.

Income Potential

$25,000 and up.

Type of Business

Primarily out-of-the-home.

Target Market

Working couples, singles, busy families, employees working late at offices.

Success Tips

Jen McColl, who handles promotions for Small Potatoes Urban Delivery (SPUD) <www.spud.ca>, North America's largest organic home delivery service, says:

> Our experience figuring out how to attract new customers with a very nominal budget has taught us that word of mouth is the very best form of marketing. To succeed at word-of-mouth marketing you need 3 things: an incentive or thank you for customers who refer you to others, dedication to customer service excellence, and the ability to track how customers heard about you.
>
> Nearly 40 percent of our business comes from customers telling friends about us. We offer a $25 gift certificate to any customer who refers another to us once that new customer has paid for their initial delivery. This $25 is a tremendous cost savings: The average cost to attract one new customer from print advertising (in newspapers or magazines) has been a whopping $300 so we just don't advertise this way anymore.
>
> We couldn't have this success rate without developing excellent rapport with our customers. We have succeeded in creating a personalized, friendly service with a vision that customers can get behind. Newsletters, regular e-mails, a Web site that offers more than just a catalogue and friendly, easy-to-access phone service are key.
>
> Our computer database tracks how customers hear about us. When someone refers five or more people to us, we send them an additional gift to thank them. We also send thank yous to customers who stay with us, high-order customers, and so on. Without a good information system, we wouldn't have the ability to offer this level of acknowledgement and service quickly and efficiently.

Note: This is an out-of-home grocery delivery business that needs a warehouse. If your home-based food delivery business is in demand, of course, depending on your finances, your facilities, and zoning and food licensing regulations, you may very well have to move out of your home base.

Franchises, Distributorships, and Licenses

See the regular issues of such print publications as *Entrepreneur* <www.entrepreneur.com> and *Home Business* <www.homebusinessmag.com> magazines (find at newsstands and bookstores) and their Web sites for listings of business opportunities and franchises related to food delivery.

For More Information

Manual

How to Start and Operate a Meal Delivery Service, by Rob Spina, 2000. Order through Legacy Marketing, 403 Hobart Drive, Laurel Springs, NJ 08021; <www.legacymarketing.net>.

Additional Business Ideas

- Start your own restaurant truck. You go to offices, companies, and factories' parking lots or lounges and serve soups, sandwiches, hoagies, coffee and other beverages, and sweet rolls.
- Start a home-based meal planning and preparation service. After an initial interview with a family, you will customize, shop, and prepare several meals a month for them. Other clients include those recuperating from illnesses or hospital stays or those with special diets.

94
JUST DESSERTS

Few people have time to bake or prepare special desserts for guests, dinner parties, or special celebrations. If you love preparing special desserts, pies, or cakes, you may find your services much in demand. Contact party or wedding planners and caterers and offer a menu and samples of your best recipes. You may also be able to supply restaurants and food delivery services that will order from you.

Jane Mitchell has had a home-based, specialty-dessert business for 10 years. Her specialties are a dozen different varieties of cheesecakes; rich layer cakes; and other specialty desserts. She has had so much business that she has had to make the choice between turning down orders or expanding. For the time being, she has chosen the first so she can have time to be with her twin teenage son and daughter.

Start-Up Costs and Financing Sources

- $2,000 to $4,000 if you already have a licensed kitchen (or access to one); more if you will remodel or modify a kitchen for your purposes.
- Personal savings, small business loan.

Marketing and Advertising Methods and Tips

- Distribute brochures listing your desserts at the main offices of schools and colleges, corporate offices, local men's and women's clubs.
- Contact restaurants and caterers.
- Join your local chamber of commerce for referrals and networking.
- Donate a dessert to a nonprofit organization. Mitchell donated one of her cakes for a graduation ceremony for women who had completed a six-week job skills program at a local community college.

Essential Equipment

Commercial mixer, various pans and baking utensils, containers for carrying and protecting desserts, vehicle for deliveries. Office supplies, computer and software for creating a database of customers, recipes, and connection to the Internet for customer communication and Internet marketing.

Recommended Training, Experience, or Needed Skills

Talent for baking. Enroll in cooking courses at local vocational schools and culinary institutes, experience in working at a commercial bakery.

Income Potential

$10,000 part-time; $22,000+ full-time, and more if you have cooking assistants.

Type of Business

Primarily in-home.

Target Customers

Small restaurants and cafés, individuals, institutions, organizations, clubs, and community groups holding special events and dinners.

Success Tips

Mitchell says, "Don't compromise your original vision." She uses only the freshest ingredients, even raising her own chickens for fresh eggs. "Thank your customers by asking for their feedback, proving you value their opinions," continues Mitchell. "I always call my customers the next day after I have delivered my desserts to them. I want to hear their comments—both positive or negative—to make sure my desserts are of the quality they expect. My prices are higher than grocery store baked goods, so I want to make sure my customers believe they are getting their money's worth. Many customers also thank *me* because they are thrilled I include free delivery of my desserts."

For More Information

Refer to "For More Information" in the Catering entry, page 409.

Association

American Institute of Baking (AIB)
1213 Bakers Way
Manhattan, KS 66502
<www.aibonline.org>

Resource site with information related to baking and the commercial baking industry.

Books

In addition to the books listed, look for ideas in the cookbook section of your local library for good, out-of-print books as well as in cookbooks produced by organizations for fund-raising purposes.

Bakery for Profit, by George Bathie (London: Intermediate Technology Publications, 1999).

The Great Holiday Baking Book: Over 250 Recipes for Occasions Throughout the Year, by Beatrice A Ojakangas (Minneapolis, MN: University of Minnesota Press, 2001).

Turn Your Kitchen into a Goldmine, by Alice and Alfred Howard (New York: Harper & Row, 1981). Out of print, but worth looking to see if it is in your public library.

Additional Business Ideas

- Jams and jellies. Grow the fruit and make your own to sell to specialty shops or by mail order.
- Breads and muffins. Sell all kinds, including lowfat ones.
- Christmas cookies. Sell by the half-pound and whole pound.
- Handmade candies. Refer to BizyMom's e-book *Bizy's Guide to Making Sweet Profits with Homemade Candy,* by Chrisshawn Simpson-MacLeod. Visit <www.bizymoms.com> for ordering information.
- Decorated cakes. Refer to BizyMom's e-book *Bizy's Guide to How to Create a Profitable Cake Decorating Business from Scratch,* by Stacy Robinson.

95
SELLING A FAMILY RECIPE

We've all heard stories of people who have taken an old family recipe and developed it into a company making mega-bucks. But before you invest any money into marketing your grandmother's cookies or banana nut bread, food specialty experts and entrepreneurs urge you to take the time to thoroughly research this industry and all that is involved in getting a new food product into stores and eventually into the hands (and mouths) of consumers.

If people rave over your special condiments (horseradish, mustard, sauce) or brownies, cookies, or cakes made from recipes that have been handed down in your family, you may have a specialty food that will bring you profits. You must, of course, make sure the recipe was not taken from a copyrighted source.

Your food item has to be unique to compete with big companies that can spend millions on research, development, and marketing, as well as the thousands of other specialty food businesses. If you (and others that you have given samples to) believe your product is the best, then you should go ahead with a business plan.

After perfecting your product, you will need to design (or have someone else design) a food label and packaging. You will also need a food handler's license and other permits, as well as Food and Drug Administration approval if you plan to ship the food by mail order. Your home office must be set up to fill orders by mailing list customers and/or specialty food retailers and suppliers. If you are successful at selling one food product, consider adding additional products later.

Start-Up Costs and Financing Sources

- Depending on your ingredients, packaging, leasing of a commercial kitchen, and so forth, costs can run from $10,000 to $24,000 and up. Writing a thorough business plan will better help you prepare for the expenses involved.
- Personal savings, small business loans.

Pricing Guidelines

Pricing your food product will be a continuing process as you balance covering your costs and staying in the same price range as your competitors' products. Specialty foods are often priced higher than similar manufactured products because customers value them as unique.

Marketing and Advertising Methods and Tips

- Rent booths at food trade shows.
- Send direct mail with samples to specialty food retailers and suppliers.
- Give away lots of free samples.
- Set up a Web site.
- Send out direct mailings and visit food stores and shops.
- Try to get your products in five to 10 different kinds of stores and talk to the retailers to see if they are pleased with the sales of your product. When that has happened and if your food has been on store shelves for a year, you can consider exhibiting at the trade shows sponsored by the National Association for the Specialty Food Trade.

Essential Equipment

A licensed kitchen in, or attached to your home (as is permitted by regulations) or access to one; cooking equipment needed to produce your product; packaging; vehicle for your deliveries; computer with billing and order processing/inventory software and home office equipment and supplies.

You may be able to rent a commercial or an organization's kitchen to get started if you are not permitted to cook in your home facilities.

Recommended Training, Experience, or Needed Skills

Experience and a background in commercial cooking is helpful; marketing your product is the key to success here. Either enroll in product marketing classes or budget your money to hire an expert to help you promote your products.

Income Potential

Depends, again, on the demand for your product(s). Income could range from $5,000 to over $100,000 if your items are sold nationally.

Type of Business

Primarily in-home, except when attending trade shows.

Success Tips

- Study the success stories of food specialty entrepreneurs.
- Literally thousands of new food products are introduced each year, so you will have to constantly study and evaluate your competition, the specialty food industry, as well as always looking for ways to reach new customers.
- Attend trade shows and while there get a copy of food catalogs to compare your product with others that are similar to yours. At the shows, you should also talk to food brokers, retailers, and suppliers to get tips and to see where your recipe would fit in the market.
- Carin Froelich, owner of Ingleby Farms <www.peppersauces.com>, says the competition is very fierce in this market, and there is competition from the overseas market as well. Froelich and her family, however, are not giving up. She says with a laugh, "These are the facts . . . although through all the hardships, Ingleby Farms will still persist in the world of specialty foods."

For More Information

Associations

The following associations sponsor food trade shows.

The Canadian Association of Specialty Foods (CASF)
P.O. Box 96509
Maple, Ontario Canada L6A 1W5
<www.finefoodalliance.com>

CASF's goal is "to foster and strengthen the specialty-food industry in Canada."

National Association for the Specialty Food Trade (NASFT)
120 Wall Street
New York, NY 10018
<www.fancyfoodshows.com>
<www.specialty-food.com>

NASFT online catalog of featured specialty foods products. Note: You must have had your food products in stores for one year to qualify for membership.

Book

From Kitchen to Market: Selling Your Gourmet Food Specialty, by Stephen F. Hall (Dover, NH: Upstart Publishing, 1996).

Legalities

Check with your state's or province's (Canada) departments that handle food licensing to see if you are permitted to cook from a home kitchen and what regulations you must follow. Certain states, like Kansas, Minnesota, and Vermont, have programs to support specialty food entrepreneurs. There are other labeling laws to which you must adhere. For information, go to the Food and Drug Administration's site <www.fda.gov> and click on the "Foods" icon.

Additional Business Ideas

- If you have marketing experience in the food industry, you could concentrate in marketing campaigns for the specialty food products of entrepreneurs and small companies.
- Start a mail order business and catalog (print and with an online Web site) featuring specialty ethnic and cultural foods.

Other Businesses

96
ENGRAVING

Engraving is used for both identification and decoration purposes. If you have experience in handling engraving tools (or have the patience to learn), an engraving business may be the venture for you. You could start with a simple electric engraver and take the time to learn the techniques of engraving. Then when you feel you have the basic skills mastered, take on simple projects and work up to more complicated ones.

Start-Up Costs and Financing Sources

- $40 to $80 for a simple electric engraver on up to $4,000 to $5,000 for an air-driven, handheld drill engraver. $900 to $1,200 for advertising and office supplies.
- Personal savings, line of credit at your bank.

Pricing Guidelines

Go by industry standards and your time and supplies used. Of course your prices will be higher if you are commissioned to do any custom orders. If you are an established artist, you can charge what the market will bear.

Marketing and Advertising Methods and Tips

- Place an ad in the business telephone directory.

- Place classified ads in the local newspaper.
- Print promotional materials—business cards, flyers.
- Send direct mailings to shop owners and auto dealers, insurance agencies, inventory specialists.
- Present samples of your work to jewelers and gift shops.
- Rent booths at artist and craft shows.
- Join a creative artists group for networking.
- Exhibit your work at museum shows and public artist displays, set up at public and college libraries, in bank and office lobbies.
- Set up a Web site to display photos and samples of your work, prices, and contact information.

Essential Equipment

Engraving tools. Also products if you sell engraved items.

Recommended Training, Experience, or Needed Skills

- Practice on your own glass and wood items.
- Work as an apprentice with an engraver and/or in a jewelry shop.
- Practice to be skilled so that your work is of professional quality.

Income Potential

$350 to $600 or more per week, more as your skill and reputation increases.

Type of Business

In-home, except for marketing presentations.

Target Market

Contact insurance companies to find out what items should be engraved for identification purposes and target shops that carry such items, including bridal shops, jewelers, trophy shops, hunting shops (engraving of guns), auto shops, gift shops, and galleries.

Success Tips

Elizabeth Dolbare, engraver-artist, offers this tip: "Find a great Web address that fits your business and try to link your address to as many other business that you would be working with. I have found that my Web address <www.scrimshaw-engraving.com> explains everything I need to convey about what my business is."

For More Information

Books

The Jewelry Engravers Manual, by R. Allen Hardy, with John J. Bowman (Mineola, NY: Dover Publications, 1994).

The Thames & Hudson Manual of Etching & Engraving, reprint, edited by Walter Chamberlain (New York: Thames & Hudson Publishing, 1992).

Engraving Tools

Basic electric engravers: *Dick Blick's Art Materials Catalog,* Dick Blick Art Materials, P.O. Box 1267, Galesburg, IL 61402; <www.dickblick.com>.

Engraving tools and other graphic transfer systems; supplies: Profitable Hobbies, 517 South Commerce Road, Orem, UT 84057; <www.paragrave.com>. Send an LSASE for full information or visit the Web site.

97
FREELANCE WRITING

Researching the publishing market (books, magazines, trade publications) and finding out what type of writing is in demand is one of the most important factors in successful freelance writing. You need to know who wants the kind of writing you do. You also need to study the craft of writing. Take courses, read trade publications and how-to books, and then write and write some more until you've got the best you can produce.

Knowing how to approach an editor is crucial (usually with a query letter), as is knowing manuscript form and submission procedures. There is no guarantee your work will be accepted, but those writers who persist and work at improving their writing skills may eventually get published.

Start-Up Costs and Financing Sources

- $4,000 to $8,000.
- Personal savings, small business loan, loans from friends or family.

Pricing Guidelines

The *Writer's Market* (see "For More Information"), an annual directory of book and magazine publishers, lists average payments for writing projects. Magazine articles: pay by the word (a few cents per word) or up to $2,000 for a midsize article. Books: advances can range from $300 (for booklets) to $12,000+ (these increase as your writing reputation grows).

Marketing and Advertising Methods and Tips

- Send query letters and/or book proposals to publishers on your topic.
- Hire an agent to handle your marketing (you pay them a percentage of whatever contract you sign).
- Attend writers' conferences and talk to editors about what they look for.
- Have a media packet of your bio and published clips that an editor or publisher may want to see.
- Get referrals from other writers for the names of editors and publishers looking for writers.

Essential Equipment

Computer with your favorite word processing software, ink jet or laser printer, modem and connection to the Internet, telephone or cell phone.

Recommended Training, Experience, or Needed Skills

- Take writing courses.
- Work for a newspaper or magazine.
- Volunteer to write a newsletter for a nonprofit organization.
- Start out writing for local publications—write newspaper features to learn how to write features, interview people, and do some basic photography.

Income Potential

$15,000 to $30,000 or more, depending on if you are writing full- or part-time.

Type of Business

In-home for the writing; out-of-the-home for book signings, research.

Target Market

Start with small publishers, publications, and trade publications, which are more likely to accept your work than the big-name publishers. This does not mean you shouldn't try larger circulation magazines or large publishers at the same time.

Success Tips

- Know your genre of writing, what publishers publish your type of writing, what the current trends are.
- Present your writing in a professional-looking format (readable print, proper margins).
- Write every day! Don't just talk about it—write . . . now!

For More Information

Books

Children's Writer's and Illustrator's Market. Writer's Digest Books, annual publication of children's book and magazine publishers. Writer's Digest Books, 1507 Dana Avenue, Cincinnati, OH

45207. Publishes numerous books on all types of writing. Sponsors a book club, offers a home study writing course, and publishes *Writer's Digest* magazine and various annual market books, including *Writer's Market.*

Get Your First Book Published: And Make It a Success, by Jason Shinder, Jeff Herman, and Amy Holman (Franklin Lakes, NJ: Career Press, 2001).

How to Start a Home-Based Writing Business, by Lucy V. Parker (Old Saybrook, CT: Globe Pequot Press, 1997).

How to Write While You Sleep, by Elizabeth Irvin Ross (Berkeley, CA: Ten Speed Press, 1993).

Secrets of a Freelance Writer: How to Make $85,000 a Year, 2nd ed., rev. and expanded, by Robert W. Bly (New York: Henry Holt & Company, 1997).

Writer's Guide to Book Editors, Publishers, and Literary Agents, 13th ed., by Jeff Herman (Roseville, CA: Prima Communications, 2002).

Home Study Course

Distance Education and Training Council
1601 18th Street, NW
Washington, DC 20009
<www.detc.org>

Write for a brochure of schools offering home study courses on writing or visit the Web site.

Magazines and Newsletters

Children's Writer Newsletter: The Newsletter of Writing and Publishing Trends, 95 Long Ridge Road, West Redding, CT 06896; <www.childrenswriter.com>.

The Writer, 120 Boylston Street, Boston, MA 02116.

Writer's Digest, Writer's Digest Books (see address under "Books").

Writers' Journal, Minnesota Ink, 3585 North Lexington Avenue, Suite 328, Arden Hills, MN 55126.

Web Sites

Following are just a few of many sites pertaining to the freelance writing market!

< http://writerexchange.about.com >

Freelance Writers' forum.

< www.freelancewriting.com >

Freelance Writing—Markets, newsletter, and industry news.

< www.freelancing4money.com >

Freelancing 4 Money—Newsletter; free and paid editions of writing opportunities; e-books.

< www.inscriptionsmagazine.com >

Inscriptions magazine—Job listings available through a paid-only subscription ($5/year). Excellent resource for professional writers of all genres.

< www.writedirections.com >

Write Directions—Online classes, resources, newsletters and more

< www.writersweekly.com >

WritersWeekly—Excellent freelance writing e-zine with markets, articles, e-books and more.

Additional Business Ideas

- Freelance editing.
- Self-publishing. With the desktop publishing systems available today, more and more people are bypassing the query/proposal route and self-publishing their own booklets, manuals, newsletters, and books. Patricia C. Gallagher < www.teamofangelshelpme.com > has written and self-published six books. She's promoted her books on nearly 200 radio and television shows, including the *Oprah Winfrey Show* (twice), CNN, and the *Sally Jessy Raphael Show*. This young mother went on a 9,100-mile book tour (with three of her children and pregnant with her fourth). Gallagher was even able to have James A. Michener write an endorsement on the inside cover of her book *For All the Write Reasons* (see below). Other books that have been self-published are *What Color Is Your*

Parachute? (4.3 million copies sold), *How to Keep Your Volkswagen Alive* (2.2 million copies sold), and *Simple Things You Can Do to Save the Earth* (3.5 million copies sold).

The following will provide you with additional information:

The Complete Guide to Self-Publishing, 4th ed., by Tom and Marilyn Ross (Cincinnati, OH: F & W Publications, Inc., 2001).

For All the Write Reasons: Forty Successful Authors, Publishers, Agents, and Writers Tell How to Get Your Book Published, by Patricia C. Gallagher (Richboro, PA: Young Sparrow Press, 1992); $24.95 check or money order to Patricia C. Gallagher, P.O. Box 806, Richboro, PA 18954.

The Small Publishers Association of North America
P.O. Box 1306
Buena Vista, CO 81211
< www.spannet.org >

98

HOME ART (OR CRAFT) OR MUSIC SCHOOL

If you have training in art, music, dance, or physical education and exercise, you may want to open your own home studio or school like these women did:

- Musical kindergarten. One older woman has operated a musical kindergarten from her home classroom for many years. The children start at 2 1/2 years of age and go for a two-year (weekly) program that teaches them the basics of musical notes, songs, and simple instruments. At the end of two years, there is a graduation, complete with miniature caps and gowns.

  A $40 registration fee is charged as well as a monthly fee ranging from $30 to $55. Class sizes average 10 to 12 students. Classes last about an hour or so, depending on the students' age level.

- Art studio. Bonnie, an artist and mother of three, opened her own children's art studio in a former farm outbuilding. It already had a bathroom and sink, so with a few touch-ups and an investment of about $500 in supplies, she opened her business. Her advertising costs were about $750, but she says, "I've never had to advertise again. I get my business through word of mouth and have a waiting list."

  Bonnie takes students from 6 to 18 years of age and teaches classes four days a week from 2:30 P.M. to 10:00 P.M. She says, "I go to work when everyone else's workday is over, but I love the convenience of having my business near my family." She charges per month, for a weekly 1½-hour lesson; $10 more per month for more advanced classes. She averages about 60 students a month. Of course, she checked zoning requirements and has a permit to operate the school on her property.
- If you are skilled in an art or a craft, you can hold lessons in your home like Sylvia Landman's Sylvia's Studio, which is a home-based teaching, design, and writing studio serving the craft industry. Sylvia says, "Never skimp on preparation and organization when working from home. Together, these form the framework for success in any home-based enterprise."

  Sylvia has written four full-length books dealing with starting and maintaining a home-based business in crafts and quilting. She also teaches full-time online for Quilt University.com and prepares others to teach, write, and sell their crafts through her online courses.

  You may want to open a similar studio or hold other lessons at your home. Do not forget to check with your insurance agent for liability coverage needed and your zoning officer for any permits required.

For More Information

Books

Growing Artists: Teaching Art to Young Children, by Joan Bouza (Albany, NY: Delmar Publishers, 1997).

Making Money Teaching Music, by David R. and Barbara Newsam (Cincinnati, OH: Writer's Digest Books, 1995).

E-Book

How to Operate Your Own Home-Based Teaching Studio, by Sylvia Landman. Visit <www.bizymoms.com> for ordering information.

99

MAIL ORDER

The mail order industry is a multimillion dollar business—as attested to by all those catalogs you receive yearly in your mailbox! Mail order is a broad term for selling products or information—either a manufacturer's or your own—through the mail. It can be your main business or a sideline to your business, as it is for one woman who owns an antique store but who also sells a manufacturer's lace curtains in her shop and through mail order to customers across the country. She advertises these curtains in a national country-style magazine and sends a free color brochure to prospective customers, who can then call her toll-free number to place an order.

Even though numerous mail order catalogs show up in your mailbox, there is still room for more! In tune with our modern lifestyles, the mail order industry has made shopping convenient and easy.

Though many people have made millions of dollars in this business, many have also lost money. Make sure you take the time to study experts' advice and the business methods and tips of those individuals who have had success in their mail order businesses. It is a good home-based business because of the flexibility in work hours, the ability to work from the home, and the potential to make high profits. The formula for success is to pick a good product or products, find the right customers, and have the money and/or marketing strategy for reaching those customers.

You may want to start your business part-time and on a small scale, and then build it up as you learn (and earn) more.

Start-Up Costs and Financing Sources

- Can average anywhere from as little as $200 to $5,000 to as much as $16,000 to $70,000.
- Personal savings, small business loan.

Pricing Guidelines

Go by recommendations quoted by experts. See "For More Information," later in this section.

Marketing and Advertising Methods and Tips

- Start with small classified ads in publications (that your own market research reveals are the best to reach your potential customers). These will generate leads to which you can send more promotional materials that more fully describe your product(s).
- Buy mailing lists from list brokers (investigate to make sure they are worth the money).

Essential Equipment

Promotional materials (including flyers or catalogs listing your products); computer with mail order software; mailing supplies, including mailing permit; area for assembling and packaging (unless you use drop shipment, where you send orders you receive directly to manufacturers); business phone line and/or toll-free number for ordering; supplies and appropriate tools for creating your product—unless you buy your items from other manufacturers to sell.

Recommended Training, Experience, or Needed Skills

- Study mail order manuals and books.
- Attend workshops and seminars on mail order business management.
- Work in a mail order company.
- Have a carefully planned marketing strategy.
- Be cost-effective with all aspects of your business.

Income Potential

Can range from a few hundred or thousand dollars to $70,000 or more a year.

Type of Business

In-home.

Target Market

Those that you gather for your own compiled mailing list; those that respond to "free information" ads; those you sign up at trade shows; those that have already purchased something from you; referrals from customers.

Success Tips

- Start slowly and build steadily as you begin to make profits. Do not jump into producing your own catalog until you have a reliable mailing list of at least 10,000 names.
- Follow local, state, and federal regulations concerning mail order businesses.
- Give your customer the best product for the best price and offer the best service you can.
- Encourage repeat orders with a regular newsletter and/or e-zine with helpful tips and your latest specials.
- Georganne Fiumara, founder of Mothers' Home Business Network <www.homeworkingmom.com> and the author of *How to Start a Home-Based Mail Order Business,* says, "Choosing the right product to sell is the first and most important step for anyone who wants to start a mail order business. The ideal product will be easy to describe, desired by a well-defined target market, affordable to ship, and can be sold for at least 4 times your cost to produce or purchase."

  Fiumara adds, "Do you have expertise in any field? If so, you can transform your knowledge into an information product. Selling information in the form of newsletters, books, booklets, audiotapes, or videotapes, will also allow you to have exclusive rights and full control of your offering."

For More Information

Associations

Direct Marketing Association
1120 Avenue of the Americas
New York, NY 10036
<www.the-dma.org>

Offers professional development, training seminars, workshops, library and information services. Sponsors an annual conference and exhibition and carries a direct marketing publications catalog.

National Mail Order Association
2807 Polk Street, NE
Minneapolis, MN 55418
<www.nmoa.org>

Newsletter, *Mail Order Digest,* and helpful information.

Federal Government Offices

Department of Commerce
Office of Consumer Affairs
1620 L Street, NW, #17
Washington, DC 20036
<www.doc.gov>

Provides information and booklets on importing/exporting, advertising, packaging, labeling, and product warranties and servicing.

Federal Trade Commission
Division of Legal and Public Records
6th and Pennsylvania Avenue, NW
Washington, DC 20580
<www.ftc.gov>

Oversees truth in advertising and the mail order industry. Order the *Mail Order Rule* booklet.

Book

How to Start a Home-Based Mail Order Business, by Georganne Fiumara (Old Saybrook, CT: Globe Pequot Press, 1996).

Software

Mail Order Wizard, by NewHaven Corporation, Columbia Center Building, Suite 864, 5600 North River Road, Rosemont, IL 60018; <www.newhavensoftware.com>. Write for prices and information about their software for mail order businesses.

Direct mail products, by MySoftware <www.elibrium.com>. Organizes names, addresses, contact information; can print out labels, postcards, bar codes, and more.

Start-Up Guide

Entrepreneur's Start-Up Guide, *Mail Order Business.* For pricing and ordering information, visit <www.smallbizbooks.com> or call (800) 421-2300. $69.50 plus shipping.

Additional Business Ideas

Mailing list business. See *Mailing List Services on Your PC,* by Linda Rohrbough (Blue Ridge Summit, PA: Windcrest/McGraw-Hill, 1994).

100
SIGN PAINTING

This business can be run on a small or large scale. Signs are still being created by artists with sandblasting or carving techniques, but today computers may be used to produce letter stencils for commercial banners, in addition to etching and silkscreening techniques.

Having artistic talent and training or sign-painting experience is a plus. You should also be able to communicate well with your customers and help them in planning a design for their sign that will best portray their business's unique style.

Nancy, a young mother and artist, has painted signs, logos, and scenes on trucks, a YMCA fitness center, and a stagecoach, to name a few. She first meets with her customers and comes up with a mental picture from the ideas given her. Then she will draw several preliminary sketches until one is approved. Nancy says, "My business is seldom boring because I never know what I will be called to do. It's great getting paid for doing what I enjoy!"

Start-Up Costs

$2,000 to $5,000 for basic supplies and advertising (more if you purchase a computer).

Pricing Guidelines

Compare the prices of other sign-painting businesses. Go with industry standards and recommendations (see "For More Information," later in this section). Some sign painters charge $25 to $30+ an hour for a drawing; $40 an hour for lettering; and $55 or more an hour for a mural. Your price will depend on the time involved, the materials, and the size of the project. Work up a written estimate and sketch for your customer. If you do get the job, then charge for the sketches—and make sure you keep the sketches.

Marketing and Advertising Methods and Tips

- Advertise in the business telephone directory.
- Leave your business cards at paint stores and office supply centers.
- Place classified and display ads in your local newspaper.
- Send direct mail to new businesses (watch for legal notices publicized in your local papers).
- Join your local chamber of commerce.
- Paint your business name and address on the back of your signs.
- Donate a sign to a community auction or paint a sign for a nonprofit event when you first start to get free advertising.
- Set up a Web site with photos of your signs.

Essential Equipment

Good set of brushes and other basic art supplies, promotional materials (make sure they illustrate a sampling of your artistic skills), paints, special tools like an electro pounce or sandblast stencil, computer (as needed).

Recommended Training, Experience, or Needed Skills

- Take art and design courses.
- Have artistic skill or sense of design, plus a mechanical aptitude.
- Apprentice with a master sign painter, if possible.
- Work in a sign-painting shop.

Income Potential

$25,000 to $75,000, depending on the population density in your area, your production methods, and types of signs.

Type of Business

In-home, except for marketing and meeting with customers.

Target Market

New businesses, satisfied customers who want additional signs or decorations (send them direct mailings of new ideas), non-profit organizations when announcing fund-raising events, garage sale holders, seasonal home boutiques.

Success Tips

- Make sure you calculate your time adequately when figuring out your price quotes.
- Keep original sketches and photos of completed projects in a portfolio to show prospective customers. Also keep a record of the time spent, materials used, and the surface you painted to better estimate the costs of future projects.
- Buy paints and materials as you need them for each project.
- Give your customers a choice of two or more signs (with price differences), a simple one and a more detailed one.
- Never stop learning new techniques and ways to improve your skills.

Franchises, Distributorships, and Licenses

Franchises

See the regular issues of such print publications as *Entrepreneur* <www.entrepreneur.com> and *Home Business* <www.home

businessmag.com> magazines (find at newsstands and bookstores) and their Web sites for listings of sign-making business opportunities and franchises.

For More Information

Book

Practical Sign Shop Operation, rev. ed., by Bob Fitzgerald (Cincinnati, OH: ST Publications, 2001).

Magazines

Sign Business, National Business Media, P.O. Box 1416, Broomfield, CO 80038; <www.nbm.com/signbusiness>.

SignCraft, P.O. Box 60031, Fort Myers, FL 33906; <www.signcraft.com>.

Supplies

Dick Blick's Art Materials, P.O. Box 1267, Galesburg, IL 61402; (800) 447-8192; <www.dickblick.com>. Sign-making supplies, kit, and other relevant items.

Additional Business Ideas

- Make wood signs. Take evening woodworking courses at local vo-tech schools to learn basic router machine skills. See *Making Wood Signs,* by Patrick Spielman (New York: Sterling Publishing Company, 1981).
- Rent out lawn or yard signs. Create and paint special occasion yard signs and rent to nonprofit organizations or consumers to announce special events or celebrations (births, birthdays, etc.).
- Cut out and paint seasonal lawn or yard signs. Create, design, and paint seasonal signs—scarecrows, witches, pumpkins; Santa Claus and reindeer; Easter Bunny; humorous characters and figures—to decorate lawns and gardens. Sell at craft shows or from your own lawn.

101
TAX PREPARATION SERVICE

Most of us do not look forward to filing our income taxes every year, but others see it as a part- or full-time income opportunity. If you know income tax filing procedures or are skilled in accounting and good with figures, this may be a good business for you. Of course, most of your business will be from January to April 15, every year, but many professional tax preparers work for their clients year-round: they file any necessary extensions, help clients keep their records in order, and provide other services that make it easier to file each year's taxes.

If this business venture interests you, talk to professional tax preparers, study tax preparation manuals, and survey if there is a need for a preparer in your community.

Start-Up Costs and Financing Sources

- $6,000 to $8,000.
- Personal savings, lines of credit from your bank, loans from family or friends.

Pricing Guidelines

Check with other preparers to see what the going rate per form is. Begin with basic charges for the simplest forms, and then figure a fee for preparing each schedule and additional form. Your fees should be based on the number of forms that the IRS requires to be filed, not based on your client's refund or payment. Some professional preparers charge from $50 to several hundred dollars, depending on the number of forms and time involved in preparing a client's tax return.

Marketing and Advertising Methods and Tips

- Place an ad in the business telephone directory.
- Post flyers on community bulletin boards.
- Place classified ads in the local newspaper.

- Hand out business cards to family and friends to pass on to others.
- Encourage word-of-mouth referrals.
- Put up road signs (if permitted by zoning) by your home office.
- Send direct mailings to business associates.
- Volunteer to assist mature adults at senior adult centers for good publicity and referrals.

Essential Equipment

Calculator, tax forms, tax reference manuals, miscellaneous office supplies and equipment, business telephone line with answering machine or service, fax machine, computer hardware and software for electronic filing, home office setup to receive clients (unless you rent office space during the tax season).

Recommended Training, Experience, or Needed Skills

- Enroll in tax preparation courses and seminars. You may qualify to be an enrolled agent by the IRS. An enrolled agent is a person who has earned the privilege of practicing, that is, representing taxpayers, before the Internal Revenue Service. See a local IRS office or visit the Web site <www.irs.gov> for more information.
- Take accounting courses at local schools or community colleges.
- Take home study courses (see listings later in this section).
- Work for a tax preparation service.
- Need to have attention to detail and be accurate, honest, and patient.

Income Potential

$45,000 to $65,000.

Type of Business

In-home business, unless you rent a temporary office during the tax season.

Target Market

Retirees, couples with complex filing schedules (medical expenses, divorced or separated, rental property owners), small business owners.

Success Tips

- ✤ Make sure you have the proper training, experience, and license to be a professional tax preparer.
- ✤ Be current on each year's tax law changes and new forms to be filed. Check with local accountants and bookkeepers for locations of tax forms or updates.
- ✤ Contact your local tax and IRS offices and inform them you are a licensed tax practitioner. Ask if they would supply you with the tax forms and instructions.
- ✤ Make copies of all prepared returns for you and your client. Put copies in your files.
- ✤ Explain each line on the form to your client and have him or her sign and date it and return it in the proper envelope.
- ✤ Check and recheck each form you do. Do not be afraid to check with the IRS if you have any questions.
- ✤ Esther Stockwell, CPA, of Duneram Consulting <www.duneram.com> (which offers accounting and tax services), says her success tip is this: "We offer the cheapest fees and promise the fastest delivery to our clients."

Franchises, Distributorships, and Licenses

See the regular issues of such print publications as *Entrepreneur* <www.entrepreneur.com> and *Home Business* <www.homebusinessmag.com> magazines (find at newsstands and bookstores) and their Web sites for listings of related tax preparation business opportunities and franchises.

For More Information

Associations

Online Tax and Accounting Sites Directory <www.taxsites.com/associations.html>. Extensive listing of national, state, and international tax associations.

Book

Bookkeeping & Tax Preparation: Start & Build a Prosperous Bookkeeping, Tax, & Financial Services Business, by Gordon P. Lewis (Ukiah, CA: Acton Circle Publishing Company, 1996).

Home Study Courses

National Tax Training School
P.O. Box 767
Mahwah, NJ 07430
< www.nattax.com >

Is an accredited home-study school offering tax preparation courses.

Web Site

< www.handrblock.com >

H & R Block—Tax Web site.

Tax Reference Guide

J. K. Lasser's Your Income Tax 2002, by Stewart Welch III and Harold Apolinsky (New York: John Wiley & Sons, 2001).

Tax Offices

Internal Revenue Service
4300 Caroline Avenue
Richmond, VA 23222
(800) 829-1040
< www.irs.gov >

Write or call for Publication #910, *Guide to Free Tax Services.* You can choose free tax publications concerning the business use of your home and other tax information booklets. Or call your local IRS office. Look in the white or blue pages of the telephone directory to find your State Department of Revenue, which can provide information on state taxes. Check with your clients' city, town, borough, or township revenue offices for local taxes to be paid.

Additional Business Ideas

Tax consultant-planner. Help individuals and couples with tax planning for retirement.

Part III

Additional Resources

Additional Resources

Associations for Women Working from Home

Home-Based Working Moms (HBWM)
P.O. Box 500164
Austin, TX 78750
< www.hbwm.com >

For moms (and dads) working from home. Newsletter, networking information, and more, including a work-at-home kit < www.workathomekit.com > .

Mother's Home Business Network
P.O. Box 423
East Meadow, NY 11554
< www.homeworkingmom.com >

Home business guidance. Features a newsletter and resource guide.

Business Associations for Women

American Women's Economic Development (AWED) Corporation
216 East 45th Street, 10th Floor
New York, NY 10017
< www.awed.org >

Committed to helping women start and grow their own businesses. Based in New York City but also works with organizations elsewhere in the United States and internationally that want to develop programs for women entrepreneurs based on the AWED models.

Center for Women's Business Research (formerly the National Foundation for Women Business Owners [NFWBO])
110 Wayne Avenue, Suite 830
Silver Spring, MD 20910
< www.womensbusinessresearch.org >

Nonprofit organization, "the premier source of information on women-owned businesses . . . worldwide."

The National Association for Female Executives (NAFE)
P.O. Box 469031
Escondido, CA 92046
(800) 643-NAFE
<http://nafe.com>

National Association of Women Business Owners (NAWBO)
1411 K Street, NW, Suite 1350
Washington, DC 20005
<www.nawbo.org>

National organization exclusively for women business owners with chapters in many major U.S. cities.

U.S. Women's Chamber of Commerce
2415 East Camelback Road, Suite 940
Phoenix, AZ 85016
(888) 96-WOMEN
E-mail: <info@uswomenschamber.com>
<www.uswomenschamber.com>

Women Incorporated (WI)
8522 National Boulevard, Suite 107
Culver City, CA 90232
<www.womeninc.org>

"A national nonprofit organization designed to improve the business environment for women through access to capital, credit, business discounts and products, and financial services."

Home Business (and Related) Associations

In addition to the associations listed here, check the *Encyclopedia of Associations* in your local library to find national trade associations in your area of business.

American Association of Home-Based Businesses
P.O. Box 10023
Rockville, MD 20849
<www.aahbb.org>

"A national, nonprofit association dedicated to the support and advocacy of home-based businesses." Does not sell or endorse any business opportunities.

American Home Business Association
4505 South Wasatch Boulevard, #140
Salt Lake City, UT 84124
< http://homebusiness.com/FLAX >

Various membership benefits and resources for home-based business owners.

Home Office Association of America
P.O. Box 51
Sagaponack, NY 11962
< www.hoaa.com >

Send an LSASE for information on membership information and benefits.

National Association for the Self-Employed (NASE)
2121 Precinct Line Road
Hurst, TX 76054
< www.nase.org >

Small Office Home Office Association International (SOHOA)
1765 Business Center Drive, Suite 100
Reston, VA 20190
< www.sohoa.com >

"Specializes in providing products and services to our members—the small office and home office professionals—that will help them run a more effective and successful business."

SOHO America
P.O. Box 941
Hurst, TX 76053
< www.soho.org >

Government Resources

Federal

Bureau of Consumer Protection
Division of Special Statutes
Sixth and Pennsylvania Avenues, NW
Washington, DC 20580

Provides information on the labeling of textile products or wool clothing.

Bureau of the Census
<www.census.gov>

Provides population statistics helpful for market research.

Bureau of Labor Statistics
<www.bls.gov>

Provides data on various industries.

Consumer Information Center
P.O. Box 100
Pueblo, CO 81009
<www.pueblo.gsa.gov>

Send for a free Consumer Information Catalog. You can order free or low-cost information on many topics, including small business information, or visit the Web site.

Cooperative Extension Service
<www.reeusda.gov>

Call your county seat for the phone number and location of the office in your county. Part of the Department of Agriculture, this service usually works in conjunction with a university. Provides information and services in the areas of agriculture and home economics, in addition to small businesses and crafts marketing.

Internal Revenue Service (IRS)
4300 Caroline Avenue
Richmond, VA 23222
(800) 829-1040
<www.irs.gov>

Write for tax publications concerning business use of your home or call your local IRS office or visit the Web site.

Office of Women's Business Ownership
Small Business Administration
409 Third Street, SW, 6th Floor
Washington, DC 20416
(202) 205-6673
<www.sba.gov/womeninbusiness>

Send for a free packet of business information of interest to women or visit the Web site. This office also helps to support the more than 200 Women's Business Centers located across the United States. For location and business start-up information, visit <www.onlinewbc.gov>.

Register of Copyrights
Copyright Office
Library of Congress
10 First Street, SE
Washington, DC 20540
<www.loc.gov/copyright>

Provides information on obtaining copyrights.

Service Corps of Retired Executives Association (SCORE)
409 Third Street, SW
Washington, DC 20416
<www.score.org>

A nonprofit association funded by the SBA, made up of mostly retired men and women who worked in business management. Services are free, and SCORE provides small business counseling and low-cost business seminars. Write for SCORE contacts in your area, call your local SBDC (see listing later in this section), or visit the Web site <www.score.org> to search for an office nearest to you.

U.S. Small Business Administration
409 Third Street, SW
Washington, DC 20416
<www.sba.gov>

This is the primary source for government assistance for small businesses. SBA regional offices and Small Business Development Centers offer free or low-cost assistance, seminars, and workshops. Also available are many helpful publications, plus:

- SBA Answer Desk: (800) 827-5722; (202) 205-7064, fax; (202) 205-7333, TDD for the hearing impaired. Provides referrals to recorded business topics. Ask for a free copy of the *Small Business Directory*, a listing of SBA publications and products including the comprehensive videotape *Home-Based Business: A Winning Blueprint*.
- SBA Procurement Assistance: (800) 8-ASK-SBA. Ask about government contracting for the small business. (See also *Free Help from Uncle Sam to Start Your Own Business*, by William Alarid (Santa Monica, CA: Puma Publishing, 1992).

U.S. Patent and Trademark Office
Washington, DC 20131
<www.uspto.gov>

U.S. Small Business Development Centers (SBDCs)
Small Business Administration
409 Third Street, SW
Washington, DC 20416
<www.sba.gov/sbdc>

Write or call for the SBDC nearest you or look in your telephone directory's white pages under "Small Business Development Center." SBDCs are usually at universities and are available in 46 states, the District of Columbia, Puerto Rico, and the Virgin Islands. They provide free services, counseling, and low-cost seminars to prospective and existing business owners.

State

Check with your state representative and/or state senator for free information on state agencies that help promote women's and small businesses within the state.

Also check in your local public library or bookstore for the latest edition of *Starting and Operating a Business in . . .* (there is one for each state), by Michael D. Jenkins (Grants Pass, OR: The Oasis Press).

Local

Contact your local SBDC, chamber of commerce, and county extension office for information on business start-up help in your community.

Books

Let's Go into Business Together: Eight Secrets for Successful Business Partnering by Azriela Jaffe (Franklin Lakes, NJ: Career Press, 2001).

Power Tools for Women in Business: 10 Ways to Succeed in Life and Work, by Aliza Sherman (Irvine, CA: Entrepreneur Press, 2001).

Turn Your Passion into Profits: How to Start the Business of Your Dreams, by Janet Allon (New York: Hearst Books, 2001).

Whole Work Catalog, The New Careers Center, 1515 23rd Street, P.O. Box 339-CT, Boulder, CO 80306. Write for a catalog.

Working from Home: Everything You Need to Know About Living and Working Under the Same Roof, by Paul and Sarah Edwards (New York: Putnam Publishing Group, 1999).

Working Solo Sourcebook, by Terri Lonier (Austin, TX: Portico Press, 1994); <www.workingsolo.com>.

Home Study Courses

Distance Education and Training Council (DETC)
1601 18th Street
Washington, DC 20009
<www.detc.org>

Write for a brochure of schools offering home study courses in all types of occupations, businesses, and trades or visit the Web site.

Magazines and Publications

Enterprising Women Magazine, 1135 Kildare Farm Road, Suite 200, Cary, NC 27511; <ewomenmagazine@aol.com>.

Partners for Small Business Excellence <www.smallbizpartners.com>. This Web site features excellent business-related articles and resources published in the annual (free) publication, *Small Business Success,* distributed by Pacific Bell Directory in partnership with a team of corporations, Southwestern Bell Yellow Pages, and the SBA.

WAHM.com, Cheryl Demas (editor) <www.wahm.com>. Home business and telecommuting information for work-at-home moms (WAHM).

Working Mother, P.O. Box 5240, Harlan, IA 51593; <http://workingwoman.com>. One year (10 issues) for $9.97 (U.S.), $21.97 (Canada).

Web Sites for Women's Home and Small Business Information

Mothers, Women's Business, Work-at-Home, Telecommuting Information

<www.bizymoms.com>

BizyMom's—Founded by author Liz Folger. Offers home business ideas, e-books, chats.

<www.bluesuitmom.com>

BlueSuitMom.com—Founded by Maria Bailey. Tips and advice for the working mother.

<www.generationmom.com

GenerationMom—Founded by Amy von Kaenel. Career and work-at-home information.

<www.gohome.com>

Business@Home—Provides home business information with About.com.

< www.committment.com >

Commitment—Founded by Paula Fuoco Davis. An Internet magazine presenting many topics of everyday living of interest to women, including home and small business articles.

< www.eworkingwomen.com >

EWorkingWomen—Created for women in business and for those who just want to find jobs online. It was founded by Georganne Fiumara, also the founder of the Mother's Home Business Network < www.homeworkingmom.comwork > , at-home ideas and jobs.

< www.herplannet.com >

herPlanet.com—Dottie Gruhler's site. A network of sites geared toward women's issues and their lives; including a business.

< www.thedabblingmum.com >

TheDabblingMum—Alyice Edrich's online parents magazine, a home business center with articles, links and e-books on starting a home-based business and mystery shopping.

< www.ivillage.com >

*i*Village—This a comprehensive informational site for women including profiles of successful women business owners, weekly chats with *Mompreneur's* Patricia Kobe and Ellen H. Parlapiano, plus articles and message boards for home businesses.

< www.momsnetwork.com >

MomsNetwork.com—Founded by Cyndi Webb and offers tools, resources, and networking to support moms working at home.

< http://Myria.com >

Myria—"The Magazine for Mothers," Includes many discussion boards and features including home business articles.

< www.tjobs.com >

The Telecommuting Jobs Page—Lists positions at companies looking for home-based workers. (Always check a company's references before signing any contracts.)

< www.womensforum.com >

WomensForum.com—One of the leading online communities with women's partner sites.

<www.womensenews.org>

WomensEnews—Womens's current social and business news.

<workingsolo.com>

WorkingSolo—Web site of Terri Lonier, author of *Working Solo* and other helpful small business books.

Start-Up Guides

Entrepreneur's Start-Up Guides. For catalogs or pricing or ordering information, visit <www.smallbizbooks.com> or call (800) 421-2300.

Supplies and Equipment

Contact companies listed for current catalogs.

Business Forms, Checks, Labels, Tags

NEBS
500 Main Street
Groton, MA 01471
<www.nebs.com>

Rapidforms
301 Grove Road
Thorofare, NJ 08086
<www.rapidforms.com>

Containers, Boxes, Bags, Packing Tissue

Cornell Paper & Box Co.
Robbins Container Corporation
162 Van Dyke Street
Brooklyn, NY 11231
<www.cornellrobbins.com>

Office Supplies

Penny-Wise Office Products
6911 Laurel Bowie Road, Suite 209
Bowie, MD 20715
<www.penny-wise.com>

Quill Office Products
Quill Corporation
P.O. Box 94080
Palatine, IL 60094
<www.quillcorp.com>

Viking Office Products
950 West 190th Street
Torrance, CA 90502
< www.vikingop.com >

Papers (desktop publishing, certificates, business stationery, etc.)

Paper Showcase
P.O. Box 8465
Mankato, MN 56001
< www.papershowcase.com >

Premier Papers
P.O. Box 64785
St. Paul, MN 55164

Miscellaneous Resources

Dun & Bradstreet
One Diamond Hill Road
Murray Hill, NJ 07974
(866) 719-7158
< www.dnb.com >

Can provide background reports on businesses (contact for fees); and a free "D-U-N-S" number which is part of D & B's Data Universal Numbering System that allows you, among other things, to gain a federal contract by registering with the federal government's Central Contractor Register (CCR).

Thomas Register of American Manufacturers

Multivolume listing of North American manufacturers. Found in most public and college libraries. Can assist you in finding suppliers or possible markets for your business. You can search the Web site for their listings: < www.thomasregister.com >.

Canadian Resources

Associations

Canadian Women's Business Network
3995 MacIssac Drive
Nanaimo, British Columbia V9T 3V5
< www.cdnbizwomen.com >

Women Business Owners of Canada
20 York Mills Road, Suite 100
York Mills, Ontario M2P 2C2
< www.wboc.ca >

Books

Building a Dream: A Canadian Guide to Starting Your Own Business, 4th ed., by Walter S. Good (Whitby, Ontario: McGraw-Hill Ryerson, 2000).

Internet Law and Business Handbook, by Dianne Brinson and Mark F. Radcliffe (Menlo Park, CA: Ladera Press, 2000); < www.laderapress.com > . Includes information about Canadian e-commerce laws.

Business Services

Canada/British Columbia Business Services
601 West Cordova Street
Vancouver, British Columbia V6B 1G1
(604) 775-5525
< www.smallbusinessbc.ca >

"The mandate of the Canada/British Columbia Business Services is to serve as the primary source of timely and accurate business-related information and referrals on Federal and Provincial government programs, services and regulations, without charge."

Government

Canada Business Service Centres (CBSCs) < www.cbsc.org > provide a wide range of information on government services, programs, and regulations and answer questions about starting a new business or improving an existing one. Provides contact information for each province and territory.

Web Sites

< www.canada.com >

Canada.com—Canadian information and news portal, including a business directory.

< http://strategis.ic.gc.ca >

Strategis—Produced by Industry Canada, a department of the federal government, this is a valuable resource of information for consumers and businesses. Includes information and guides on starting and financing a business, exporting, and other issues pertaining to having a business in Canada.

Periodicals

Home Business Report, 2625a Alliance Street, Abbotsford, British Columbia V2S 4G5; <www.homebusinessreport.com>; e-mail: <HBRCanada@aol.com>.

Profit magazine (print), Profit Subscriber Services, 777 Bay Street, 8th Floor, Toronto, Ontario M5W 1A7; (416) 596-5523; <www.profitguide.com>. Business information and resources for Canadian entrepreneurs.

How to Contact the Author

If you have any comments or questions, or are interested in receiving a free sample of the e-zine, *A Self-Employed Woman's Guide*, send an e-mail to <pyhuff@hotmail.com> or an LSASE to Little House Writing & Publishing, Box 286, Sellersville, PA 18960.

Index

S

T

U

V

W